Animate Form
Animate Design
Animate Thinking

Ali Khiabanian

© All Rights Reserved
All rights reserved. No part of this book may be reproduced or transmitted in any form or by any means, electronic or mechanical, including photocopying and recording, or by any information storage and retrieval system, without permission in writing from the author.

Title: Animate Form, Animate Design, Animate Thinking
Authors: Ali Khiabanian
Translator (from Persian): R. Kafouri
Editor: Negin Alizadeh

Cover design: Ali Khiabanian

ISBN: 9781947464063
LCCN: 2018913037
Publisher: American Academic Research, Reseda, CA
Prepare for Publishing: Asan Nashr,
www.ASANASHR.com

Dedicated to Greg Lynn

Whom that Changed my view to architecture.

Table of Content

Chapter 1 (digital Design & Design Process)..10
    Virtual Reality 11
    Role of Virtual Space 11
    Digital Thougth 11
    Digital Understanding 12
    Digital architecture records changes of conditions 13
    Is Digital Design Process a nonlinear Structure 13
    Design or Modeling in Computer, Witch One? 22
    What is Occurrinh or Will Happen in Near Future? 22
    What We Learn from Digital Process 23
    Important Points in Digital Architecture & Design 23

Chapter 2 (How to Make Animation) 27
    Instruction 1 28
    Instruction 2 29
    Instruction 3 30
    Instruction 4 30
    Instruction 5 33
    Instruction 6 35
    Lavasan Pedestrain Bridge 36
    Animate Design is Developted Process of Parametric Design 39
    Instruction 7 40
    How to Save Animation. 46
    Define a Specific Trajectory for Camera Motion 47

Chapter 3 (Animate Design) 100
    Why Animate Design?. 49
    First Part of Animate Design. 50
    An Introduction to Snapshot. 50

Animate Photography.. 56

Morpher... 58

Mcloth. 60

Experience of Mcloth. 63

Design of Coty Square Based on Mcloth Technique. 100

Second Part of Animate Design. 71

Animate design strongly emphasizes on repetition, variation and evolution 100
Nature Pavilion... 79

Third Part of Animate Design. 82

Fourth Part of Animate Design. 83

Fifth Part of Animate Design. 84

Experiences of Responsive Space 85

Sixth Part of Animate Design. 89

Animate Design Diagram... 100

Second Diagram of Animate Design Process. 100

Animate Design & Sketch.. 100

Chapter 4

Smples and experiences of facilities provided to designers by computer.
.... 100

Pattern Design. 100

Facad Design of Pezeshkan Tower 104

Interior Renders of Pattern Changes and Shadows.. 112

Density of Form & Shade. 116

Daylight 118

Chapter 5 (Kinetic Architecture) 119

Simulation of Kinetic Structure No. 1. 121

Simulation of Kinetic Structure No.2 122

Design of Facade of Diba Bags & Shoes Market 124

Examples of Kinetic Surfaces & Crusts 128

Flowering 129

Symmetry Tower 134

Chapter 6 (Growth & Metamorphosis) 136

Metaballs 137

Growth 139

Twist 141

Transformation 145

Metamorphosis 149

A Dance in Middle of City 153

Urban Design Elements 156

Design of trade-office tower using animate design technique............ .157
Animate Thinking 162

Thniking & Creativity Pavilion 169

The Last Words 173

Refrences 175

Potency of computer-based graphic in encountering with dynamic processes which are only displayed with animation and cannot be displayed using images is undeniable. Contrary to predetermined linear process of film, the computer-based graphic makes active presence during real-time operation, assimilation of being investigated process (in images and data) and special experiences possible for users. It is a very wide area often used in different arts in addition to cinema and extent, accuracy and variety of works which may be done in the field of animation and animated images are increasing. Animation suggests two important possibilities to architects:

First, designers and users may attend the space and move there before execution. Second, architecture is no longer a static and dynamic structure, it can move, transform, and develop, if required. The first suggest is being stabilized in architecture using attractiveness of 3D glasses. However, the architecture society is significantly far from such attitude, i.e. the second suggest, in addition to execution restrictions. There is a pressing need to codify a new method and process of design for animation. Different arts use this capability in displaying and especially designing of their works more than architects. Besides enthusiasm of the author to discover new areas, this subject is the main reason for compiling this book.

As a designer, my animation experience goes back to 2002 when I started to make short animations through combining and expanding of platonic volumes. The experiences were manifested in an animation made for my thesis, "Modern Art Museum", of project design process indicating to formation of crust and architectural space.

In design process, architecture was not supposed as a fixed structure. Rather it was supposed as a flexible, dynamic and transformable structure. Did it since had done several sketches and had ideas for the projects and needed such structure and technique to put them in practice although was not informed of the activities conducted in this regard and idea of construction parts of which can move, open, and close. Attractiveness of such discovery, at least in my mind, was so exiting that I continued it and compiled in this book through making several animations and studies.

Ali Khiabanian

www.IDUArchitects.com
YouTube Channel Name: Ali Khiabanian
Instagram: IDUArchitects

Chapter 1
Digital space & Design process

Virtual Reality

Virtual reality was brought forth from middle 1980s[1]. People encountered with apparently real images while they were made by computer and were not real. Two antonyms, i.e. "Reality" and "Virtual" were put together for the first time to create a new concept and attitude of "being" and "not being".

The space made in computers are more real and sometimes more attractive than reality of our surrounding environment. You can move in the space, decrease or increase light intensity, and change height and thickness of wall as you desire. You can change color and material of walls or change them to a worn out and destructed ones. Capabilities of computers in some fields, especially architecture, are more than our function in real world. Besides representation of architectural space and providing conditions for better and more complete recognition to complete and change other spaces, the space made in computer creates a new technique of architectural thought and creation in the architectures' mind.

Role of Virtual Space

Virtual space is not an isolated and inaccessible world rather all people may access it using required equipment (computer and related instruments) and executing simple instructions. Architectural space may be restricted to digital space. All people who can consciously imagine their presence in the space may access virtual space. This space is formed based on our imagination of its form in mind, visual or digital space. "All objects are symbolic in virtual space. They refer to the physical world to which belong in different scales and mainly through metaphor. This relation is required to help the user to direct itself in this symbolic space. Our criterion from abstraction helps us to understand available relations with our physical world, the relations indicating to forms for classification of objects of virtual space and understanding its meaning" Peter Anders says.

Every object may have one or more meaning and variable specifications in virtual space. Architecture of virtual space is certainly a coded one with unlimited symbology. Architect of virtual space is responsible to define codes indicating to meanings.

Digital Thought

---

[1] M. Amir Bani, "Contemporary Architecture" Lecture, Islamic Azad University of Qazvin, 2002-03

Digital thought means a thought realized in interaction between architect's mind and computer. The architect is no longer the only creative and deciding person of architecture creation scene, rather it has a colleague developing or affecting its work. Increasing relation of designer with each component of space and quick realization of imagines in architectural design makes the architect's mind close to 3D space where the architecture is created. It opens new horizon in mind, eyes and hands of the architect.

In a near future and real world, your eyes will see virtual events and spaces in computers in addition to the surrounding reality or you will arm your eyes to instruments and glasses to observe what is beyond reality in both real and virtual worlds. In other words, our attitude to the surrounding world as well as our understanding is being changed significantly.

Digital Understanding

Computers and other electronic systems extend our understanding of architectural space due to creating new techniques of thought and creation. They result in new and different perception of usual structures possessing the power to anticipate future and change our life style and attitude toward nature.

In addition to changing perception of available reality, two transformations are created in understanding and perception process: first, a perception we should have of virtual space, its facilities, instruments and mood, and the last but not the least, perception of relation between reality and virtual (real and virtual architecture). It is not possible to see the surrounding reality with realistic eyes without virtual perception of the surrounding reality and do not consider possibility of expressing or converting virtual space to reality.

For example, programmers and users of graphic applications aim at creation of spaces which are exactly similar to our surrounding reality. Processing capability and high realism of computers and computer software in creation of contrast, color tonality, kinds of shades and lights have been grown in recent years such that it is really difficult for experts to distinguish reality and virtual.

Digital architecture records changes of conditions.
It is instant record of combination, changes, destruction, interference, transformation and extension of form and structure in space.

Virtual architecture means electronic representation of architectural design. Virtual architecture phenomenon follows several objectives:
- Assimilation of architecture and available form
- Assimilation of being designed project to perceive and present architectural plans
- Virtual displaying or completing part of an unreal building
- Design of urban space for movies and animations

Marcus Novak believes that fluid architecture in cyber space is a substance-less architecture. It has abstract elements, tends to music, and is a changing architecture. Cyber architecture is a symphony in space during time, a symphony which is never repeated and does not continue to be completed.

Is digital design process a nonlinear structure?
Design process operates on breadthwise and there is a bilinear relation between them. Any changes affect other elements and effect of such changes comes back to the initial element. It is a back-forth breadthwise movement which increases relation between the process elements in addition to interaction. In creative design process (published by the author in "Creativity in Architectural Design Process I"), there is a vertical hierarchy and the designer is obliged to pass them one by one. This is a process followed by most architects using computers and includes most design policies of architecture studios of Iranian universities (Diagram 1, design process diagram). The diagram was designed more dynamically and flexibly. Therefore, cyclic motion during the process, return to previous stages and possibility of merging of stages or deleting a specific stage of design process are strongly emphasized. Even, it is possible to change the direction during design process, e.g. when the designer encounters with the produced structure, a more new, better and complete idea may occur to him and he may change the design process to a new direction.

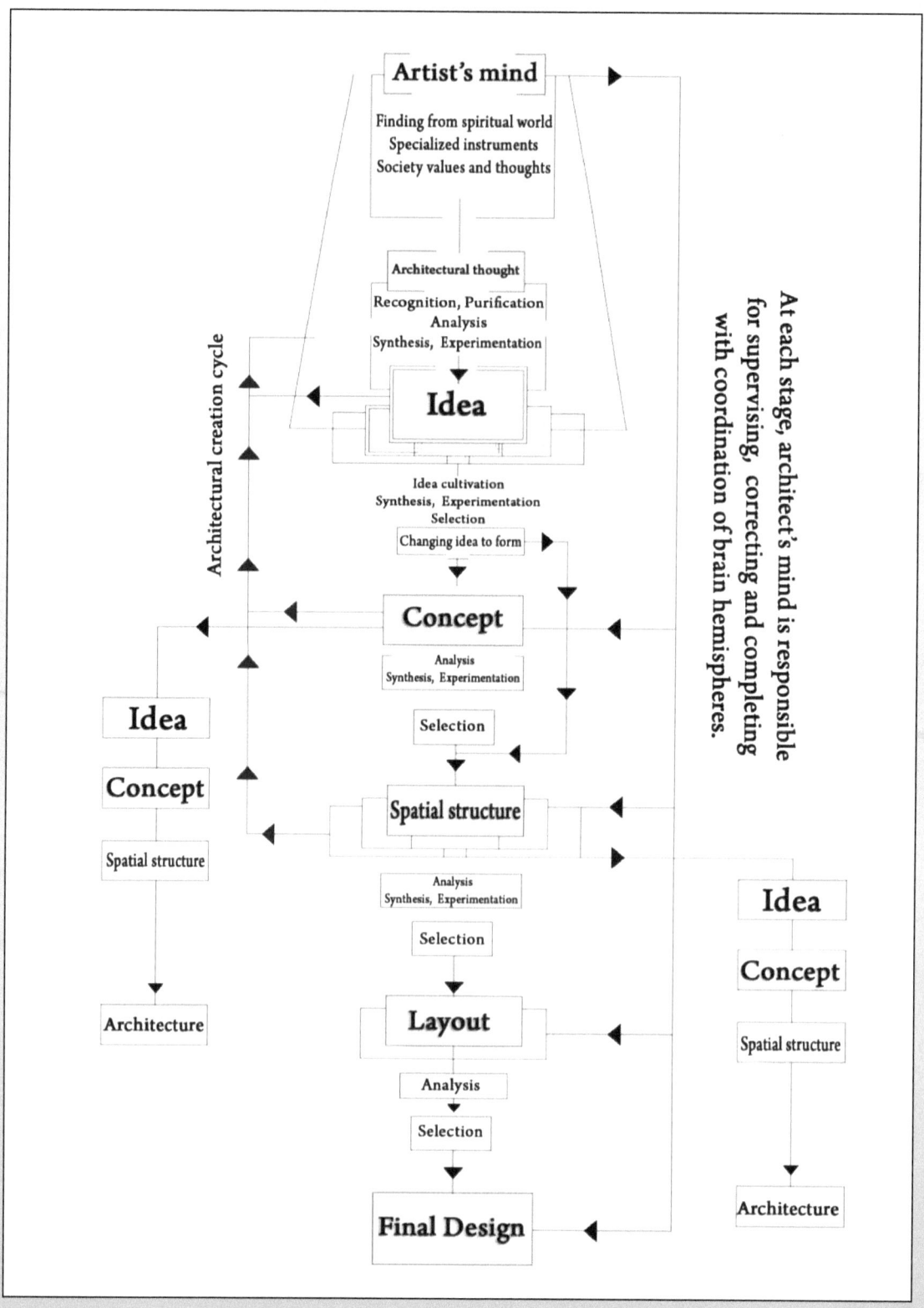

Diagram 1: Architectural design process

Using the researches and experiences of "Creativity I" book, I changed vertical structure of the diagram to a horizontal one (Diagram 2, Creative Design Process). In such case, the design diagram is not a plan and hierarchy which should be passed, rather it takes form of a trajectory which moves back and forth between designer's mind and the physical world including, sketches, 3D print, etc. No stage is preferred to another. It is a flexible system convinces you to use relations and trajectories to return and review the past stages in addition to more clarity. (Wide section of human mind may be used in future to think and design completely due to evolutionary process of human nature or technological progresses).

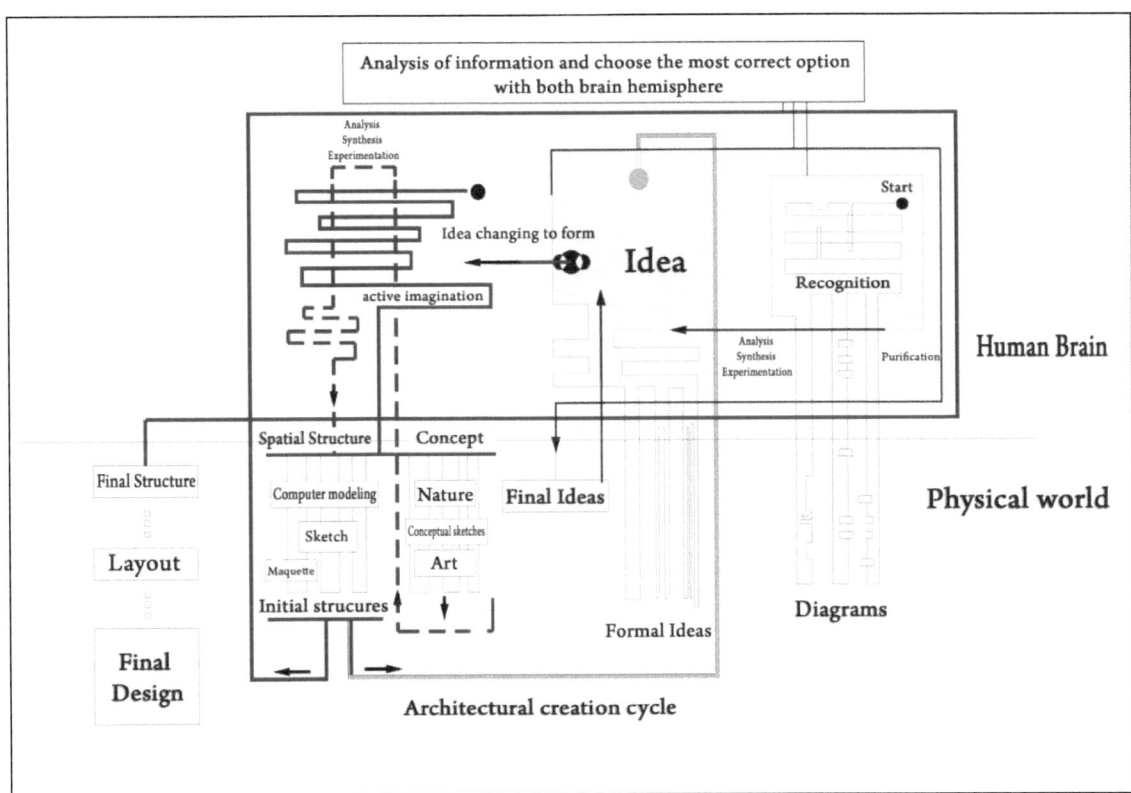

Diagram 2: Creative design process based on type of relation and interaction of designer's mind and the outer world

Comparing with digital design process, it is really difficult for the designers' mind to control and organize the components in such method where several components are involved in design process especially when the designer intends to create a new and creative work. In the above-mentioned diagrams, it is not always easy and possible to return and review the stages and evaluations specially to track effect of changes on elements and design process. As robots and manpower is required to manufacture automobiles, computers and software help architects to significantly affect accuracy and speed of design process especially in meeting requirements of current era.

Digital design is created when there is an interaction between computer and designer. However, in non-digital design, the designer is the only master-mind, determinant and decision maker. In digital design, computer and designer consult each other to make the final decision.

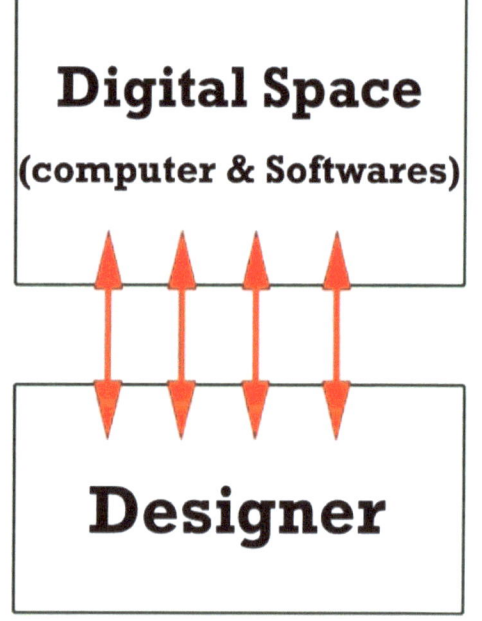

There is a breadthwise relation between the designer's mind and computer. Design processes are in more coordination and interaction and their relation is much stronger than influencing and being affected such that in diagrams of digital design process, different design stages are drawn inside rectangles and they are connected as molecules, they can replace each other or leave the process.

Diagram 3

In fact, computers can supervise over, control and concurrently think about several things in a time much shorter than human mind. This is a notable specification which should be used. Even, we should try to promote our mind capability to have such a performance and analyze several issues concurrently. Therefore, classification of events occurring in computers thinking process is really difficult and time consuming. For this reason, I use "Concurrency of design stages" phrase in computers instead of classification of design stages. In the diagrams 3, 4, 5 and 6 which are gradually completed, a specific cooperation of designer and computer are demonstrated and outputs are considered for decision making and intervention of the designer to, for example, evaluate the ideas or forms produced by software and specify the form or idea to be developed by the computer. In contrary to classic design processes, specific hierarchy could be supposed for digital design. Sometimes in creative design process (as mentioned in "Creativity in Architectural Design process I[1]"), structure and concept stage are merged or the concept stage is deleted.

Even, information of recognition stage sometimes results in a specific structure in interaction with the site and weakens idea and concept stages such that ideas are formed in the recognition stage and directly lead to spatial structure or even the initial design due to powerful or limited specifications of the project site. In digital design, however, important and critical changes beyond merging or deletion of design stages are observed. In such design, design process stages are interwoven and do not follow specific hierarchy. Rather, they act according to the governing situation and affect each other. For example, you can enter a new component such as "wind" during the design process. The computer will verify its effect on all conducted activities- not only the completed stages- and form of the building may significantly change and affect the site design. As another example, changing height of the building may affect total structure and elements of the building including door and window.

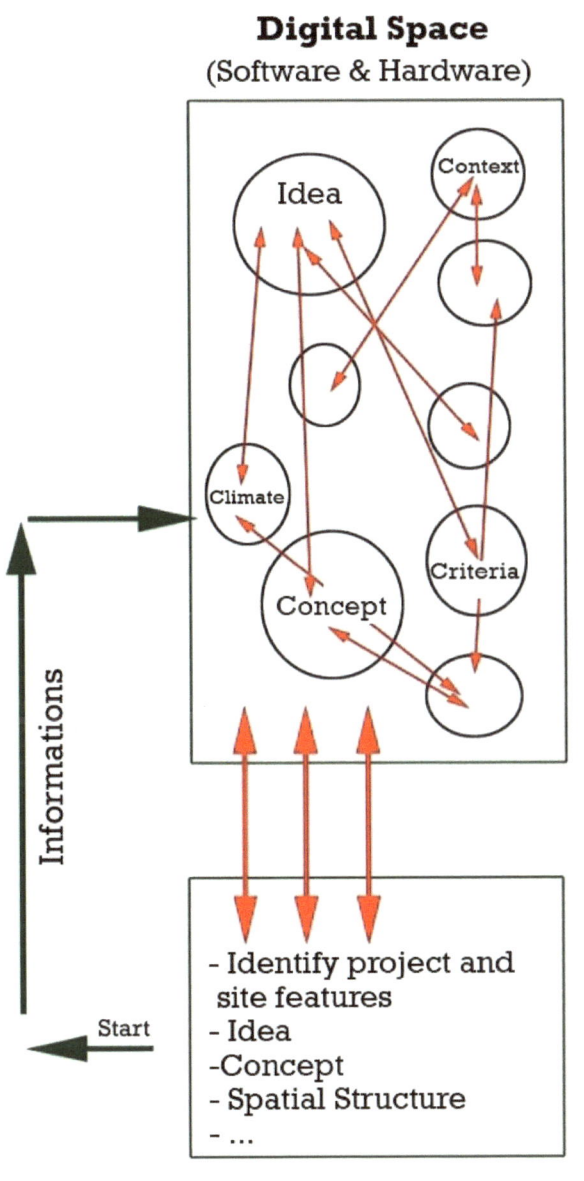

Diagram 4

1- To learn more about the design process diagrams, refer to "The role of brain hemispheres in architectural design" (translation of creativity in Architectural Design process I, I I)

From beginning of design process when it receives information about project recognition, site and designer's ideas, the computer begins its thinking and analyzing process and is capable to offer different ideas, structures and forms concurrently or in a short time span. In initial design stages, kind of the applied material is even important and the computer warns us about some execution restrictions. When the designer changes or increases information, the images presented in computers are also changed or completed (Khiabanian, 2012). The stages and components involved in design process in computers memory are very close and work with high coordination and dependency like an animated organism its components are accurately related to each other.

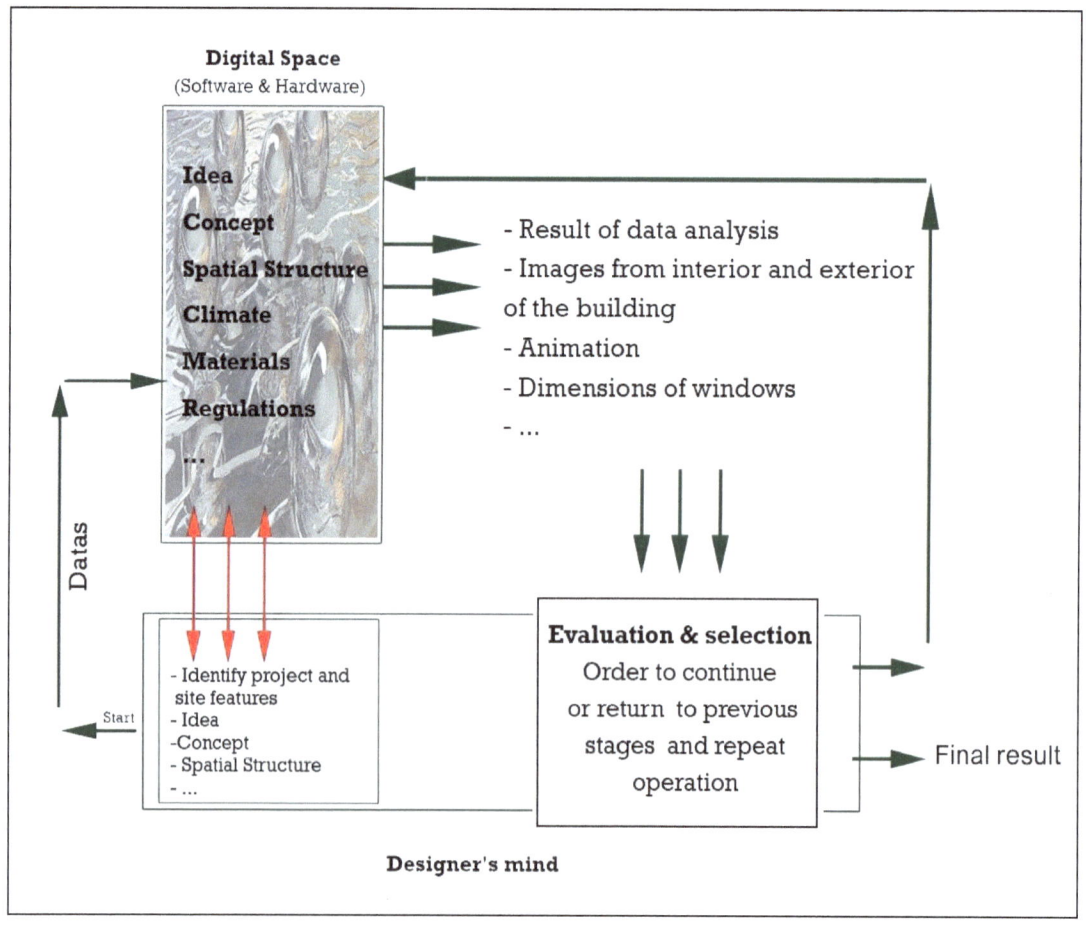

Diagram 5 (Digital Design Process)

If design stages and the works which should be done by the designer are considered as components with their special requirements, restrictions and limitations, it may be stated that digital design process is a process of cooperation and concurrency of forces varying from the employer's requirements and regulations of municipalities to structural and aesthetic restrictions. Each of them are forces which are moving and changing to find their accurate position in a wide area created by computers and digital facilities (e.g. 3D print and digital glasses). In other words, digital design process records changes of position of forces, i.e. accurate and on-time record of ideas, forms and created spaces and control of forces during the process to create the best response.

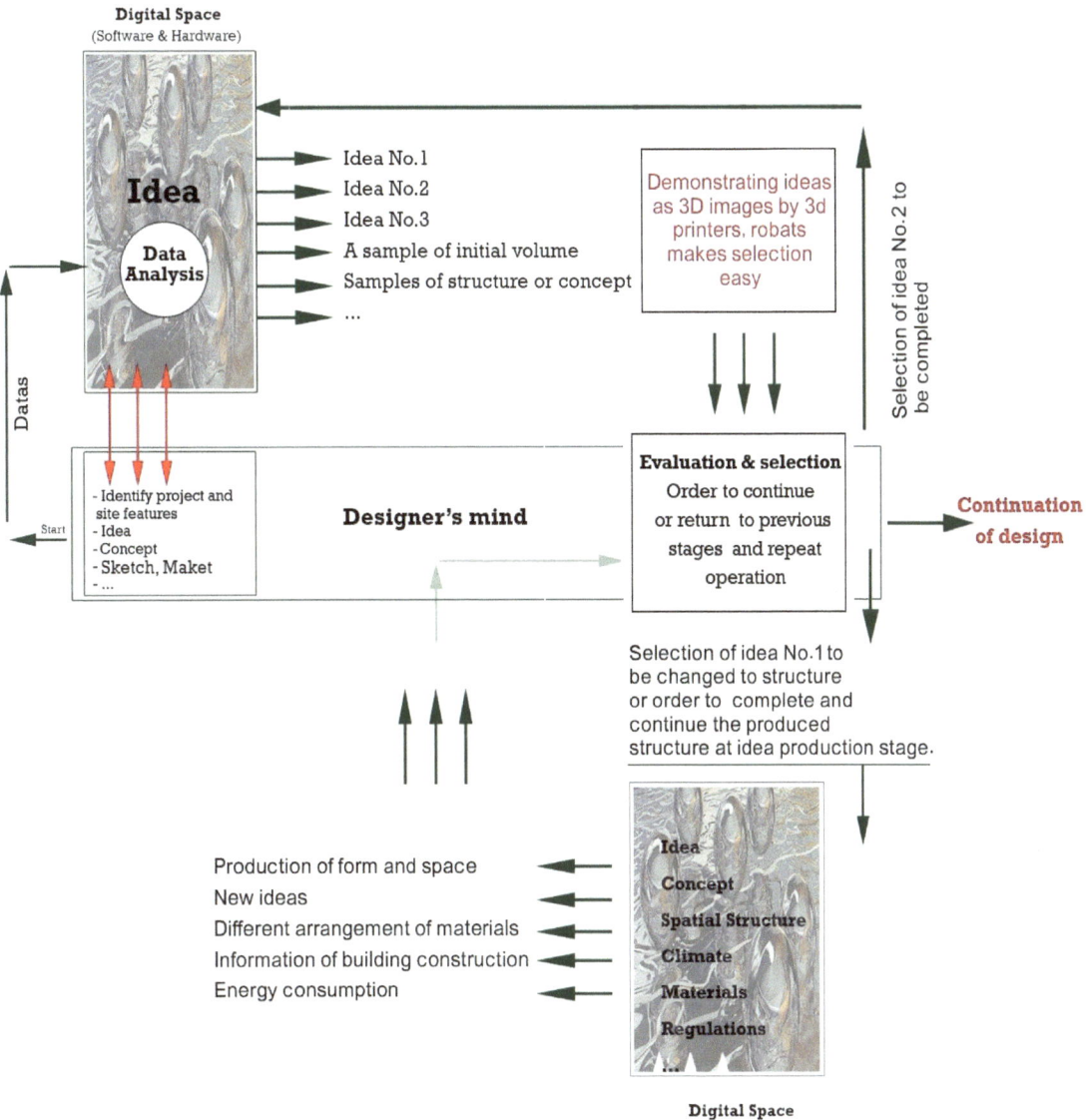

Diagram 6: Full view with more details of digital design process

However, reality of digital design process is far beyond!

The designed 2D diagrams indicate to two-dimensional and linear nature of digital design process while the design process occurs in a multi-dimensional space. Time component- as the fourth dimension in digital design- creates different conditions of non-digital design and only by human mind and hand due to possibility of calculation, effect of intensity and location of sun, displaying depreciation, and moving inside the space. Diagram 7 shows a weak and general scheme of 3D structure of design process.

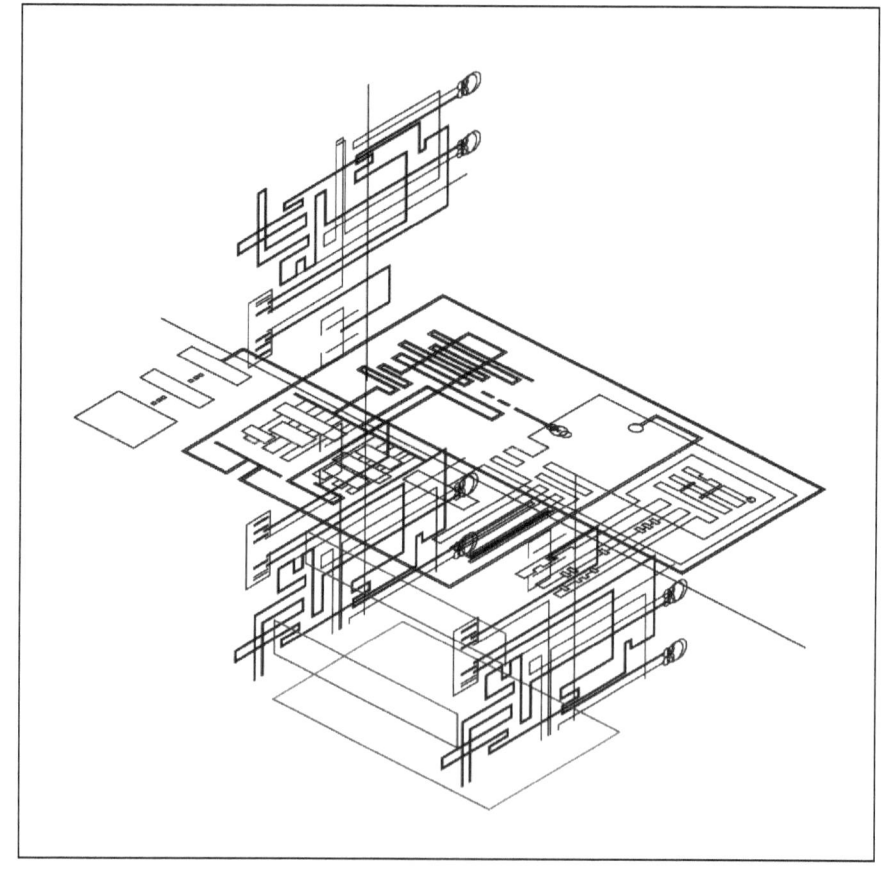

Diagram 7

In a detailed scheme, however, digital design process is a minimized structure or model of galaxy and world surrounded by a space of waves, forces, energy, data, planets and stars formed based on requirement and definition of project and space attitude and are interacted. However, it should be remembered that the planets are made of bubble. They are very flexible and may merge with other bubbles, explode, scatter in space, and attach other field of data and force. The "picture 1" which is modeled by the author demonstrates the mentioned process.

Picture 1

Design or Modeling in Computer, Which One?

The author believes that digital design is often a nonlinear structure while modeling in computer is often a linear process. What happens in a designer's mind differs from what occurs to a person who, for example, wants to make a computerized model using models or sketches. Mentality of such person has a high pictorial resolution of the project which will be done. For this reason, he/she knows the plan and the orders to use. However, the designer encounters with several components which should be included, assessed and valuated in design. There are several answers for a designer and the final results may be a combination of them. This is true for all kinds of design, whether digital or analogue. Although the author tried in "Architectural Design Process" books to present a specific process of design, it should be accepted that personal and specific process of the architects in so called analogue design change for several times. It becomes more complex in digital design and keeps the designer away from a specific and logical design trajectory due to wide data and operational range as well as increasing of components (e.g. light, climate, motion in space, etc.) which was given important role and manifestation owing to advancement of technology.

Digital design has another face and is not only limited to use of designed orders and plugins. Scripting and algorithm design, especially in recent years, along with appearing of plugins such as Para 3d, Grasshopper and MCG (Max Creation Graph) in 3Ds Max software requires a specific linear process in most cases so that the designer may model his/her mental images in computer.

What is Occurring or Will Happen in Near Future?

Technology in the field of architectural design and construction has been progressed so quickly that new events and news are expected in all moments. Digital design, with all endeavors made for specification and documentation of a design method, is very unstable and depends on software and hardware progresses and it is not possible to present a definite design method. 3D glasses are of the most important innovations in this regard and try to evolve and remove imperfections to enter design process. I believe that these glasses will create such a revolution in design process in future years that we will throw away our computers and tablets. 3D glasses create a complete interaction between software and designer and mitigate the barriers and obstacles found in the mentioned processes. Designer becomes part of the operating system or design and modeling software. For example, "Extrude" order is no longer needed to elevate cube roof, designer's hand does the same and even all tasks recommended in "Modify" menu of 3Ds Max software. Moving hand and fingers, we can bend, rotate, substrate, or cut our form.

If your design method changes, digital design diagrams and manuals found in next pages will be helpful in coherence of your mind and your thought method in encountering with and using technology and will release you from being absorbed and trapped in design process.

What We Learn from Digital Design Process:

- Reciprocal and dynamic relation among the components leads to evolution of design effect
- Enhances creativity and power of mind of the designer
- Changes capacity of the designer's mind from what it is to what is unimaginable and directs his/her to discover passive and even impossible phenomena
- Develops mental archive of the architect concerning plurality and diversity of architectural ideas and structures
- The designer's mind may act more dynamically and accurately than before
- (Note: The above-mentioned cases will be realized through practice if there is an interaction between the architect and computer. Unfortunately, lack of accurate understanding about function of computer and how to communicate with it results in lazy mind of designers and students.
- Digital works are created with high scientific accuracy
- Progress of representation and structural illustration is observed in architecture
- Computer makes it possible for us to record complex mechanisms.
-

Important Points in Digital Architecture & Design

- Computers promote accuracy and scope of action of architects to create a complete and accurate architecture. Computers should not be seen as accelerators. Production of various and infinite ideas by computers along with acceleration of design process increases architectural works rate and requires more endeavor and accuracy. For this reason, architects with powerful and dynamic minds will be pioneers of future architecture, those who can move in step with technological advancement and demonstrate high power of analysis and choice.

- When you survey in a virtual world, you have a specific location and mood. The data about you may be sent to the persons visiting the media concurrently and they can really see your character when you move. Their data may also be transferred to you, to a virtual world where different persons may enter simultaneously and communicate with each other (Fathzadeh, 2001)
- In digital architecture, creation depends on nature and facilities of the media as well as accurate and wide relation of individual with media (includes wide range of designers, programmers and users) rather than personal genius. In fact, a genius and creativity which act coincidently with virtual space will be effective.
- With cooperation of computers and electronic systems, there will be shorter creation time and more freedom of action in creation. Technique will result in more creativity of designer and several ideas, volumes and structures will be created and tested. But, when the work will be completed?
  This is an important issue which depends on mind power of architect and his/her endeavor. Design is similar to growth and bring forth of a tree and different methods of plant breeding will help its better and complete growth and fertility rather than shortening of its fructification time. The fruits bred in short times and unconventional conditions may be bigger than natural fruits in size but they are poor considering nutritional values.
- Software transfer design method to architects considering the planned structure and the architects often adapt themselves with computer options to create their imaginations. In future, the architect will neither be a person who is proficient in design tools nor a person with high creative power in combining form and creating of space.

Rather, he/she should be sufficiently proficient in media sciences, design and programming of design software. Unfortunately, architects' capability depends on tools (computers) more than ever and, in fact, computers teach us thinking method while thoughtful architects should create thinking, understanding and imagination techniques of the space, program, and train. Others will only be uses of their software using creatively and completely their thinking and architectural tools and have limited power of action in creation of architectural space, qualitatively and quantitatively. However, they think, design and make in a way designed and planned by the first group (thoughtful architects).

- In digital design process, architectural work is created as a result of interaction and synchronization between stages and subjects discussed in design not necessarily through competition in a linear course. There is a dynamic relation between elements of digital process interacting concurrently. For example, idealization and spatial structure design are not distinct. They affect each other to end of design process and lead to completion or correction of the project.
- Design ideas may be brought forth in three dimensional models of indoor and outdoor spaces easier than other design tools and techniques. It is likely that new ideas are created by form variations. Using advanced systems, it is possible to calculate effect of unpleasant winds on building structure and reduction of temperature of the building during different seasons and conditions. Interestingly, computers brought forth different models and ideas to comparison. Entering numbers and digits obtained from calculations and clicking a button, designer encounters with tens of forms and solutions which may transform our architecture.

When you work on a form or structure, computers offer you new ideas considering the made variations. These ideas affect your form again and change direction of mental process of the designer. This is due to fluidity of the space where the designer works. Every action of the designer is like a force imposed to the whole subject rather than a special point. It is noteworthy that the designer may change rate and range of the force effect. In manual design, the whole volume is not changed when part of the volume is changed (drawn or erased). The designer evaluates and applies variations upon his/her discretion while computers offer alternatives to the designer before he/she makes any decision. For example, omitting an angle of a drawn line leads to quick change of the volume and adapts itself with new conditions (Picture 2).

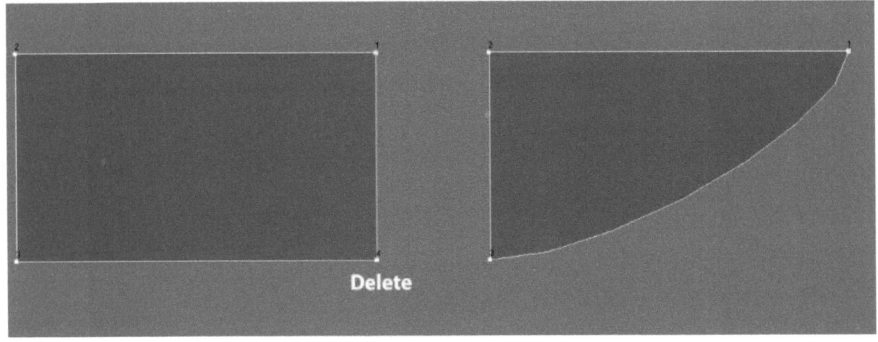

Picture 2

- In case of mind reinforcement and complete proficiency to design software, the architect may use spatial design method while he/she is dominant over indoor and outdoor space of the project. Volume and form design is not distinct from indoor spatial design and they are done concurrently and variations of each of them over another may be observed and evaluated.
- Plan, cross section, and volume are not designed in specific stages of design process. Rather, they are developed and completed while they are interwoven and affect each other- from the first line drawn in computers.

- The designer is relatively aware of results of his/her work and anything may happen until the last moment when he/she finishes design and turns off the computer! (Khiabanian, 2013)

Chapter 2
How to make animation

To better understand the forthcoming discussions and operationalize design technique, this section instructs you how to make an animation using 3Ds Max software. Contrary to the conventional method, I prefer to practically make an animation before description of theoretical discussions, quality and function of instructions. Once the subject is understood, detailed explanations will be provided.

- **Instruction 1**

Do the following stages in order:
1. Draw a cube.
2. Turn on "Auto Key" button below (it will be red).
3. In opposite, insert "100" instead of "0". (Picture 3)

<Picture 3

4. Move the cube in direction of X axis and place it in "B" point.
5. Turn off "Auto Key" button.
6. Press "Play" button at below right corner so that your cube is moved between A and B points. (Picture 4)
Note: When "Auto Key" button is on; all changes of the volume are recorded as animation variations. Therefore, take care to turn it on and off when required.

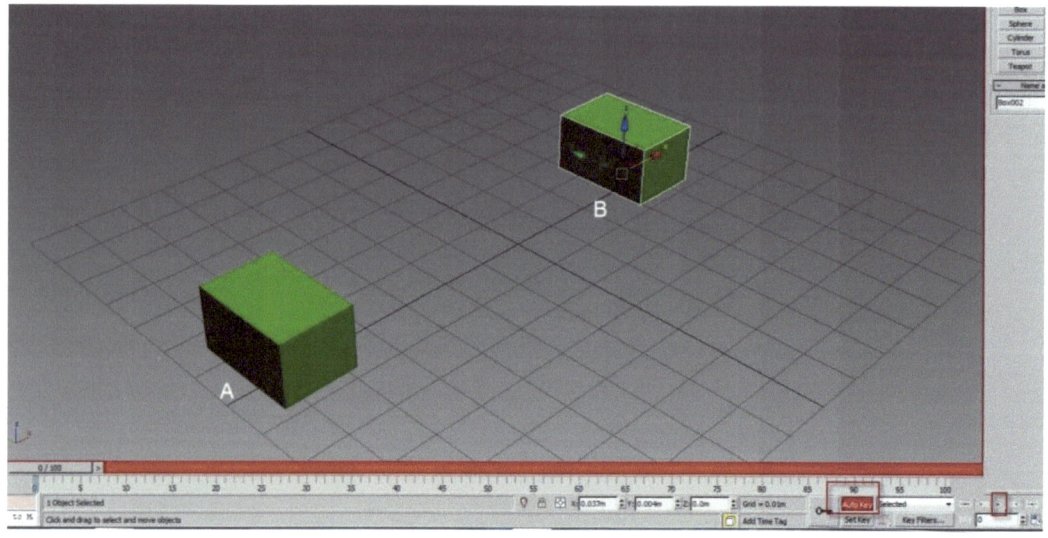

Picture 4

- **Instruction 2**

Here, the above animation will be completed and developed. Do the above stages in order. Change height of the object after placing of the volume in B point (after step 4). (Picture 5)

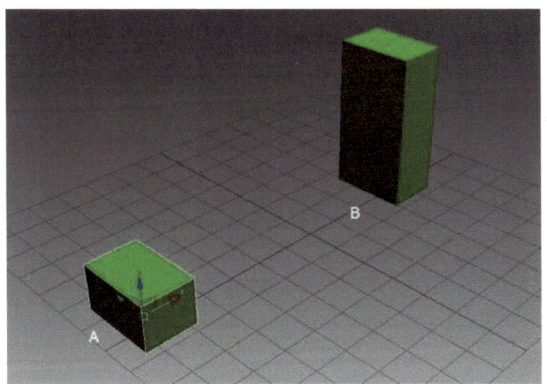
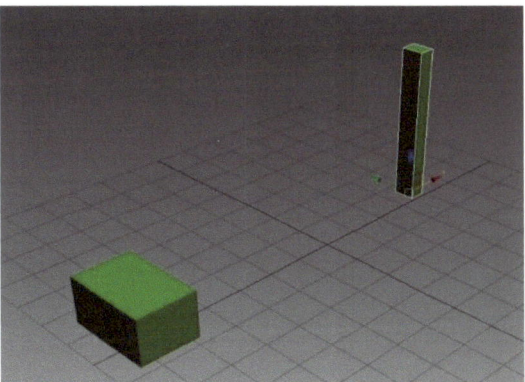

Picture 5   Picture 6

Press "Play" button. Height of your cube will increase while it is moved (picture 3). You can increase or decrease length and width of the object instead of changing its height (picture 7).

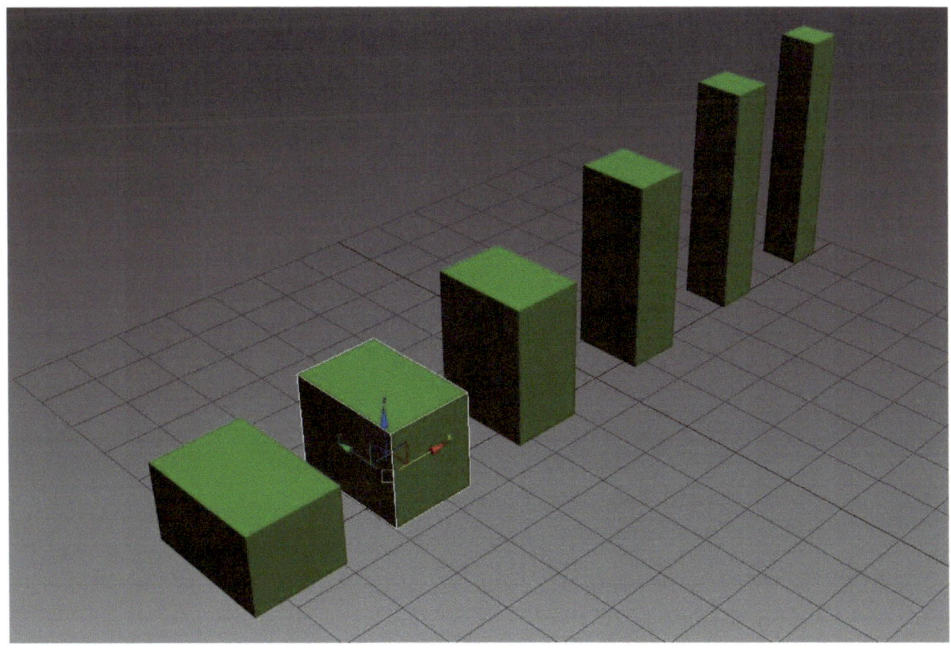

Picture 7 shows the first cube transformation stages.

- **Instruction 3**

In this stage, we will rotate the cube for 45° around X axis in addition to changing parameter of the cube. Turn off "Auto Key" button and execute the animation (picture 8).

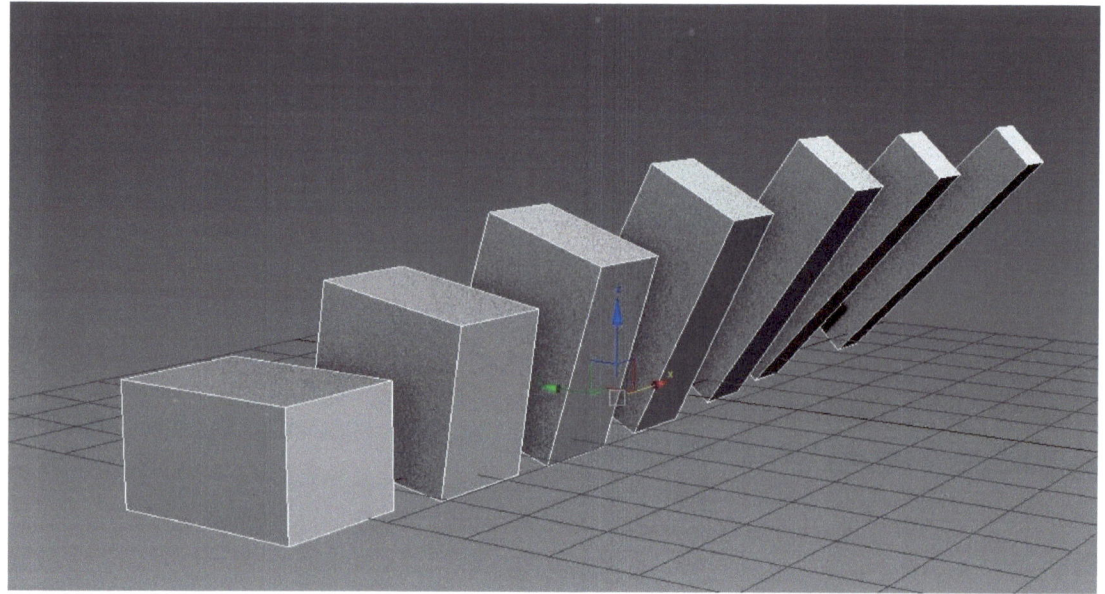

Picture 8

- **Instruction 4**

   (Making animation using "Bend" instruction)

"Bend" instruction is of "Modify" instructions used to bend objects. In this animation practice, we will bend a cube and return it to its initial state.

1. Draw a rectangular cube and increase its vertical segments.
2. Turn on "Auto Key" button below (it will be red).
3. Insert "50" instead of "0" inside the rectangular (picture 8).

Picture 9

4. Execute "Bend" instruction and insert "90" for "Angle" so that the object is bent.
5. Again, Insert "100" instead of "50".
6. In "Bend" instruction, insert "0" for "Angle".
7. Turn off "Auto Key" button.

8. Press "Play" button. You will see that your object bends and returns to vertical state (picture 10).

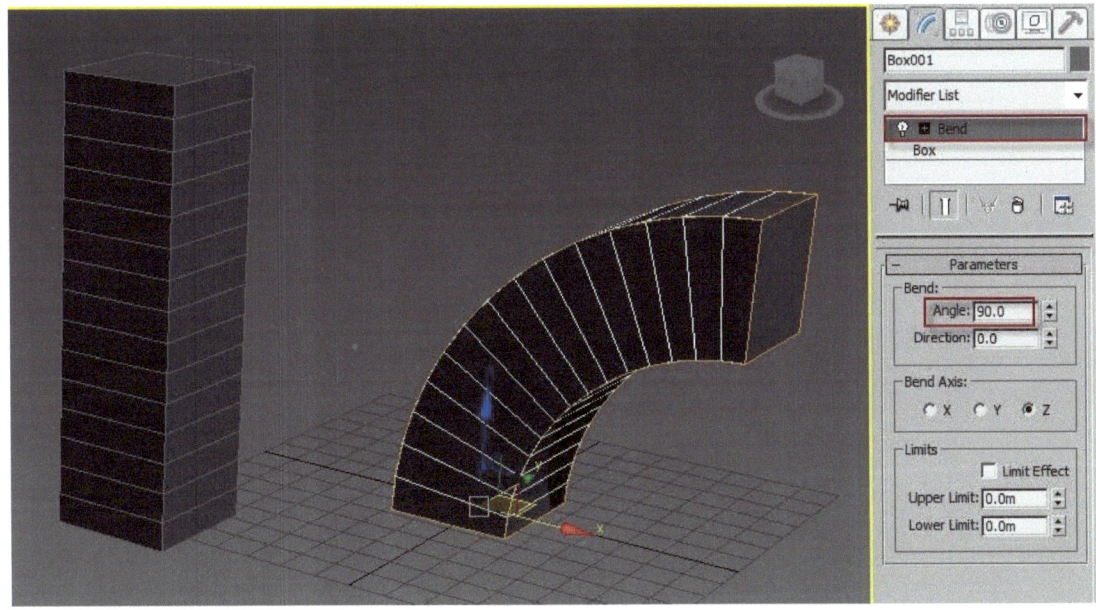

Picture 10

Knowing about the process and practically experiencing animation making, the related parts are described.

According to the following picture, numbers "0" to "100" indicating to duration of animations and frames are seen below of 3Ds Max plane. This is called "Track Bar". Each number is regarded a frame and every 25 frames is one second, i.e. you need 250 time frames to make a 10- second animation. The key where "0" and "100" are located over it is called "Time Slider" used for changing time and select the desired frame. Moving it, your animation will move. Instead of typing your frame number- instead of "0" on left hand- you can place your "Time Slider" on your desired frame (picture 11).

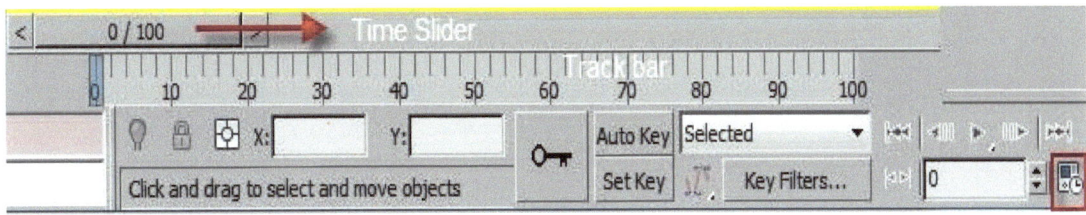

Picture 11

To change time of animation, press the clock-like icon located at right hand below. In the window, you can increase or decrease "End Time" (picture 12). Time management considering motions and variations of objectives is an important issue in making animations. Time should be managed in a way that animation is seen with a balanced speed. For example, it is better to move camera with a fixed speed in architectural animation and avoid from moving it slowly and fast (except to special occasions). Also, it is better to coordinate speed of camera movement with that of objects and other cases which will be known after acquiring experiences and making several animations.

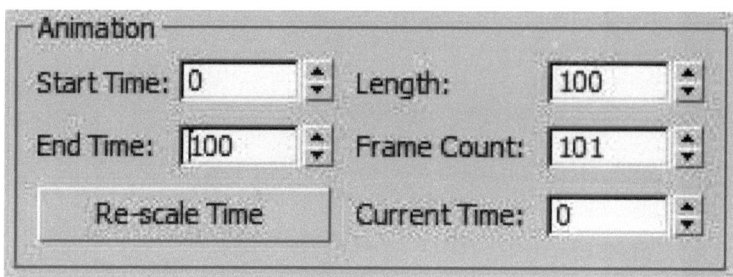

Picture 12

Until "Auto Key" button is not activated, you will be in a normal state of modeling in 3Ds Max. Once "Auto Key" button is selected, all your practices in 3Ds Max will be recorded in animation making system of the software. Thus, turn off the button when you do not want your variations being recorded in animation. According to previous instructions, time interval for the event which is going to happen to an object, camera, light, etc. should be specified in making animation. In other words, you should specify your frame below before exercising any instruction or change. Once "Auto Key" button is activated, any changes, for example, in volume parameter will be saved in the software memory on the frame.

For example, in instruction 4 (please review stages 3 and 4), 90° variations of "Angle" is recorded in frame 50 and a black square appears on "50" indicating to changing of the object on that time. Of course, bending of the object was began from "0" and reaches to 90° bend in frame number 50 through gradual bending.

- **Instruction 5** (making animation using Wave instruction)

1. Draw a plan with 40*40 segments.
2. Select "Wave" from "Modify" menu and exercise following values according to the picture.
3. Turn on "Auto Key" button and put "Time Slider" on frame 100.
4. Put "Phase" (indicating to number of movements of the wave and varying from "Minimum" to "Maximum") on "4". (Picture 14)
5. Turn off "Auto Key" button and press "Play" button.

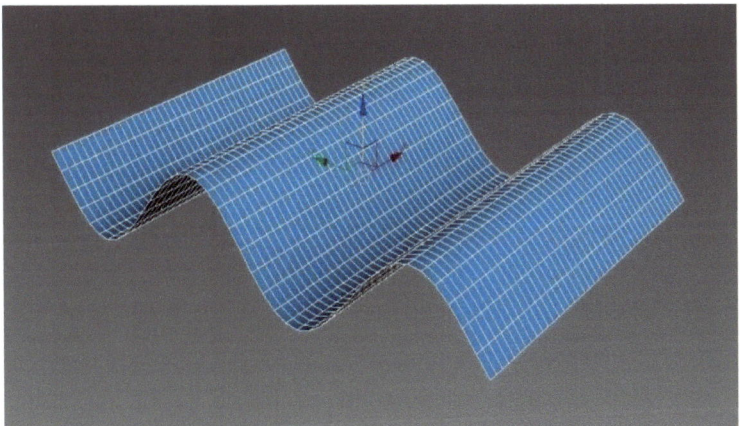
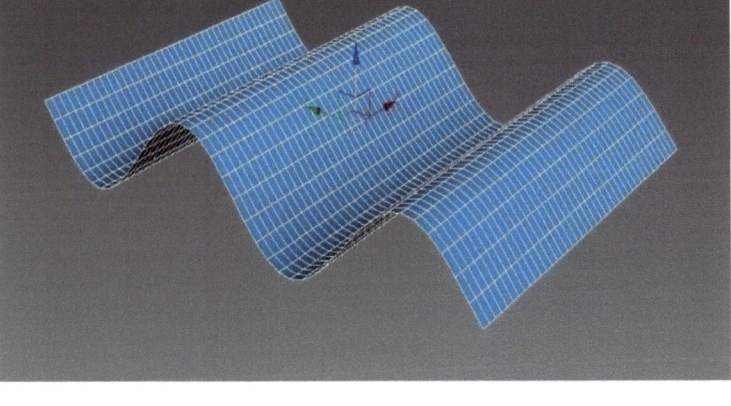

Picture 13- Wave   Picture 14>

The drawn plane will vary in form of wave movement and produces different structures which is worthy to be studied from form and spatial viewpoint. This is of initial instructions of 3Ds Max software and most architectural users know it. However, less people know about its capability to design an architectural volume. After construction of buildings such as Paul Klee museum by Renzo Piano in 2005 in Bern, Switzerland, and other buildings, attention of the architects working on parametric design was attracted to capabilities of this instruction more than ever (picture 15).

Picture 15: Paul Klee museum by Renzo Piano, adapted from http://fineartamerica.com

Infinite pictures or renders obtained from a wavy plane during making an animation is really important. The pictures play an important role in better recognition of location of turning point of arches, their contact with earth and other cases affecting more accurate design of the project. The following pictures show wavy plane transformation in the instruction 5 (Picture 16).

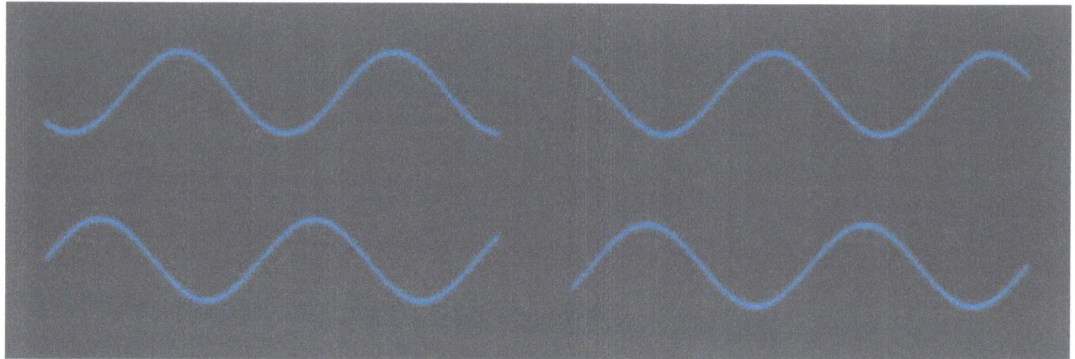

Picture 16

Stimulating designer's curiosity is a special feature of 3D software. It provides conditions where designers are encouraged to obtain more experiences. While I was placing previous pictures, it occurred to me to combine the curves. An interesting result was obtained, an idea to design view of the buildings where you can create various samples through moving Time Slider. It will consume significant time if they are drawn manually or using computer (picture 17).

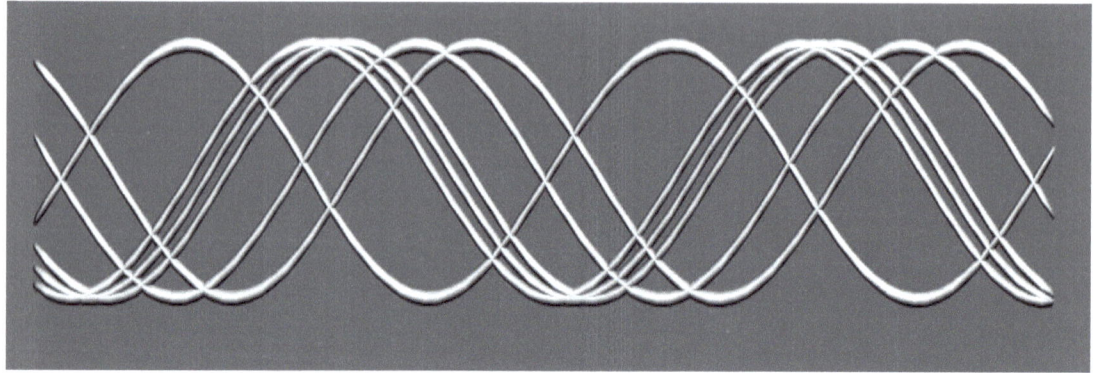

Picture 17

Instruction 6

At first, we should know how to use "Twist" instruction (picture 18):

1. Draw a cube with several segments and select "Twist" from "Modify" menu.
2. Increasing "Angle", the object will turn around itself.
3. Selecting X, Y and Z axis, you can change turning direction of the object.

In these experiences, we try to create a new structure from inside of the cube, a structure indicating to form and spatial power of the cube in changing to a new structure (Picture 19) (Khiabanian, 2012).   Picture 18- Twist >

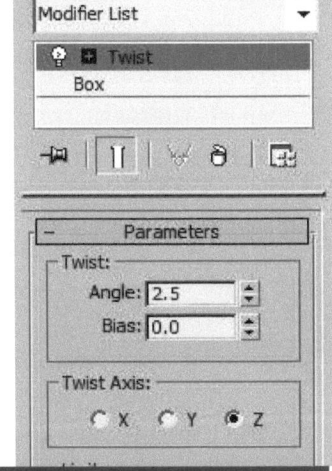

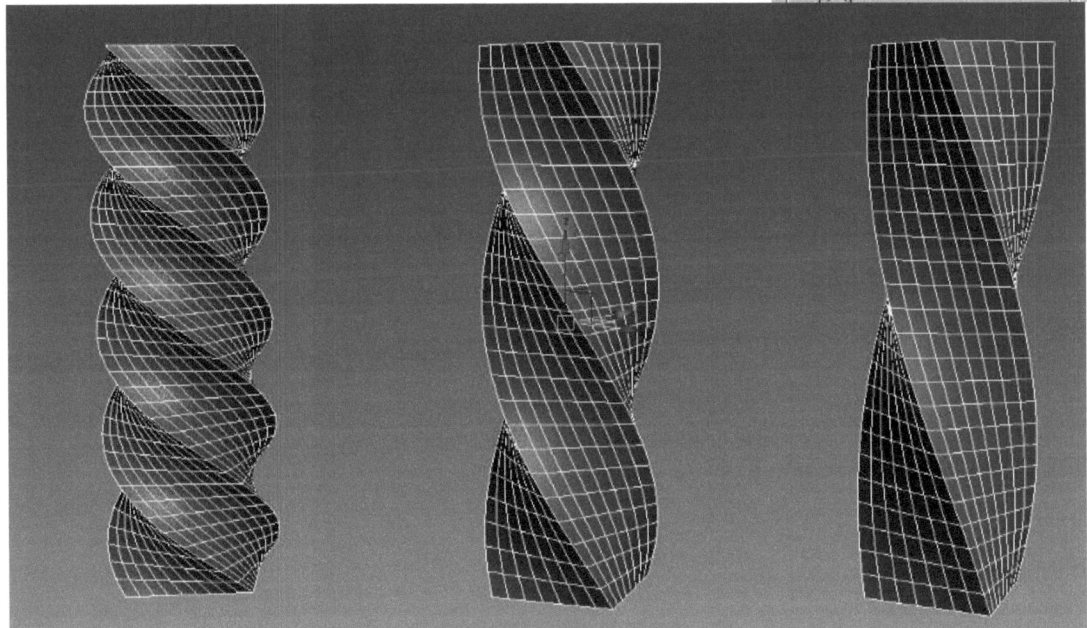

Picture 19

To make cube turning animation, you can change "Angle" after specifying the frame. Pressing "Play" button, the cube will begin to turn and will take states similar to what is seen in the above picture. Increasing or decreasing the turning angle, you can temporarily see possible states of cube transformation. However, parametric variations are recorded when the animation in made and you can review and study them for several times.

Lavasan Pedestrian Bridge

Lavasan pedestrian bridge is another example of using or at least effect of "Twist" instruction in design. This 49m bridge was designed by Hoor Architecture Office. Eng. Amir Taleshi was the responsible architect and Ms. Leili Abedini and Ms. Shadi Khakbaz were of colleagues of the plan. It is a creative design executed well by Saber Kooshan Atieh Company (Picture 20, taken by Mohammad Dehghani).

Picture 20

At present, strong effect and presence of software in all design fields is undeniable and more samples may be discussed in this regard. However, there is an important issue, i.e. attribute of designers to facilities and mental structure of software and programmers. How a simple instruction originating from a creative mind may serve as inspiration source of most designers. Unfortunately, most architects look at software as a tool to design and three dimensional modeling of their mental imaginations or architectural models. There are few architects began their design using computers, think with computers, and let the computers to challenge their mind. We should accept computers as our colleagues and like-minded in design offices, as a person who has its own ideas or at least as a person communicating with whom may provide us with new and applied ideas, forms, and structures. Such function of design, making complex architectural works, advancement of technology, appearance of 3D printers and, the last but the most important, recording and codifying of parametric design in the recent decade which granted a special nobility to digital designers and users (as believed by the author) have prepared architecture offices and architects' mind to accept digital colleagues more than ever.

We come back to design technique of pedestrian bridges. Parametric design was used in both bridges where a rectangular cube turned because of changing of angle and created a new structure.

However, an animate look to these forms results in their development and variety, on one hand, and springs to mind that the structure can move and transform gradually, on another hand. For example, each white square indicates to passing of 3600 persons over the bridge, the bridge turns 10° after passing of 100 persons, and the second square turns after complete turning of each square. (Picture 21)

Picture 21

Or different forms of turning which may be programmed and transform the bridge gradually. (It is noteworthy that showing the pictures and expressing the ideas do not mean the projects criticize. Rather, it aims at stating facilities and capabilities provided to us by software). (Picture 22)

- Another idea springs to mind is movement of layers or frames over each other. In other words, main structure may remain fixed in Lavasan Bridge and only a square frame with a distance from the main structure rotate over it.
- The square frames may move and/or their thickness may vary.

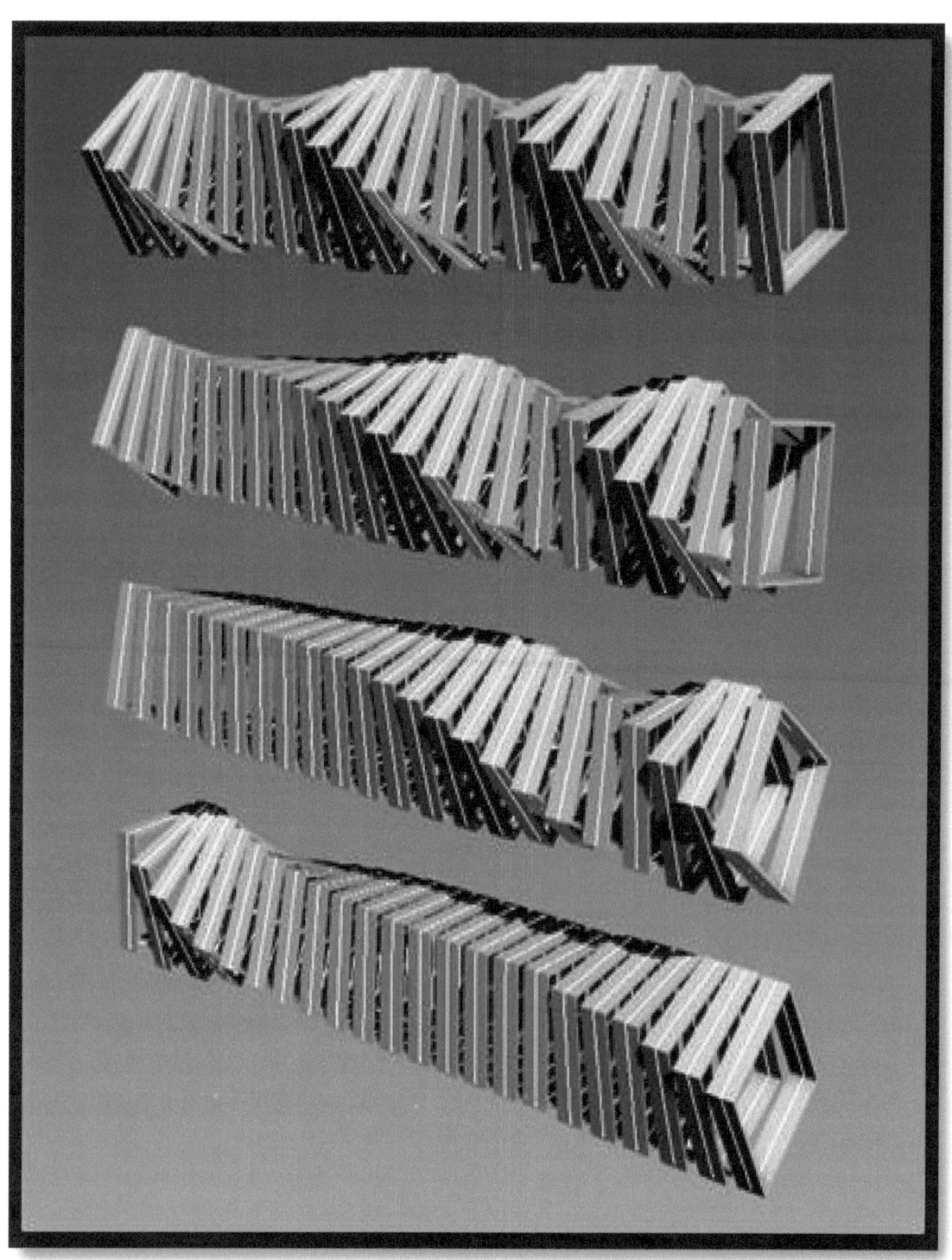

Picture 22

Animate design is developed process of parametric design

As observed, animate design is developed form of parametric design or recording of all parametric variations of the object which may be represented (the made animation may be seen for several times):
- Recording form state from movement, turning, rotation, and changing of dimensions to transformation to complex volumes and forms
- Recording light geographical location and intensity variations
- Recording of variation of intensity and transformation created over form and space by different forces
- And other cases created due to changing of values (parameter) and recording of these pictures and data such as length of shade, depth of light penetration, and dimensions of windows which will be referred more will be really helpful in design process.

The enthusiasts may study "Creativity in Architectural Design Process III" book and become familiar with parametric design and theories of Patrick Schumacher- partner and colleague of Zaha Hadid - and instructions and modifiers of 3Ds Max which make design and drawing of complex and curved volumes possible (Picture 23 shows sample of forms moved in "Creativity III" book designed using animate design method).

Picture 23

- **Instruction 7**

    (Making animation using "Edit Poly" instruction)

"Edit Poly" instruction contains several commands to change form, an important instruction used to draw machine, face, and make architectural complex volumes. To begin, draw a plane. Then, go to "Modify" menu and execute "Edit Poly" instruction.

According to the picture, if you open "(+)" at left hand of "Edit Poly", five words will be appeared (Picture 24). They make it possible for us to select different parts of the volume, move or rotate them. For example, if you choose "Vertex", you can select points and if you use "edge", you can select segments over the volumes. According to the following picture, you can use "Vertex" to select angles of the drawn plane and move it upwards. Your plane will transform. It can be done on segments inside the plane or on other objects (picture 25, 26).

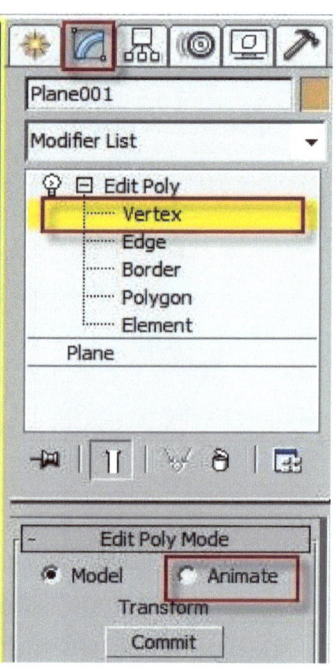

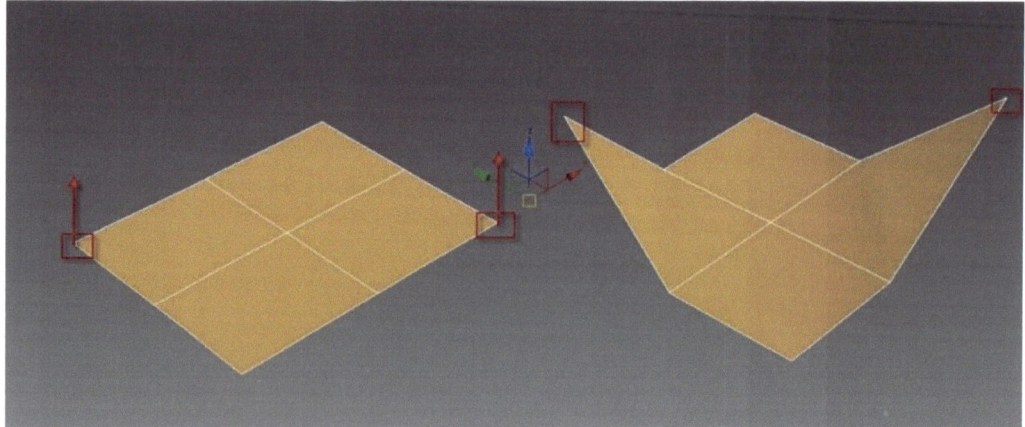

Picture 25

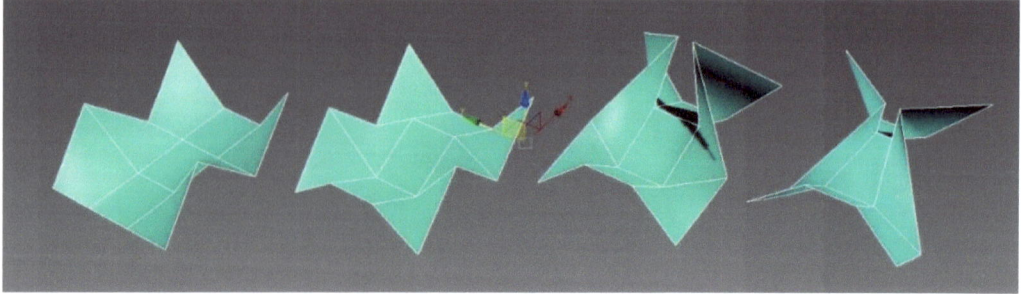

Picture 26

"Edit Poly" makes it possible for designers to deal with the volume as a plastic and transformable material and exercise their imagines of form and space over the volumes.

After practicing, this time we will design using animate technique. In other words, superficial variations will be recorded in form of animation. At first, tick "Animate" according to the picture. Then, turn on "Auto Key" button and place "Time Slider" on 100. Begin design and move or rotate the points and segments on plane. Finally, press "Play" button. You will observe changing of a surface to a broken volume. You can verify the variations from up, left, and right views, too. Then, you can select your desired volume occurred in a specific frame and complete it. Following picture shows four frames from opposite view of the animation made for final volume of the previous picture. (Picture 27)

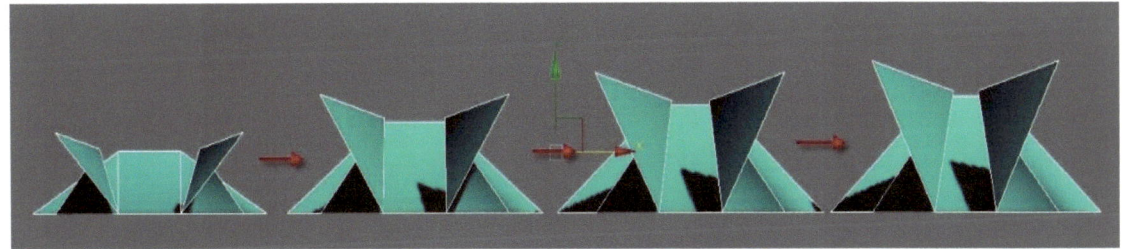

Picture 27

Note: In animate design, computerized design and modeling is based on the assumption that form lacks a static structure and the form and space may essentially move, vary and evolve.

Picture 28, 29 & 30 are another samples of design and evolution process of two parallel surfaces. Evidently, these practices and obtaining different experiences in this regard will direct us to a better and eminent understanding of form and space and its relation with time and mere theoretical study will not be useful.

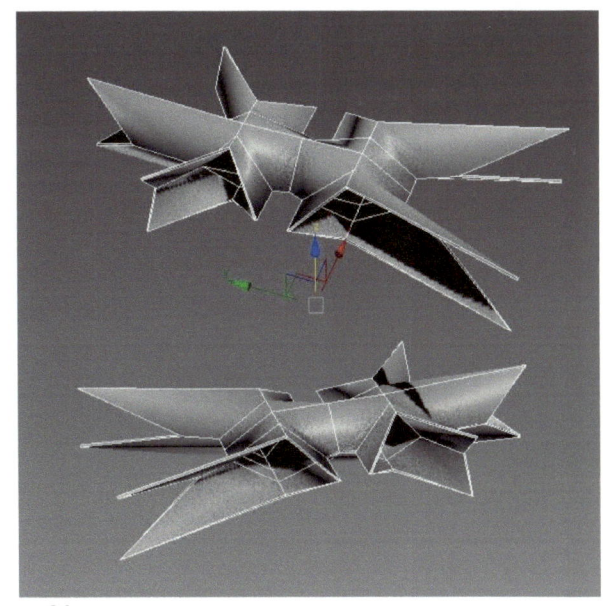

Picture 28 >

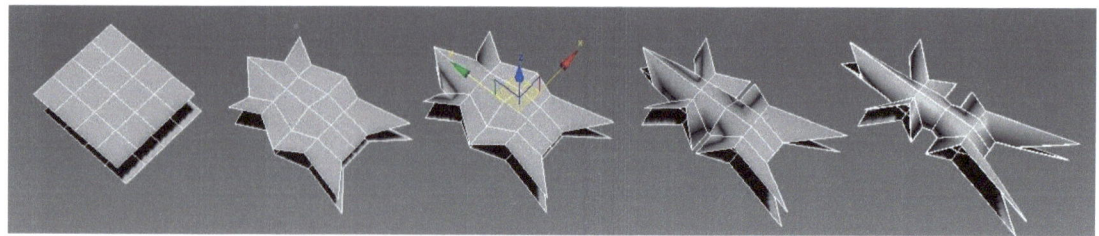

Picture 29

Picture 30

What will be mentioned in this book is only a sample of events happed or may happen in digital design process. A parametric and animate attitude to structure of software and animate design in digital world may reveal most hidden and ambiguous aspects of nature and function of form and space against ideas, technology, new materials, etc. and will direct us to consciously enter future.

Next two pages show samples of form animate for museum design. Twenty-one frames/renders were selected from 400 renders of opposite view and indoor space. Full animations of this form and other forms of the book as well as parametric and animate design trainings may be observed at **YouTube channel of the author "Ali Khiabanian"**.

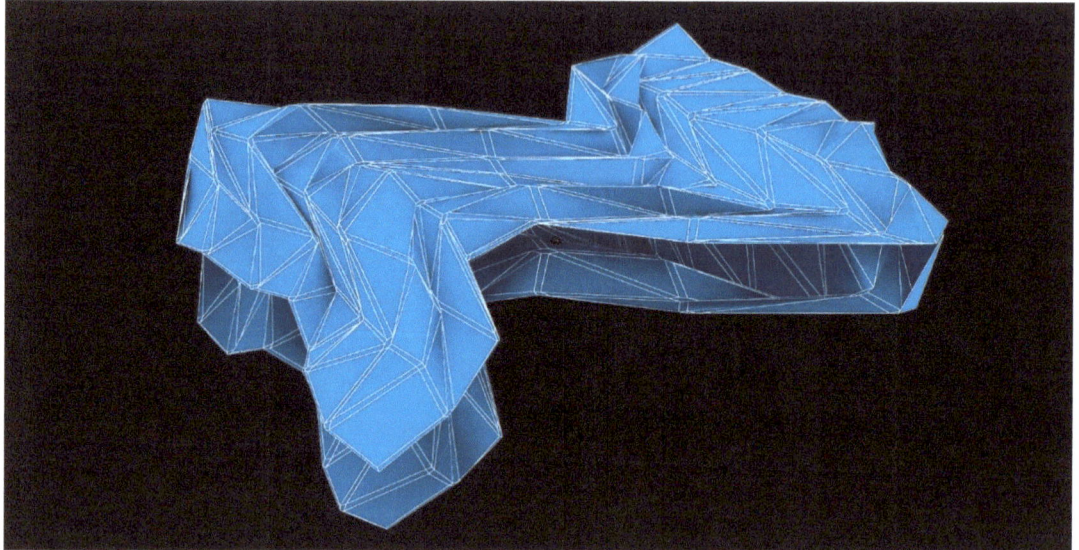

Picture 31 - (The original designed volume its structure and form will be changed in next pictures).

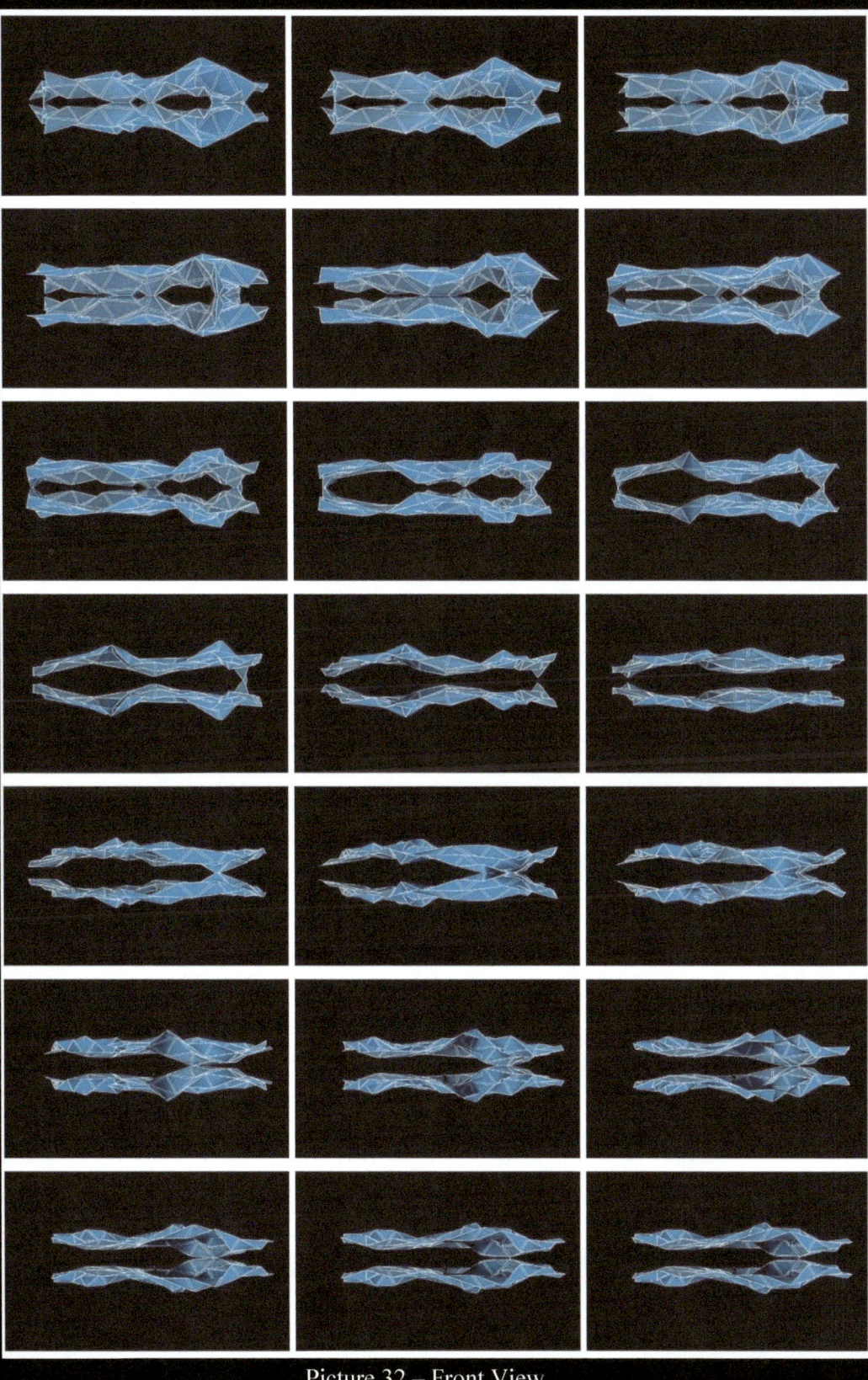

Picture 32 – Front View

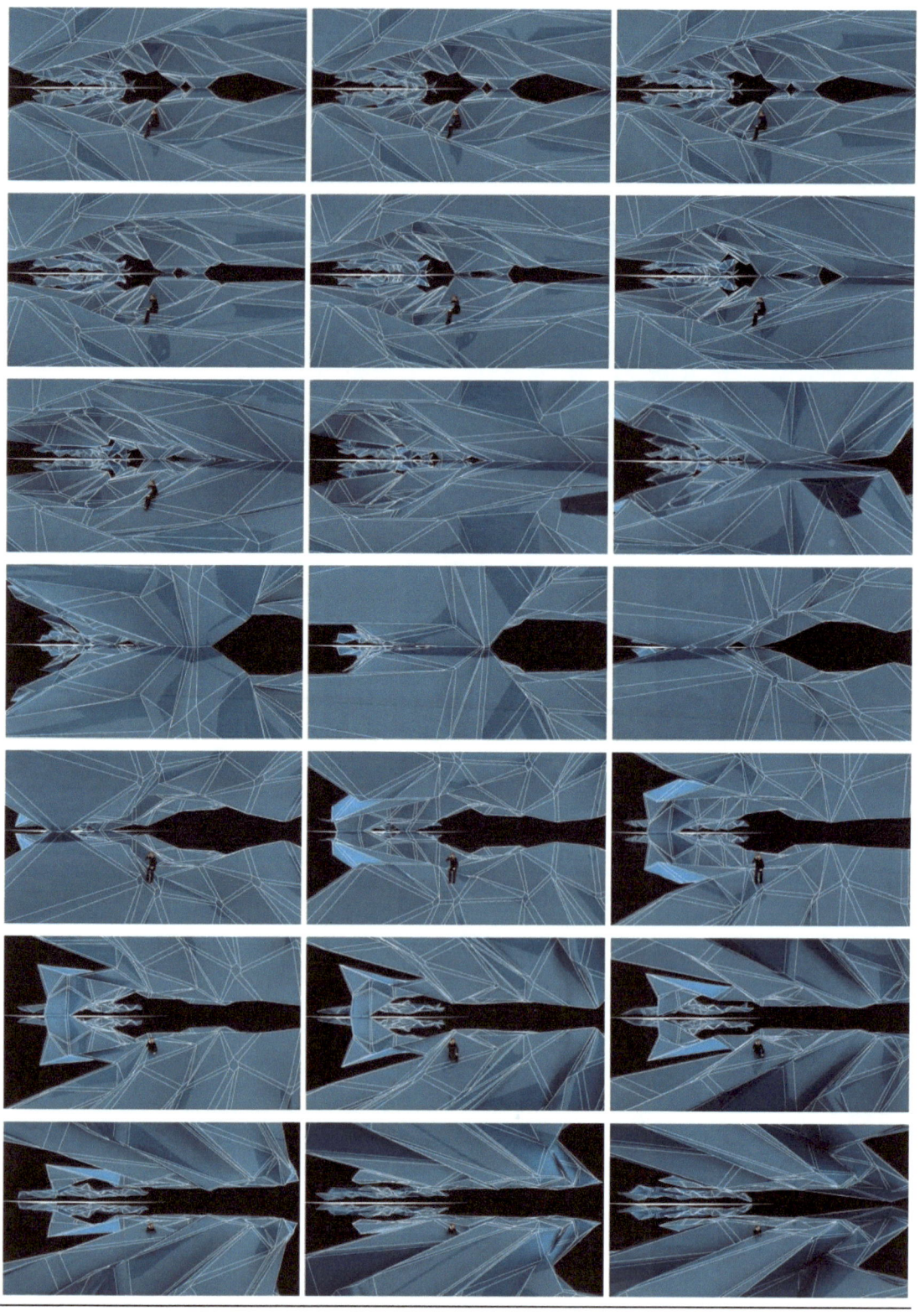

Picture 33 – Interior Renders

Magnification of some final frames of the animation

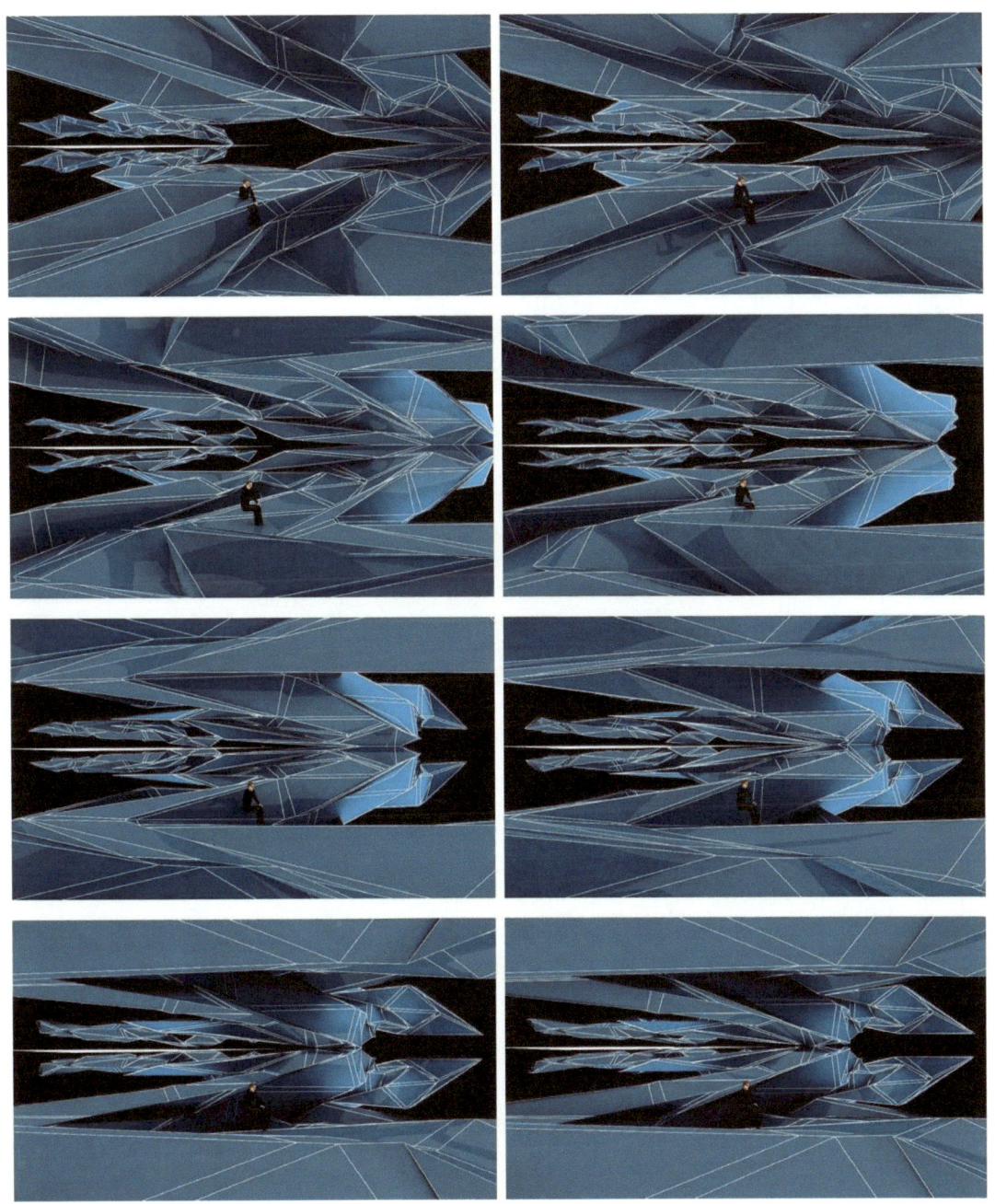

Picture 34

How to Save Animation

To save the animation as a movie, press "F10" button and select "Active Time Segment" in Common Parameters> Time Output" address (picture 35). To save the animation in a specific time interval, you can record animation start and end frame number in "Range".

It may be defined at "Every Nth Frame" where, for example, your animation will render every other five frames.

In next stage, you should specify dimensions of render plane. Select "HDTV" at "Output Size" and fix its dimensions on "1280*720".

Then, a destination and suffix should be introduced to save the animation. Press "Files" at "Render Output" and type your desired drive and name to save the animation and choose "AVI" suffix at "Save as type" section and press "Render Button" (picture 36).

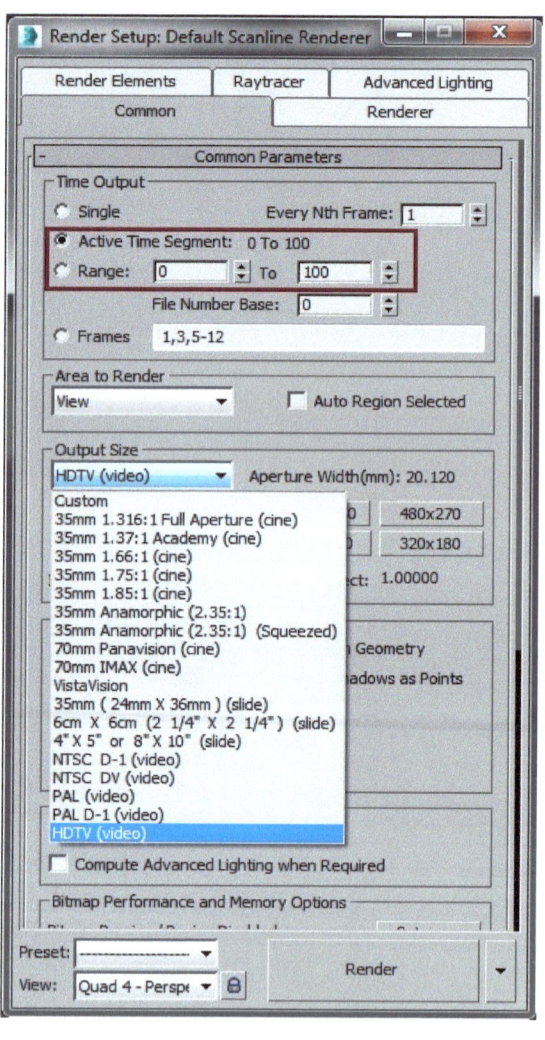

Picture 35

Your animation file will be saved as a movie and may be played by "Media Player".

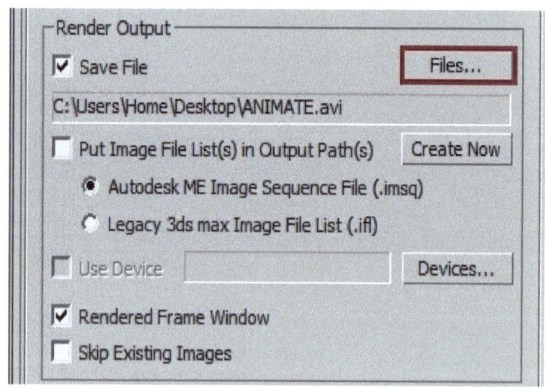

Picture 36

Define a Specific Trajectory for Camera Motion

- First, draw your trajectory for the object or space where the camera will turn.
- After choosing the camera, go to "trajectory constraint <constraints <animation".
- There will appear a dashed line. Using it, you can choose your desired trajectory.
- "Motion" will be opened at right hand of the plane. At "Parameters" section, you can use "Pick Target" to choose the object around which the camera target should rotate. (In such case, the camera target will not move. However, when the selected object is moved, the camera target will also move). (picture 37)
- To move the camera target, you can define a trajectory for it, i.e. select end of the camera, go to "Animation" menu, and complete the above-mentioned stages.
- To change the trajectory, you can refer to "Edit Spline". Your trajectory will transform and the camera will move according to the same variations through select the vertexes and moving them.

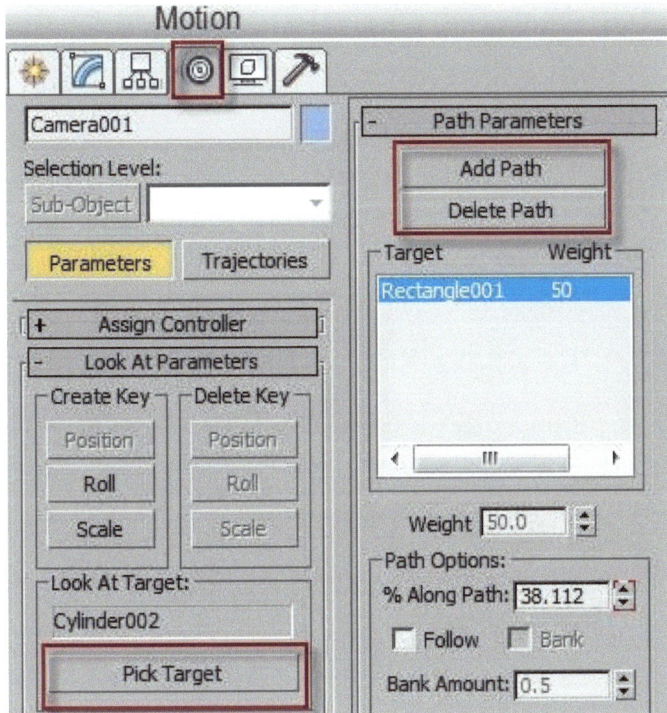

< Picture 36

- To define a new trajectory, select target or time variations of start of the camera and go to "Motion > Parameters > trajectory Parameters > Add Trajectory", according to the picture.
You are recommended to clean the last trajectory and then introduce the new trajectory using "Add Trajectory". The camera target may be moved using "Pick Target".
- You can define start point of camera motion through putting "Time Slider" on zero and changing "Along trajectory" value.
- In "Motion> Trajectories" we can use frames numbers to define the camera in a way that it passes only specific part of trajectory, for example, from frame 50 to 100. To do so, typewrite number of frames at "End Time" and "Start Time" sections. Increase "Samples" value to make camera trajectory and its motion speed more flexible. Then, press "Collapse" to see the variations.

Chapter 3

Animate Design

For better understanding of readers and offer a complete definition of animate design, this chapter was divided into six parts each of them add new concepts and points to the last definition. Unlike the usual, I avoided from presentation a comprehensive and concrete definition of the subject. Rather, I used a process which gradually adds to your perception and completes the initial definition according to "Animate Thinking" techniques (which will be referred to at end of the book).

Why animate design?

- This technique gives a new life to architectural design process like 3D printers and widens its perspective and limits of activity.

- Makes designer's thought more close to computer thought.

- Diversifies forma and space and creates more freedom of action and accuracy in plan and cross section design. Plans are not only 2D lines, rather they are walls with door and window where a designer move, controls it from different angles, changes dimensions of openings according to the space lightness and determines energy loss and depth of light penetration in spaces and during day and night.

- Makes production of new ideas which are beyond of imagination power of designer possible. They are achieved through animate thinking and interaction with computer.
- Makes it possible to being more proficient in design process and changes the object variation process (you can change or delete any desired parameters and instructions in a specific time-frame). For example, if an object in initially bent and then turns, you can prolong bending time of the object to occur concurrent with turning or after completion of turning.

- It will result in better understanding of time and quality of human presence in architectural space and his activity. With such recognition, better and more accurate decisions may be made in conformity of human and society and affect human soul with an accurate and more complete design.

- Animate design opens our eyes to a world of movement, variation and transformation and our surrounding and forms and spaces we encounter provide more possibility to convert or solve the problems.

- Animation helps to better describe and introduce conceptual and seemingly inapplicable plans.
- In a world where clouds move, trees shake, rivers run and everything is changing why we should look at form and space with a static thought. Our design method may serve like running of a river.

- using animation in presenting plans widens scope of vision of employer and provides a better understanding of the project.

First Part of Animate Design

We use pictures and movies to describe and understand animate design easily. When we design manually or by computer, the output will only be images (sequences) indicating to our form and space in different states, like pictures taken from different scenes of a movie. However, watching these pictures differs from watching the movie even if they are arranged carefully and we can know story of the movie. In the first step, animate design tries to connect designed forms (through using "Snapshot", "Morpher", etc.) or develop tools and techniques of designer to start design in form of making an animation. The technique is not only for architects and may be useful for all users, from sculptors to dress designers who use computers as much as used by architects.

An Introduction to "Snapshot"

It is a simple and applied instruction which makes passing from mental imagination to objective visualization easy and brings various ideas to design process and mind. "Snapshot" may be found in "Tools" menu at top row of 3Ds Max.

To begin, draw a rectangular cube. Place "Time Slider" on "100" and press "Auto Key" button. Then, move the rectangular cube in direction of "X" and rotate it around "Y" axis. Turn off "Auto Key" and execute "Snapshot". There will appear a table like the opposite picture. Choose "Range" option and enter, for example "10" as number of copies. This means that 10 objects will be created from transformation of rectangular cube from frame "0" to "100" (pictures 38 & 39, at the bottom).

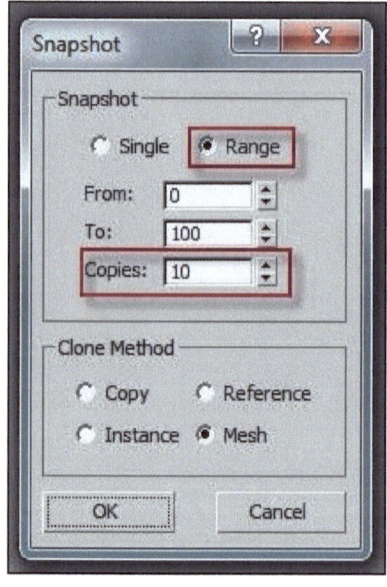
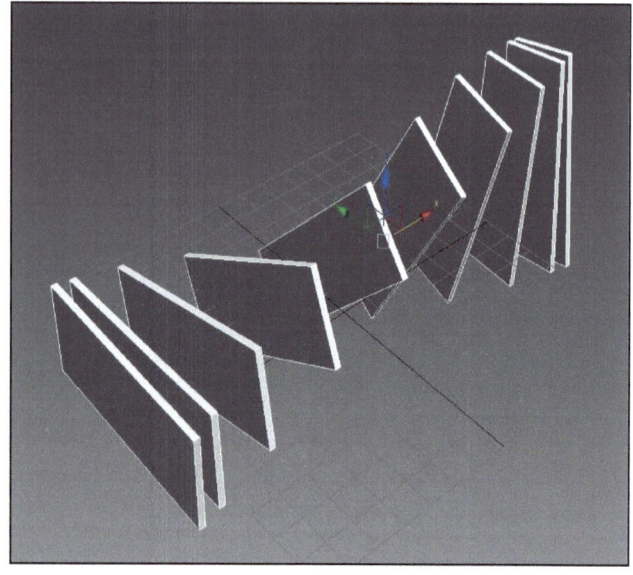

As seen, you introduce only two states of your desired volume to the software and the software fills the gap through creation of volumes which transform and gradually convert into final volume. Following example shows the original and final volumes where the original volume gradually transforms with the specified number and makes a complete structure.

Experience No.1

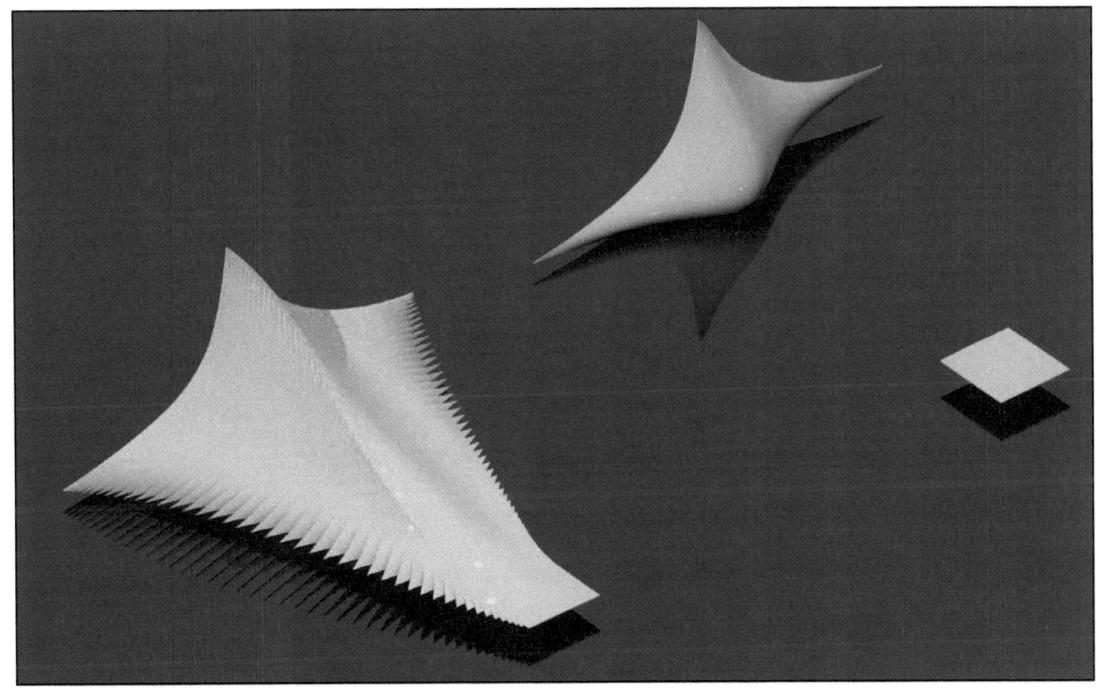

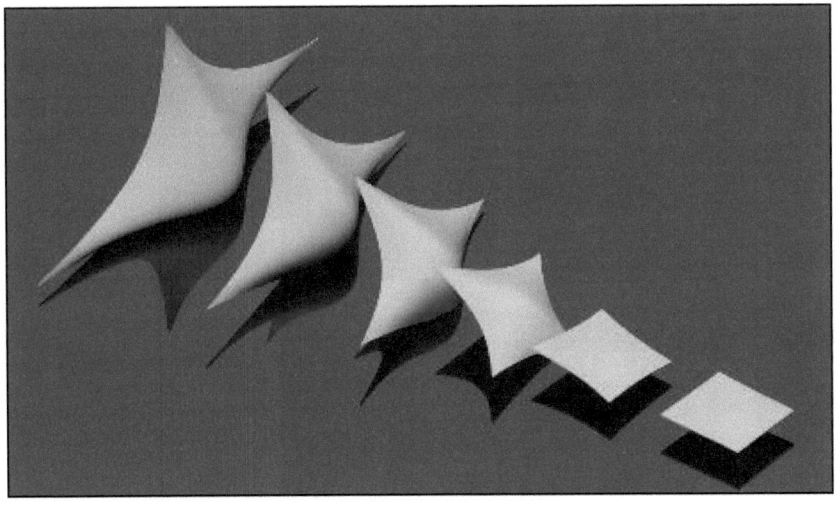

Pictures 40 & 41 of Experience No.1

Continuing the above practice- in experience No.2- we will fix the first volume and change the end volume. As seen, a different structure is made with normal variations.

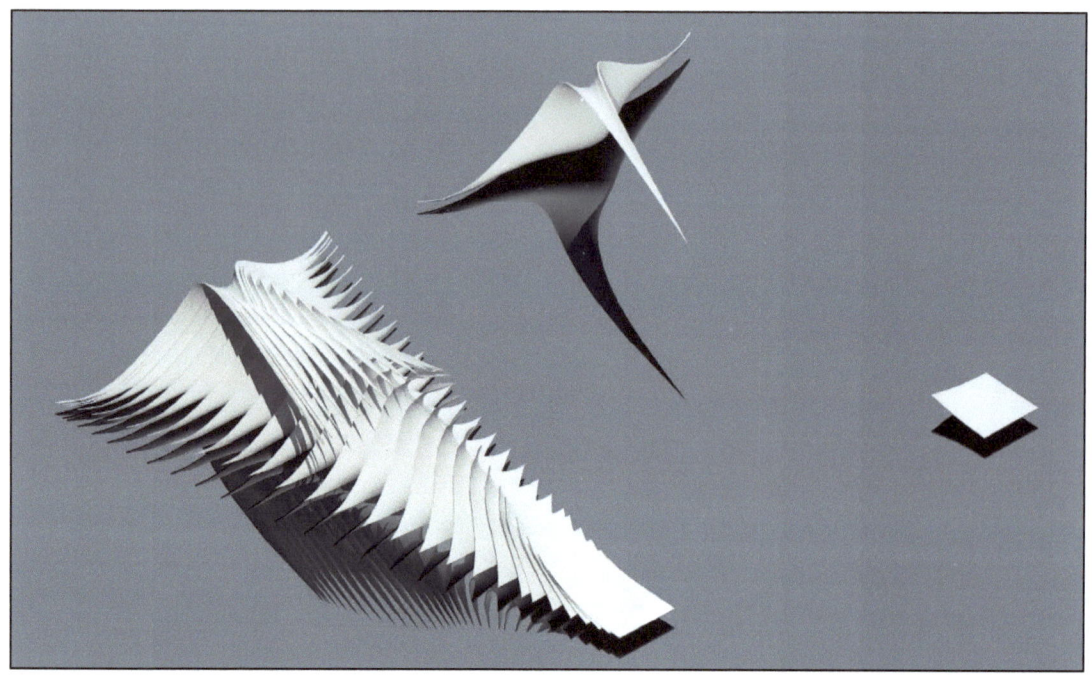

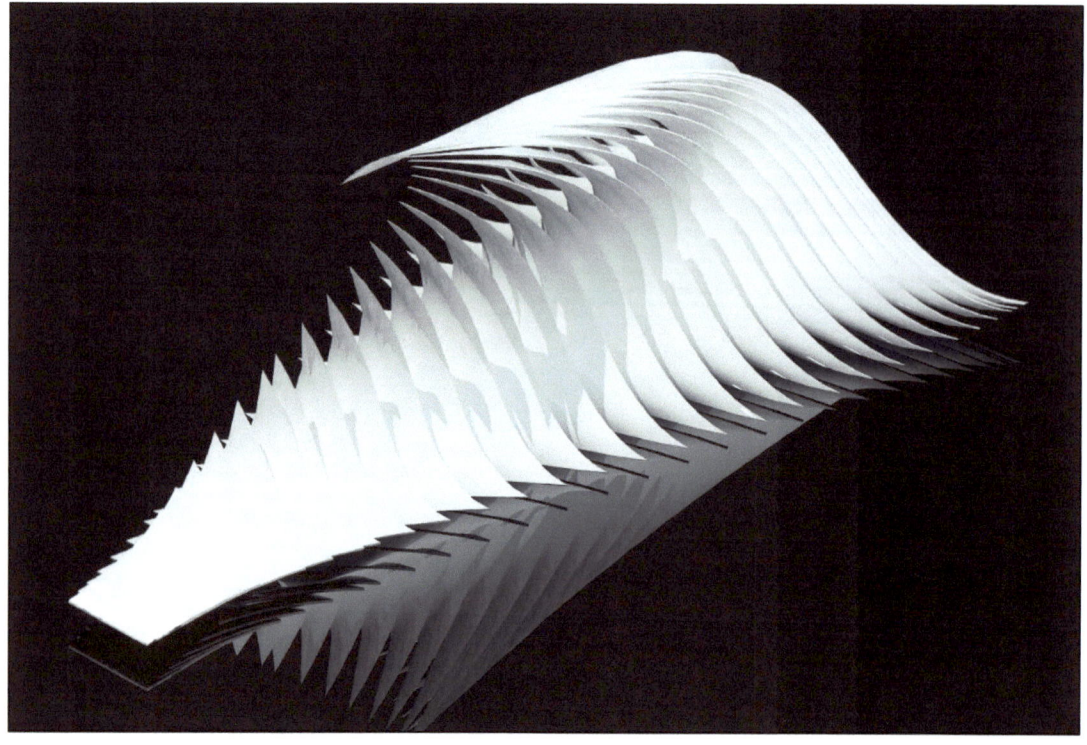

Pictures 42 & 43 of Experience No.2

Experience No.3

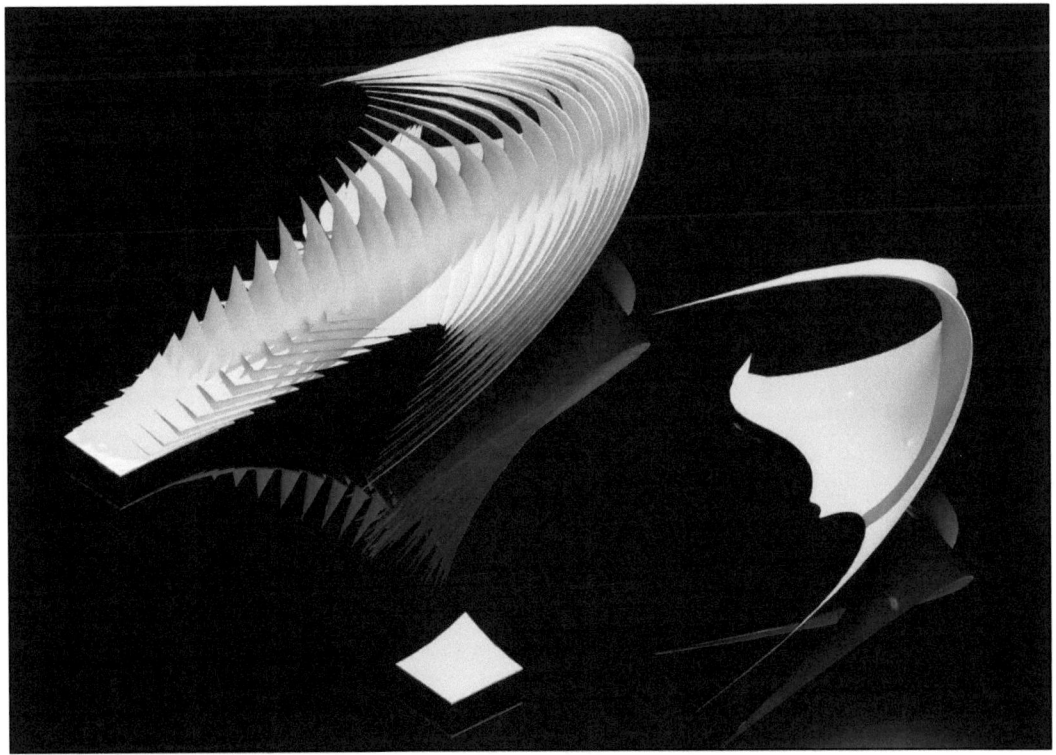

Pictures 44 & 45 of Experience No.3

Experience No.4

I confess that the volumes produced in these experiences were not imaginable even for the author before observation of final result.

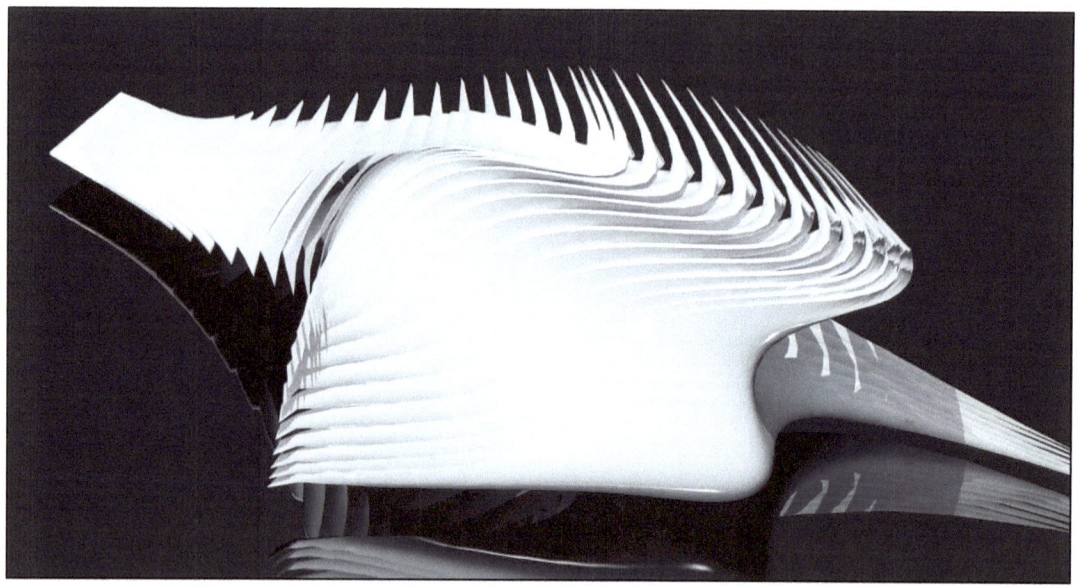

Pictures 46 & 47 of Experience No.4

This is a sample of a bench made by architecture students of University of Colombia in 2011which may be designed by "Snapshot" and use the cross sections required for cutting and making produced by 3Ds Max. (All pictures of the project, known as Polymorphic, may be visited at http://www.archdaily.com). (Pictures 48 & 49)

Picture 48

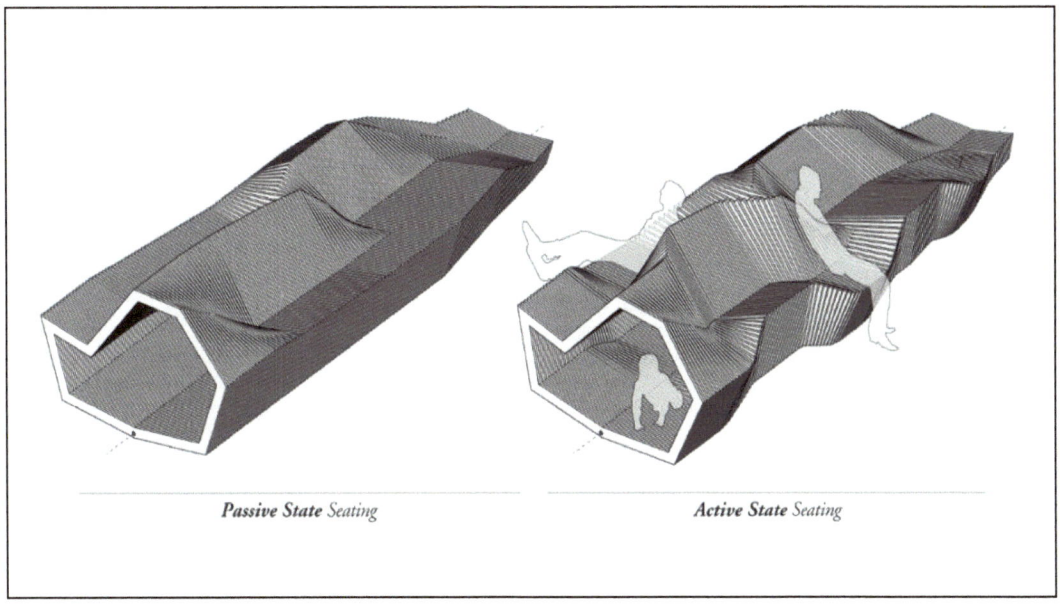

Picture 49

Animate Photography

I recommend you to look at works of Etienne Jules Marey for better understanding of "Snapshot". He was a French scientist experienced animate photography for the first time. Before innovation of video camera, a collection of pictures of motion, rotation, and dance of human and animals were produced or so called filmed in 1883. His video camera was like a gun where a long tube was used for its lenses and it had a circular treasure where the photographic glass was located. (Pictures 50 & 51)

Picture 51- (Pictures of human jump, by Etienne Jules Marey)

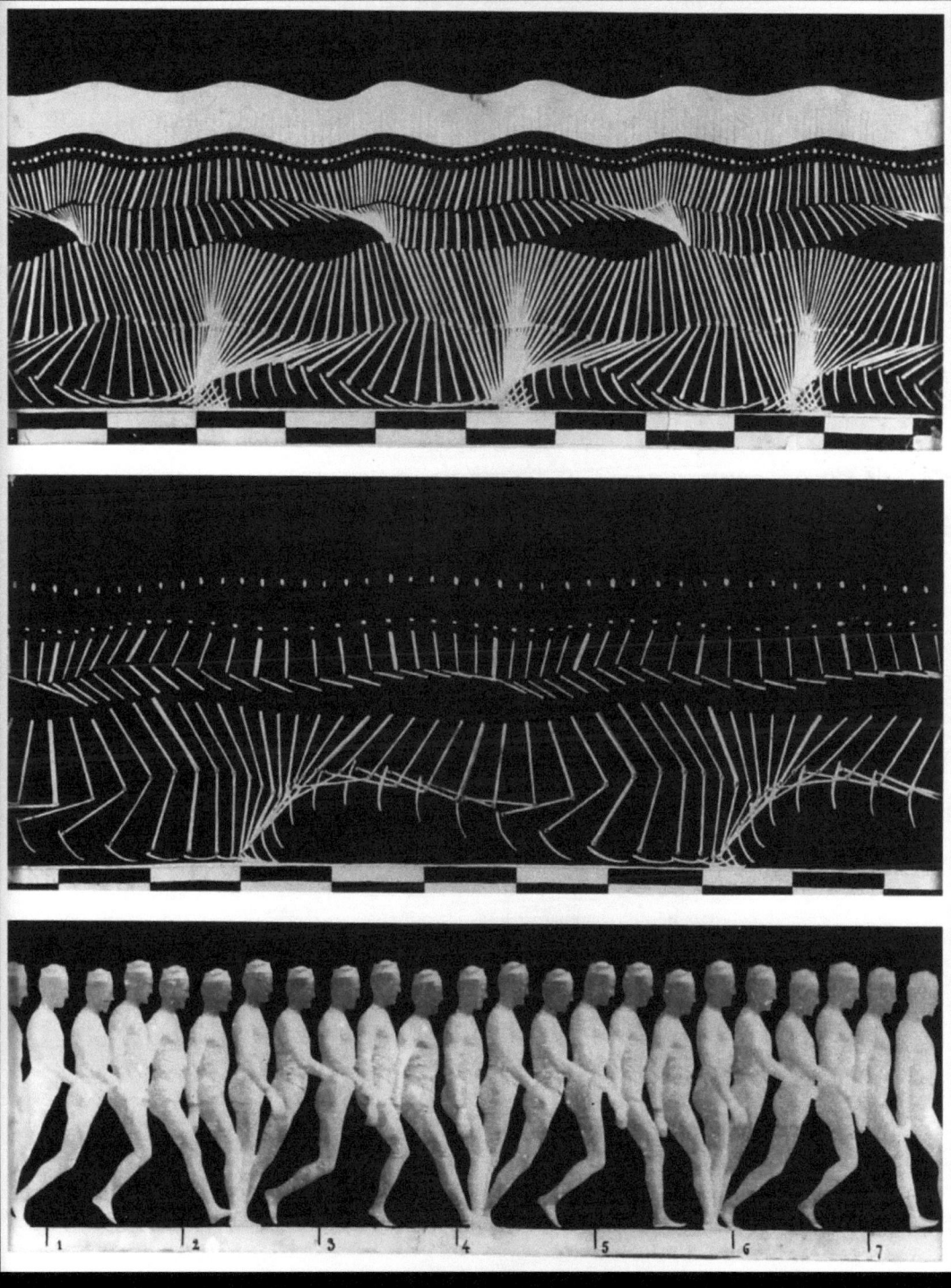

Picture 52 - (Pictures of walking man associated with pictures analysis, by Etienne Jules Marey)

Morpher

"Morph" means gradual and flexible change of an image to another using animation making techniques of computer. There are "Morphing" software and other online programs to transfer images. However, three-dimensional software such as 3Ds Max, FormZ and Maya make it possible to transfer images on volumes. The best manifestation of such transform may be seen in "Terminator II" where the spatial terminator and negative character of the film changes to different characters (Note: Software other than 3Ds Max was used in special effects and conversion of terminator).

To learn the process, draw a cube as the following picture, create two copies of it, and change the structure through moving angles of the cube using "Edit Poly" instruction. Define the first cube as the main one and two other cubes as the volumes to which it will be going to convert. An animation may be made from changing of structure of the main cube. (Picture 53)

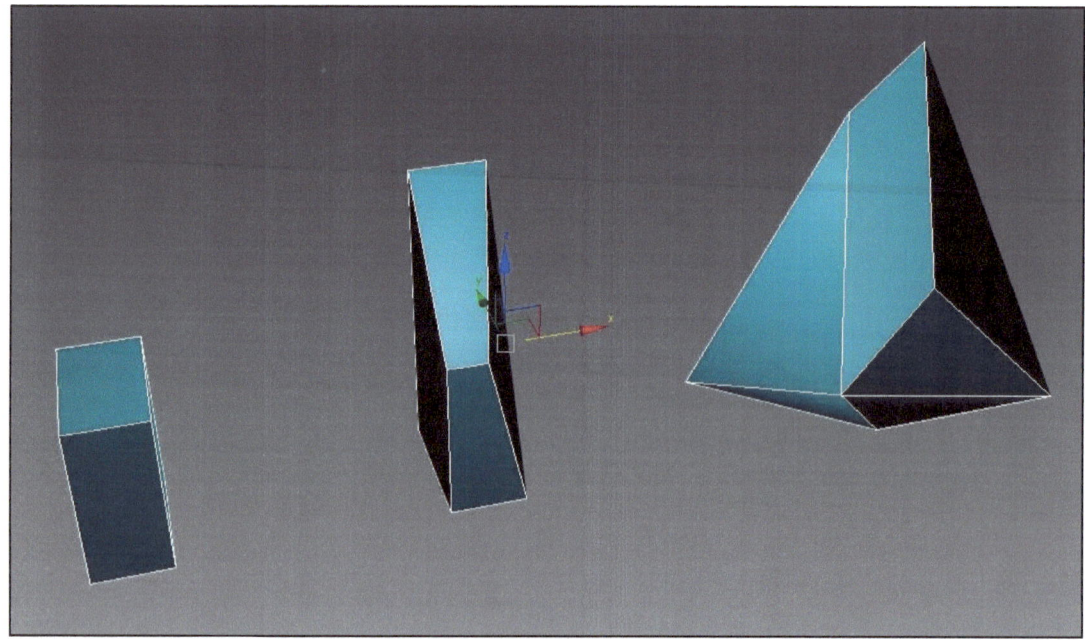

Picture 53

Do the following steps in order:
- Select the first cube and execute "Morph" instruction from "Modify" menu.
- Press "Capture Current State" button as seen in the picture.
- Typewrite name of the volume or a number like 1 in the opened window.
- The word "Empty" seen in the picture will be changed to your typewritten name.
- Then, select "Empty" (below the name you entered).

- Choosing "Pick Object from Scene", select the second volume. You can introduce the third volume to the modifier in this way. Name of your volumes will be recorder instead of the words "Empty". (Picture 54)

- Changing number which is seen opposite the volumes' name, your main volume will transform. Using this process, you can make an animation of transform.

"Morpher" is an important modifier converting different broken volumes or the curves with equal segments, in spite of its limitations.

Imaging and evaluating middle forms created through changing of a form to another is an important issue.

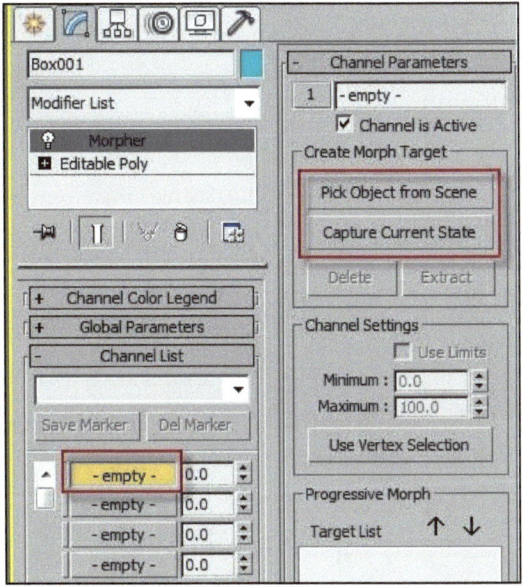

Picture 54

The author believes that appearing of such modifier is based on animate thinking as thinking about conversion, changing and evolution of volumes made the author eager to search such facilities in different software. There are different instructions and modifiers ignored by the architects during the years and now the designers turn to it and use facilities of computers more than ever due to changing of their attitude including paying attention to gradual evolution and motion.

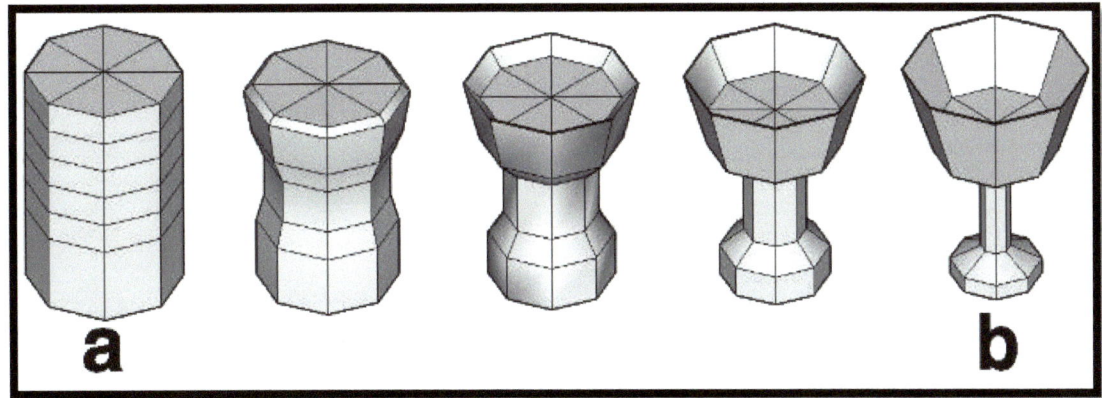

Picture 55 - An example of transform and making of a glass using FormZ software (http://www.formz.com)

Mcloth

It is very effective technique to affect or influence a form on another form. Flattening a bedcover on a bed is a simple example of this technique. In this technique, the form will be used flexibly and finely as a bedcover or cloth flattened on bed or dining table where it transforms as the bed or table or in form of objects found on the table.
Training Steps of Mcloth
1. Draw a plane with 50*50 segments. The more the segments, the more flexible your surface and the more fine and beautiful the final form. We begin with these segments to prevent from heaviness of the file and time prolongation.
2. Draw a sphere and place it beneath the rectangular surface. (Picture 56)

3. Select the plane and choose "Mcloth" instruction from "Modify" menu, according to the picture. (Picture 57)
4. Select the sphere and choose "MassFxRBody" instruction from "Modify" menu, according to the picture. (Picture 58)

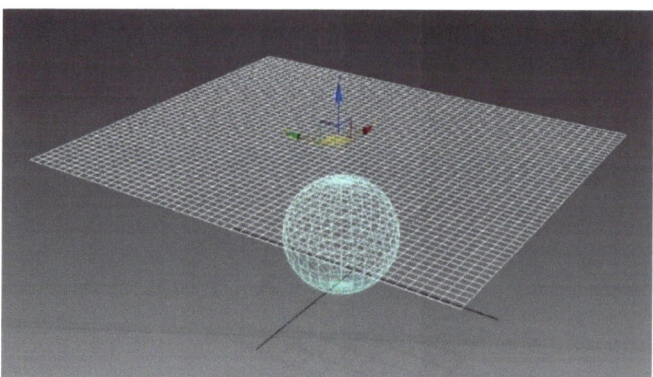

Picture 56

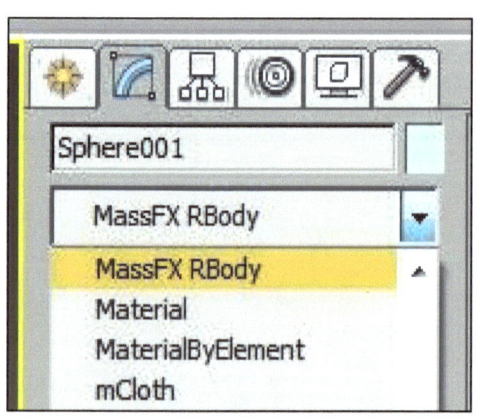

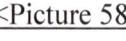

Picture 57>

<Picture 58

5. Stand under "Modify" symbol and click right. Select "MassFx Toolbar" in the opened menu so that the toolbar required to work with MassFx appears. Select the first option of left hand in the toolbar to appear a new toolbar menu, i.e. "MassFx Tools". Select "Hammer" symbol (Simulation Tools) according to the picture to open "Simulation" folder. (Picture 59)

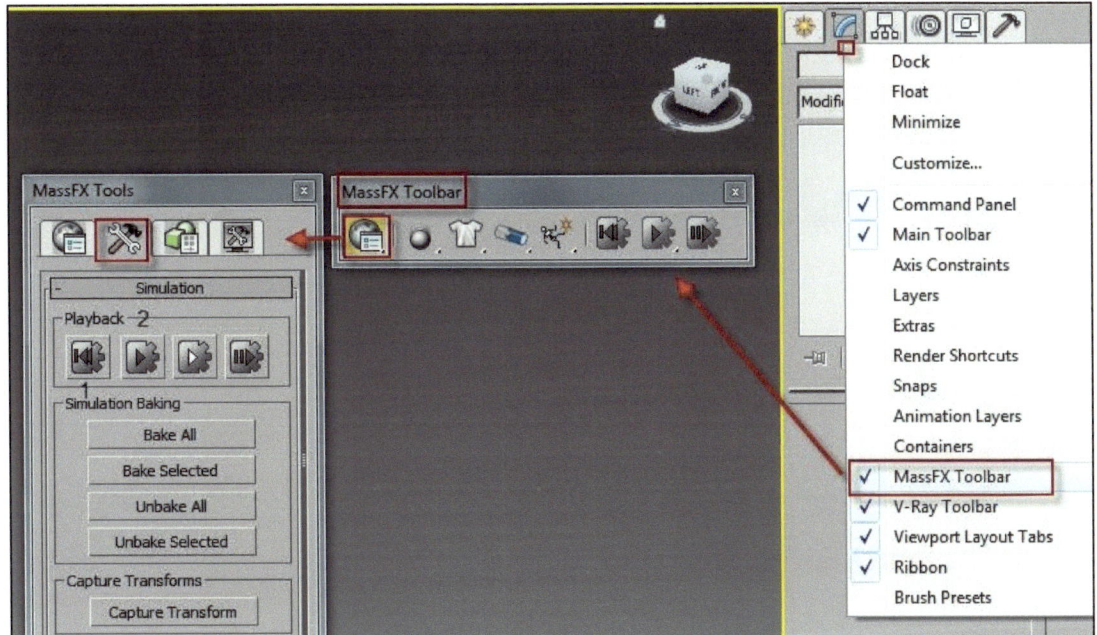

Picture 59

6. If the mentioned steps are taken correctly, your plan will begin to move through touching "Play" (Start Simulation) No.2 in picture of the step 5.
When it clashes with the sphere, it will transform like a cloth. It will take a sphere form if there are more segments. (Picture 60)

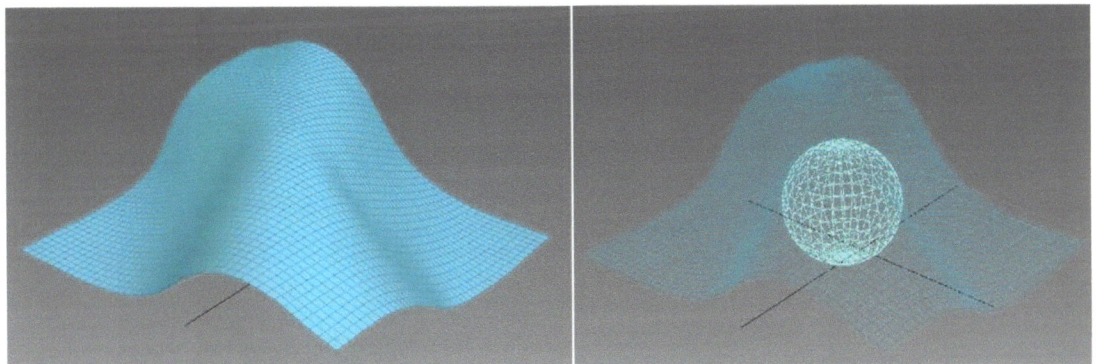

Picture 60

7. Use No.1 (Reset Simulation) to return the first state.
 8. Finally, to make an animation, press "Bake All" button and wait.
9. Remember that click "Play" on right hand angle of 3Ds Max plane to see the made animation.
10. You can use other objects instead of plane and more spheres or objects instead of one sphere.

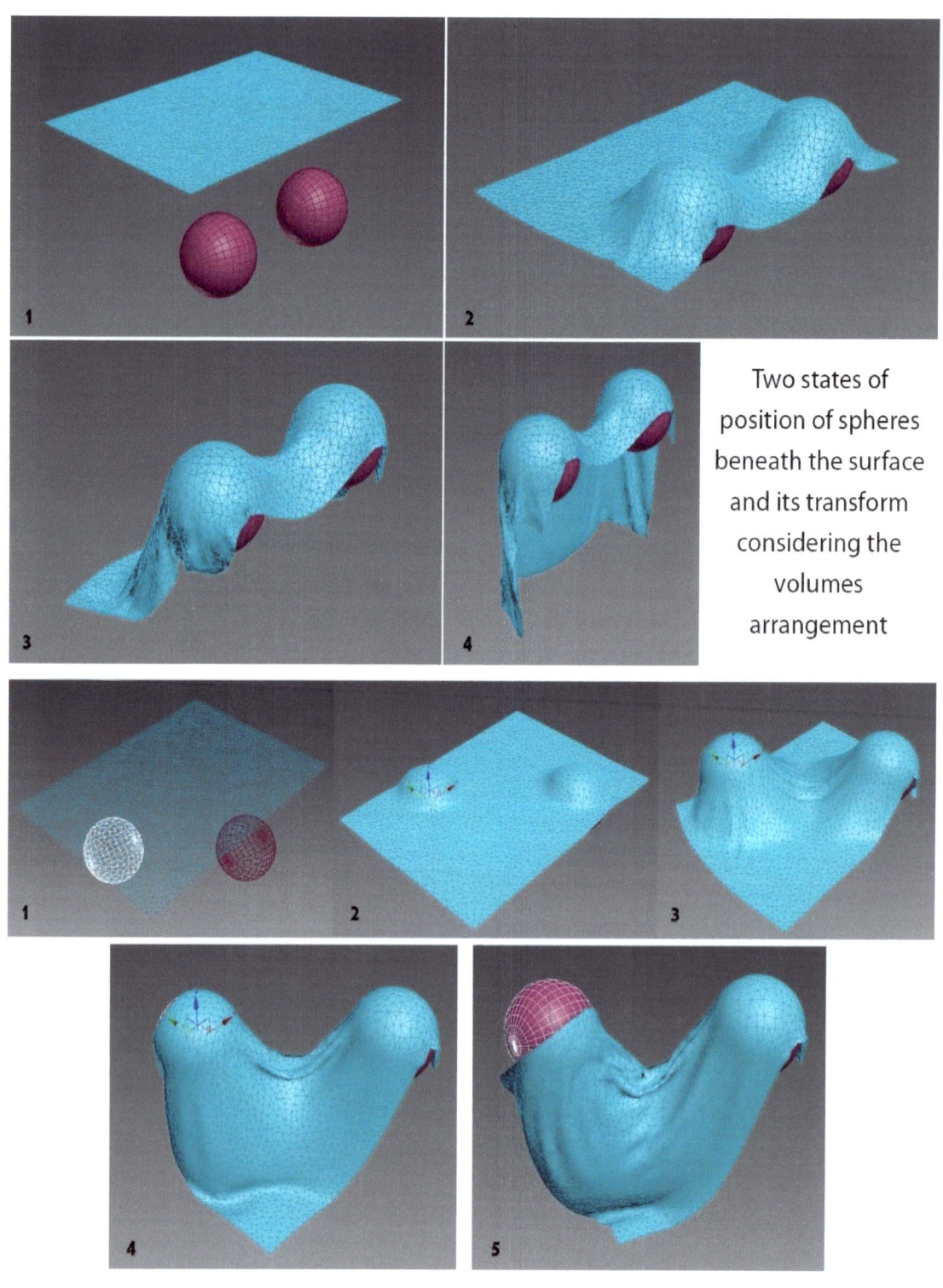

Picture 61

Experience of Mcloth in clashing with cubes indicating to buildings of a city. In fact, this practice was an introduction to design square of a city which will be described in next pages.

Following pictures show (step by step) clashing of the surface to the horizontal surface with cubes indicating to buildings. (Pictures 62 – 64)

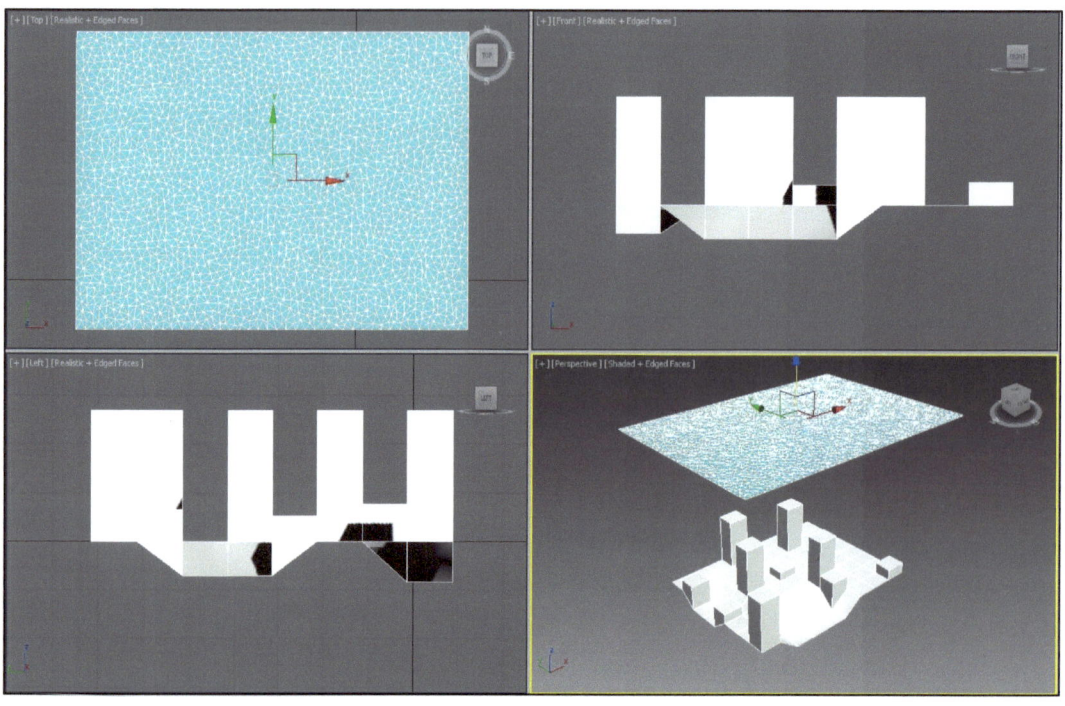

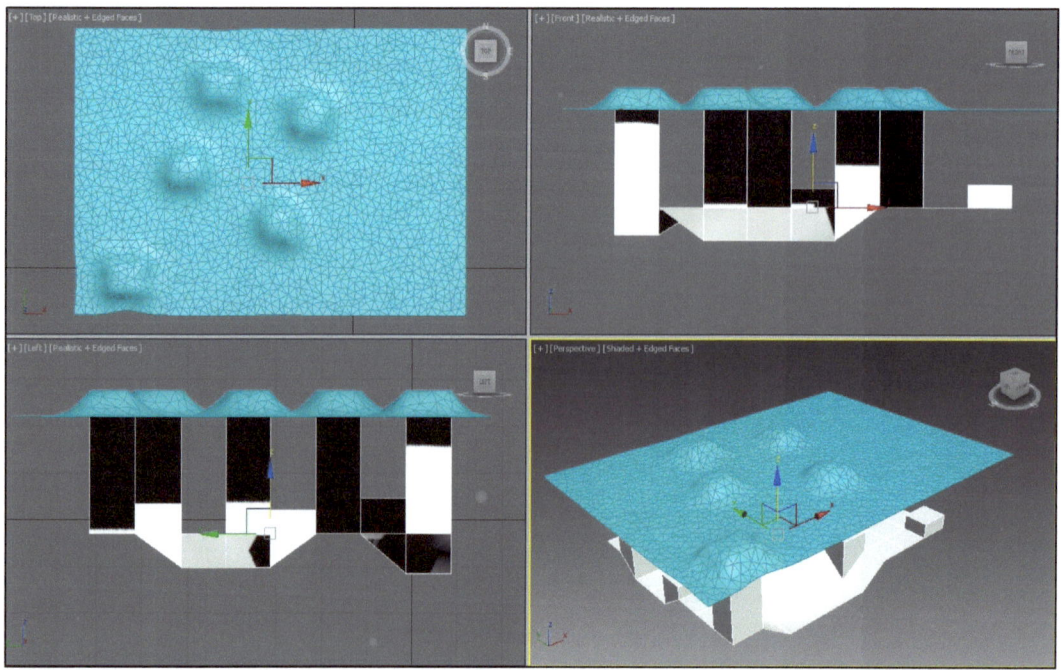

Picture 62 & 63

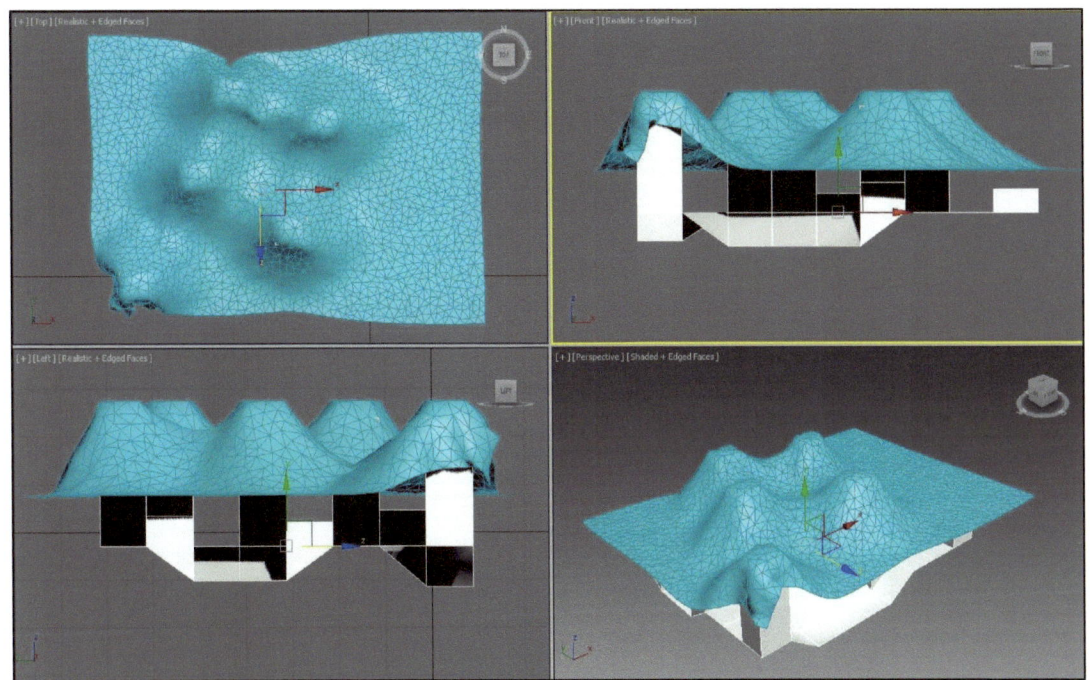

Picture 64

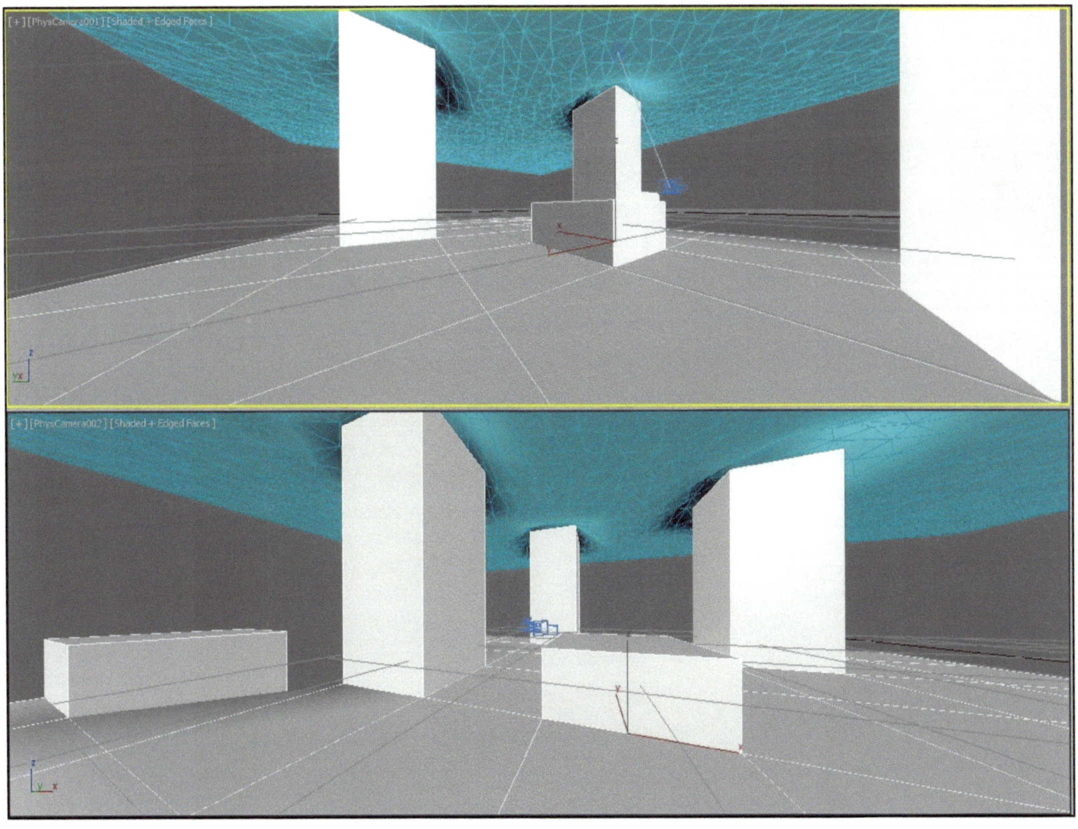

The surface transform in cashing with buildings from human perspective. (Pictures 65 – 67)

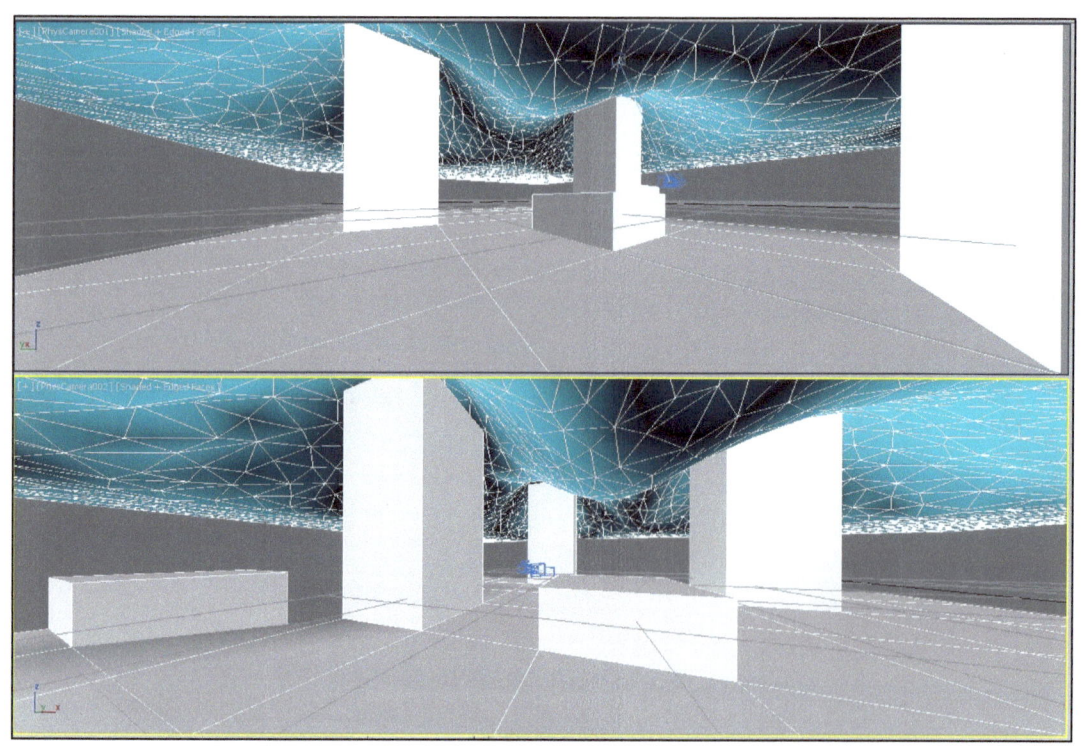

Picture 66

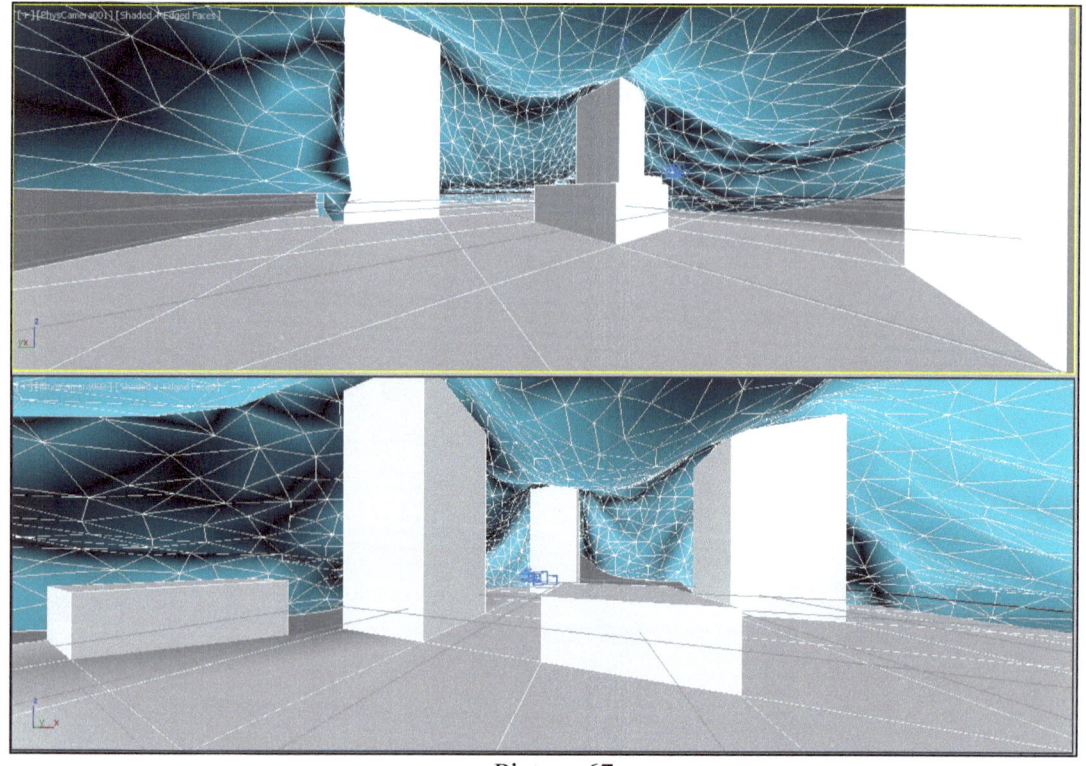

Picture 67

Design of a City Square Based on Mcloth Technique

Using the concepts of population traffic, presence and density which are supposed as forces affecting the square space, an imaginary crust was considered to record and demonstrate such variations. It is noteworthy that the project was considered as a research project in interdisciplinary office in 2008. Considering software facilities of that time, effect of some components was manually made in the imagined crust. The following diagram shows a simple model of animate thinking passing an evolutionary path to create an interaction between computer and social components. It tries to mix different urban layers and social behaviors and base output of design process on it. (Diagram 8)

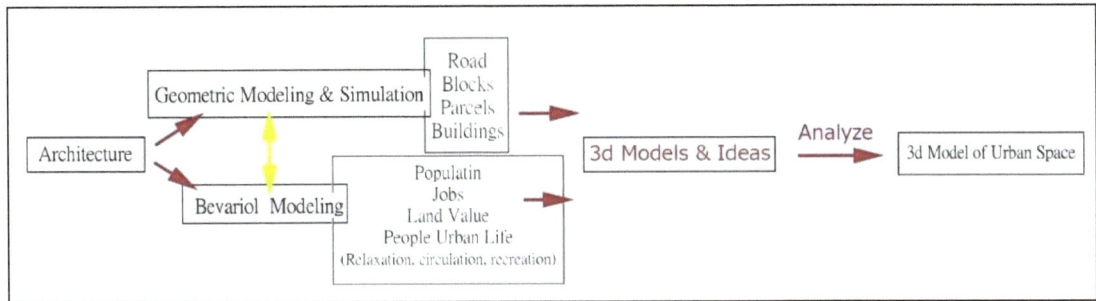

Diagram 8

In Interdisciplinary Design Universe (our office), some alternatives were designed for this project. We satisfied to the alternative No.1 due to time limits, cost and severalty of the works. To observe other projects as well as modern projects, you may refer to www.IDUarchitects.com.

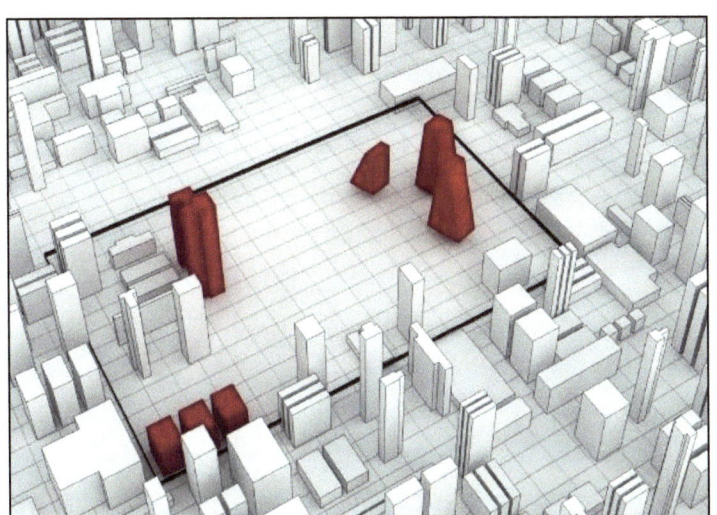

< Picture 68 - Current state of the square

Design process of project (Pictures 69- 74)

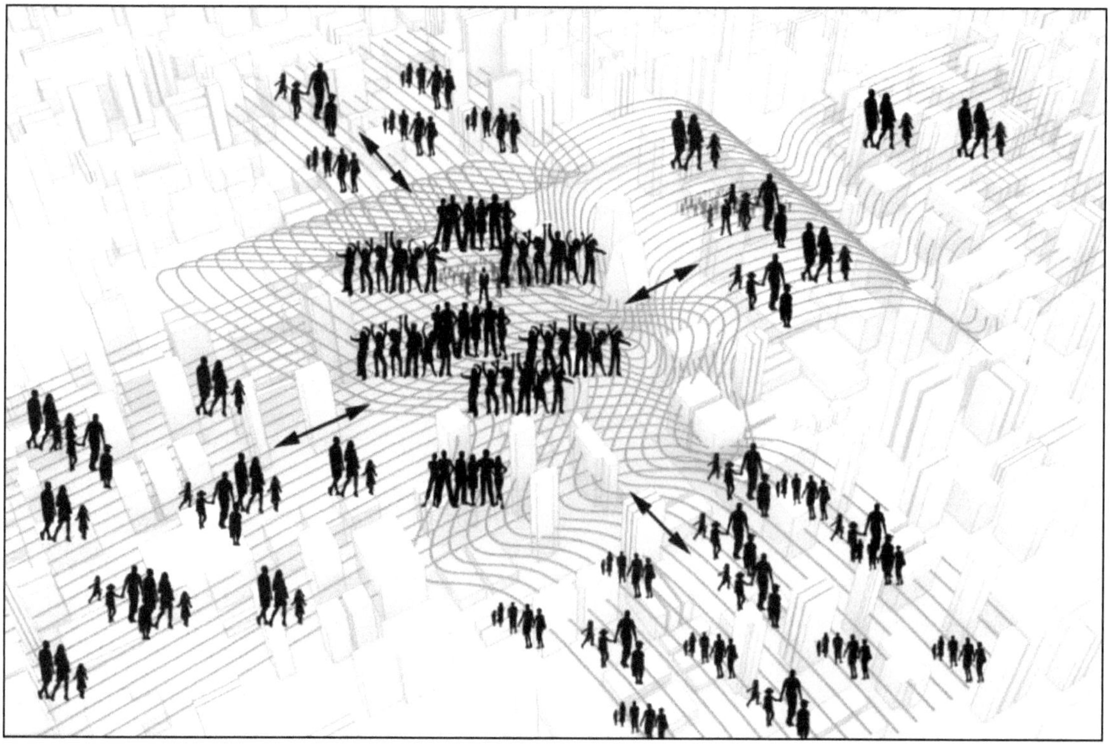

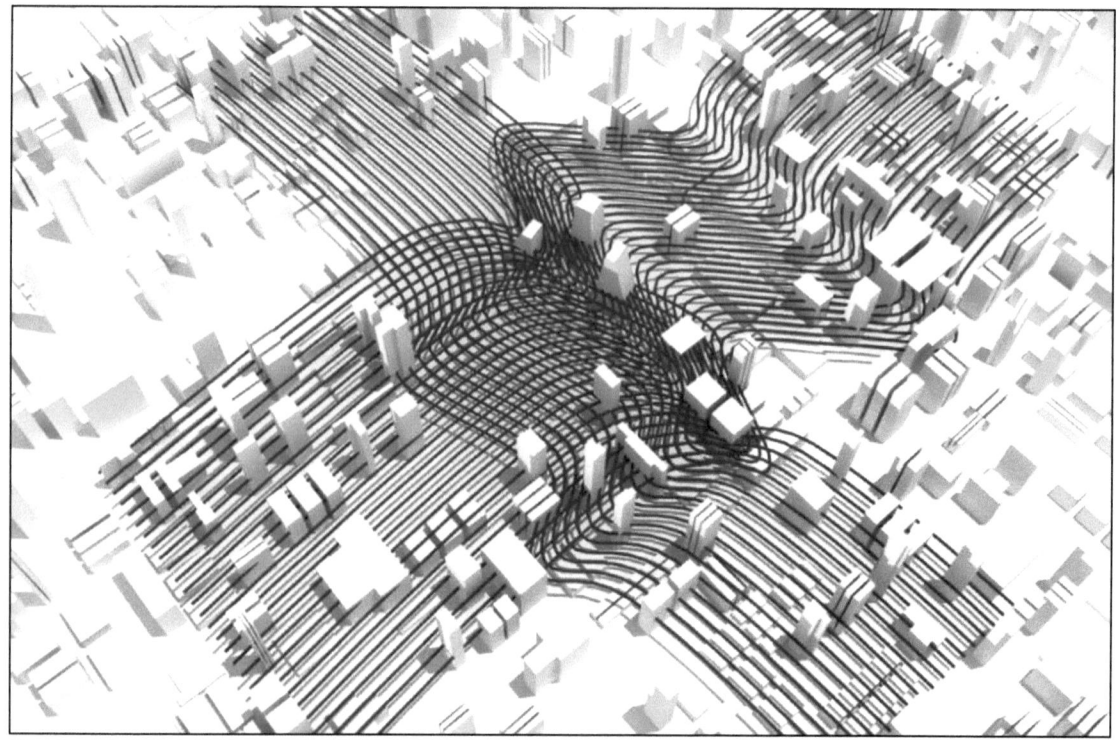

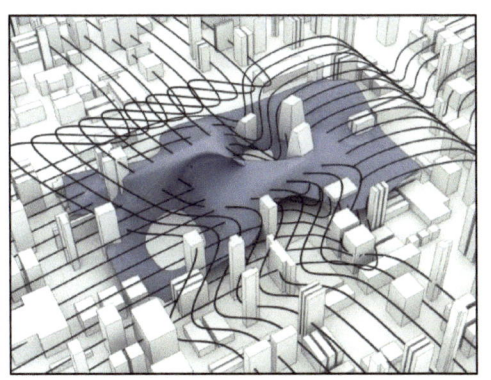
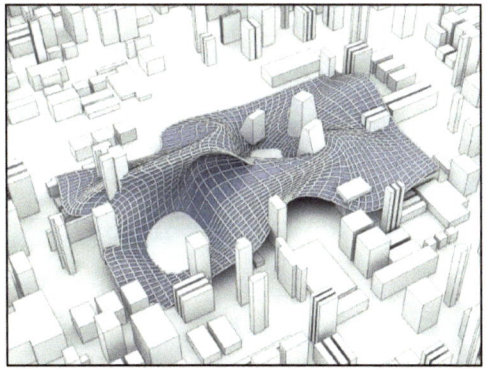

Pictures 71- 74

Selected alternative of several alternatives

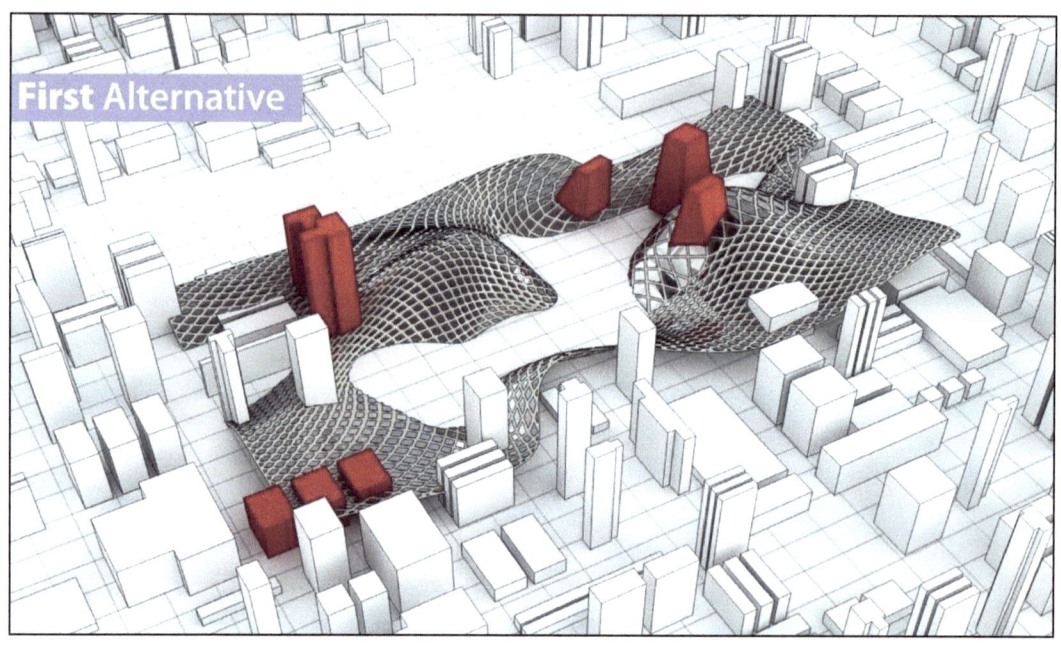

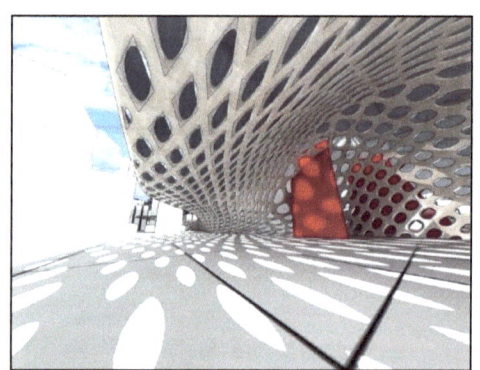

Second Part of Animate Design

Nature of space and architecture is changing from a fixed and unchangeable structure to a dynamic and fluid existence which is capable of change, growth, stimulation and transformation like living creatures. Design of such space requires different thinking and tools. Animate design is a process where form and space is being affected by different moving, varying, evolving and developing forces. In this design method, form and space are considered as dynamic rather than static. In design process, the form and space dialogue with designer, accept and analyze desires, project or land limitations and other factors and show an appropriate behavior. The project you will see demonstrates evolutionary process of formation of surfaces which grow, reproduce, combine with each other and make a generality in a complete coordination due to being influenced by each other, i.e. transformation of a surface leads to transformation of other surfaces and/or when they are reproduced they move along with the flow or curvature of the main object. (Picture 79)

Picture 79

The above explanations are completed as follows:

- Architecture may be regarded as a dynamic and living creature its form and nature changes through changing of light, furniture, presence of human and passing of time.
- Animate design is not a linear process. At any moment, design in frame 85 may be stopped in its motion trajectory between frames 0 to 100 and start a new trajectory.
- Animate design originating from animate thinking is a process of thinking mainly consisting of dynamism, gradual evolution, creativity, layer-by-layer thinking, combination and interaction between the layers. The process develops our way of thinking and comprehensively interacts with other design techniques. Animate thinking deals with convergence of forces including location, adjacency, culture, human, natural forces and requirements in a coherent and wide range and makes their strengthening or weakening, changing and accelerating possible. Convergence of forces and thoughts is an important issue placing us in a position beyond special style and viewpoint. Intentionally or unintentionally, we are involved in natural requirements and we have to use principles of sustainable architecture as an important component in design or follow principles and regulations of modern architecture design.
- Design process as well as several and various outputs in this technique is preferred to result of the work more than any other design process.
- The result is formed in interaction with computer and even the designer is not completely aware of the result.
- Changing of time and location affects form and quality of form or space.
- In this design technique, form and space behaviors are accurately evaluated using wide range of information.
- Computer and software provide several facilities. A form may be converted or changed to tens, hundreds and thousands form.
- This design technique helps us to use the original form A in order to reach forms which are out of mental imagination of the designer and they may not be created using other computerized techniques. In the project you will see, nature of a simple cube was changed and converted to a structure similar to an element, sculpture or a movable canopy. (Picture 80)

Picture 80

Following the previous project, symmetry of the original cube is located vertically and the animation is rendered with the same setting. Such copy of the original volume is only obtained in last frames and its height is changed. (Picture 81)

Picture 81

As seen, a new structure surprising the author is created only through a simple symmetry. The final structure may be regarded as a memorial building and the original structure with high potential may be used to design an office tower adapted from Iranian architecture. (Although the author is not inclined to name the designed projects to prevent from restriction of creativity of readers, he has done it in some cases to clarify the subject) (Picture 82)

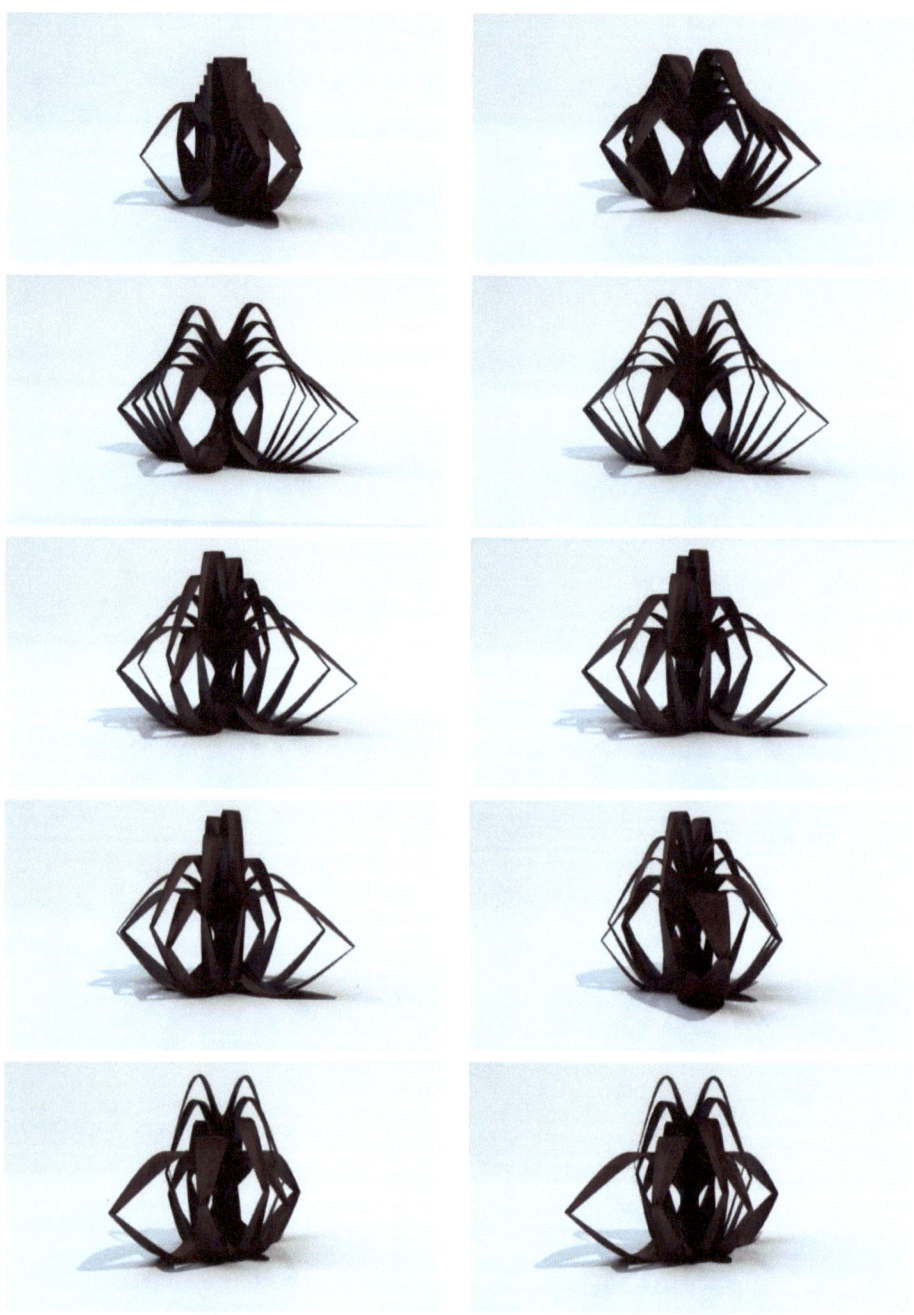

Picture 82

Animate design strongly emphasizes on repetition, variation and evolution.

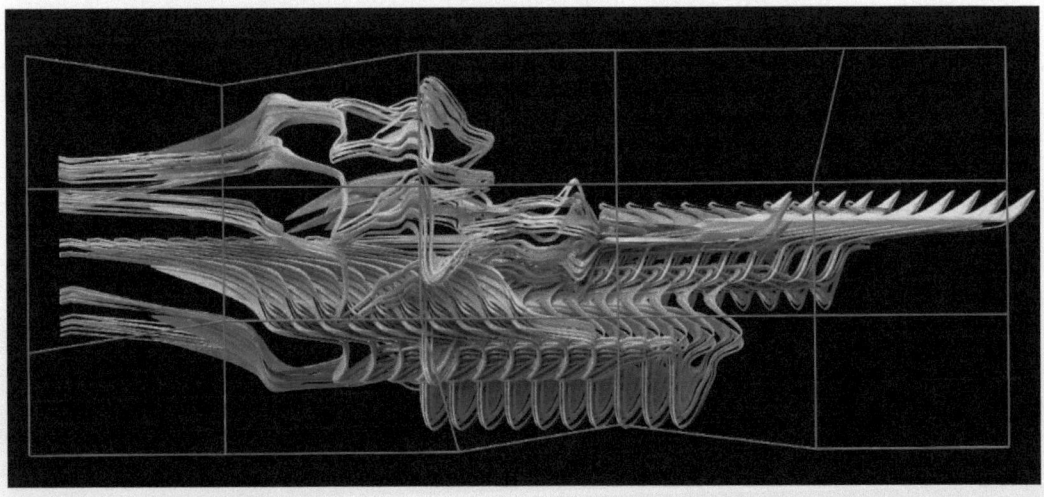

Pavilion design based on animate design process. (Pictures 83- 85)

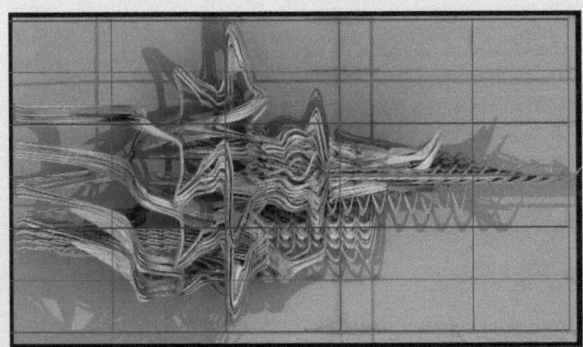

Picture 83 - Opposite view of pavilion

A space full of excitement. At first glance, it seems complex. But when we pay attention to the pavilion formation process, we find out that the repetitive forms are made of the same materials and they are transformed and interwoven through repetition.

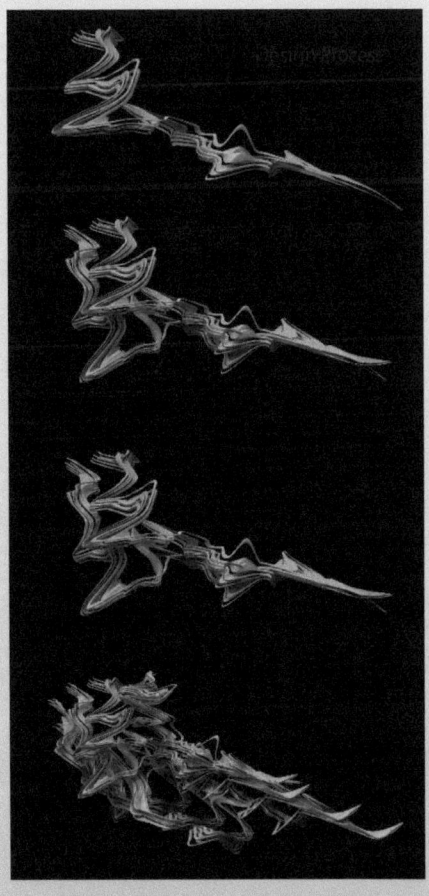

Picture 84 - Bird's-eye view

In animate design, different layers are formed from inside of the work and complete the space. It exactly occurred in the last project: when a force or motion is imposed during the process, some forms changed more than others due to their fluidity. (Picture 86)

Picture 86

- In this method, each and every frame is valuable and is regarded as an important ring and may be selected as the main form.
- In this method, your design process, forms, different locations of the building, light direction, length and depth of shades, etc. are recorded exactly and may be accessed and changed easily. In other computerized forms, however, the forms and steps produced during the work are recorded limitedly and most of them are omitted from study cycles.
- In animate design, the designer may start design easier than manual design method through assuming several concepts. Contrary to the conventional viewpoint, such assumption develops your mind. (Evidently, this method requires practice and experience. After experiencing some simple designs, the designer adapts his/her mind with a completely familiar event or, in other words, remembers it).

Nature Pavilion
(A research project in Interdisciplinary Office)

Project partner: Samira Mahoutchian

Picture 87- Site plan

Picture 88- Interior & exterior perspectives

- It provides conditions to those fascinated to parametric design and creation of complex spaces to create infinite forms and spaces using a process of production, conversion and variation.

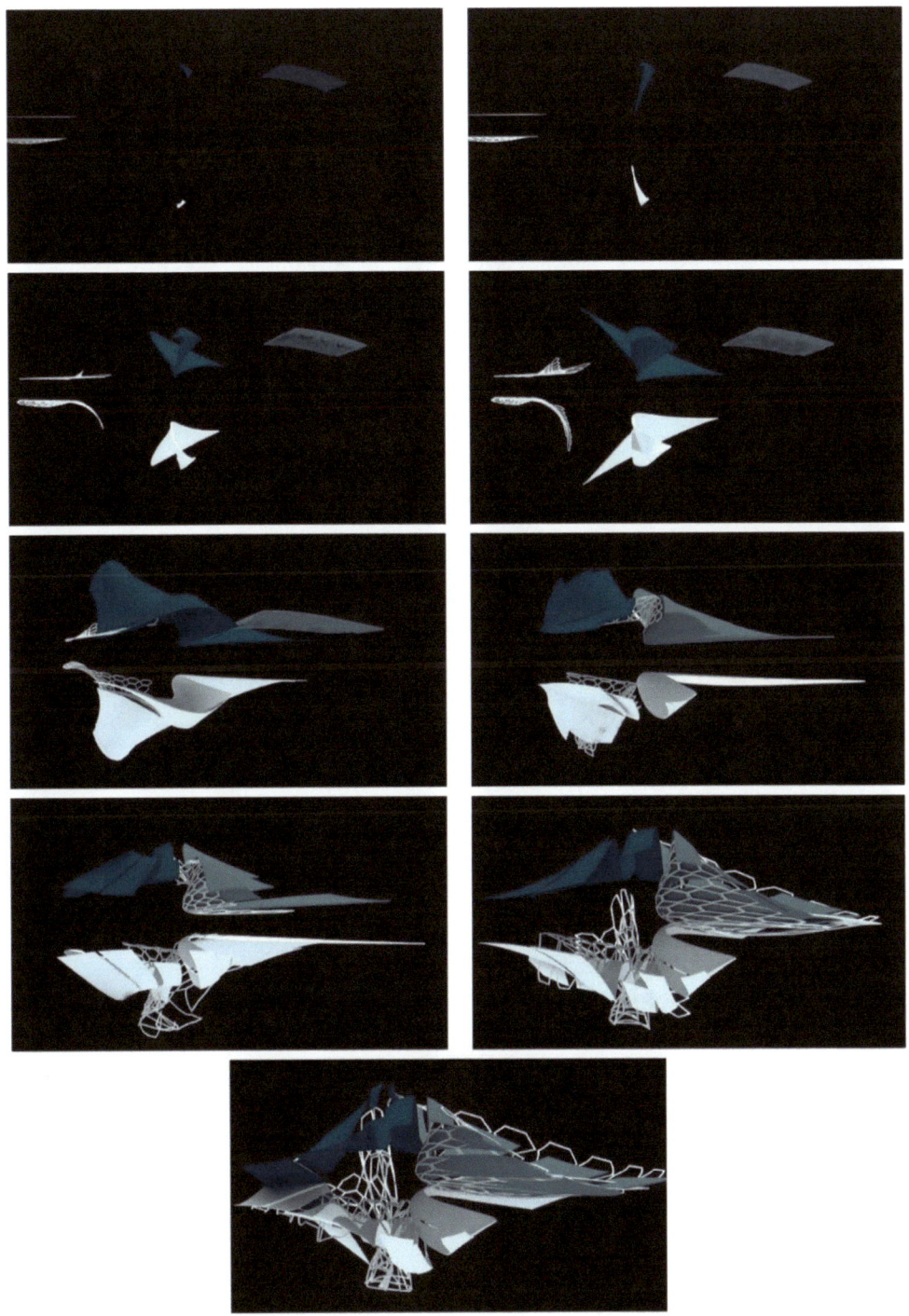

Picture 88 – Process of formation of form & space

Third Part of Animate Design

Even when plan, outside volume and indoor space are designed concurrently and control plan and volume variations with cameras from different points, we are less inclined to move inside the space, walk, and evaluate events, visual priorities and space circulation like an impartial supervisor. Animation of indoor space is usually made at the end of the project to make it attractive for buyers or for media advertisement.

Design the space through moving and attending there

Walk inside the space, move the walls, or change height of the ceiling or arrangement of lights. This is a design method evaluates and consciously changes different issues from arrangement of walls and furniture to light level through moving in the building. It may be out of mind for the readers, but in a near future the designers will work in a room equipped to simulation systems of virtual space in the real world, will observe what is designed in computer, and will move around and inside it. The employer will enter his/her home through wearing advanced glasses and will accompany the designer.

Being present in the space we design is an excellent experience, a presence which may change the space and make it possible to experience another life style. I wonder is it practically possible to experience the architectural subjects brought forth by Heidegger, being present in existence, understand it and interact with it through advancement of technology and stabilization of animate thinking which introduces the existence as intelligent phenomena.

Fourth Part of Animate Design

Study of presence, motion and behavior of human inside a space
According to the studies, most inefficiency of buildings in routine applications may not be attributed to pure technical inefficiencies rather they are arising from the fact that owners and residents of such buildings are not able to behave as supposed by the designers.

Human> Motion, Behavior> Architecture

This may be done in two ways:
A. When modeling of indoor and outdoor space of the project was completed, studio colleagues and ordinary people may be asked to wear special glasses and move in the space. Recording and evaluating of behavior and motion of people (from selecting the motion path to paying attention or ignoring parts of space or their reflex to light changes, displacing walls, and density of human in specific parts) before executing the plan may result in a relative assessment of accepting of the plan by people and success of the project.

In a project, for example, members of the design team disagreed about inciting curiosity of addressees and their non-tiredness. I suggested that to invite some people and ask them to move inside the space by camera movement and finally let us know their perception. It was done by a mouse on monitor and interesting results were obtained.

B. Human behavior in the previous or similar projects may be renovated in this project. For example, when a museum of residential complex is designed for a country with important ecological and cultural differences, this method will play an important role and will have important application in identifying requirements, interests and generally, psychological particulars of its nation.

Fifth Part of Animate Design

Animate design is an important technique in research, design and execute of responsive and adaptive architecture. As the most important issue, animate design deals with reaction and the feedback received from form and space by the addressee and designer against an action, an interaction created between form and space in both virtual and real worlds.
- Feedback of space to designer (responsive architecture or crust)
- Feedback of space to residents, visitors, addressees and even passersby
-

To better understand the subject, you are recommended to watch "responsive hexi wall fluctuates based on nearby movements" movie from www.Dezeen.com. There, you will see hexagons move according to the artist's behavior. (Picture 89 & 90)

< Picture 89- Man sitting and hexagons do not move

Picture 90 - In the picture, the artist jumps up and the hexagons bend toward up, too.

Experiences of Responsive Space

In next pages, you will see projects designed with such an approach and the pictures refer to the last two definitions. (Pictures 91-93) The pictures demonstrate transformations of a cube being affected by an external force moving on it and sucks frames of the cube body outwards (toward it). intensity of the force and its affection limit may be controlled and a special form or person may be defined instead of the force. In such case, cube will transform upon movement of a human beside the cube. Transformation of the cube depends on dimensions and motion of the person.

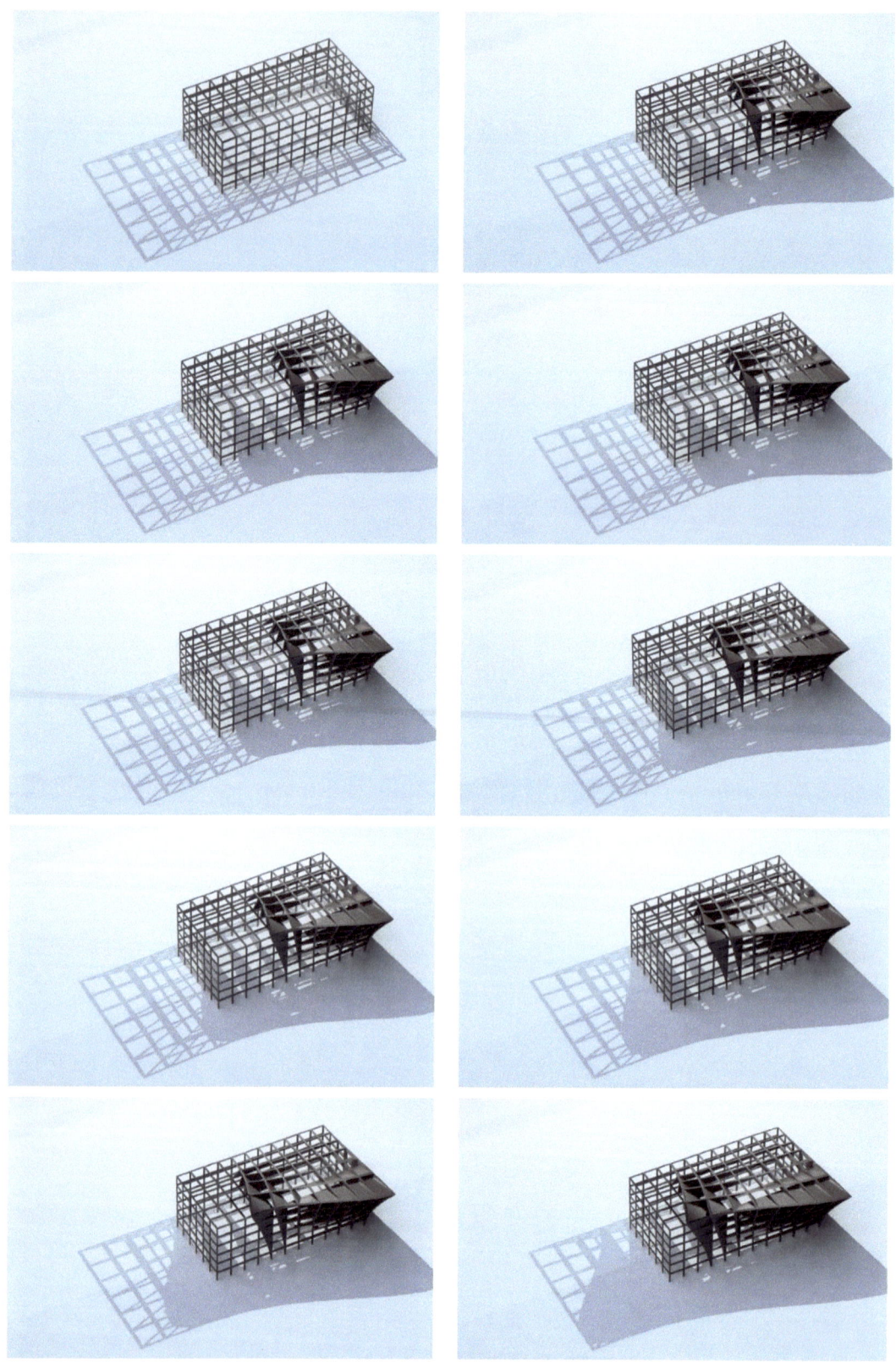

Picture 91

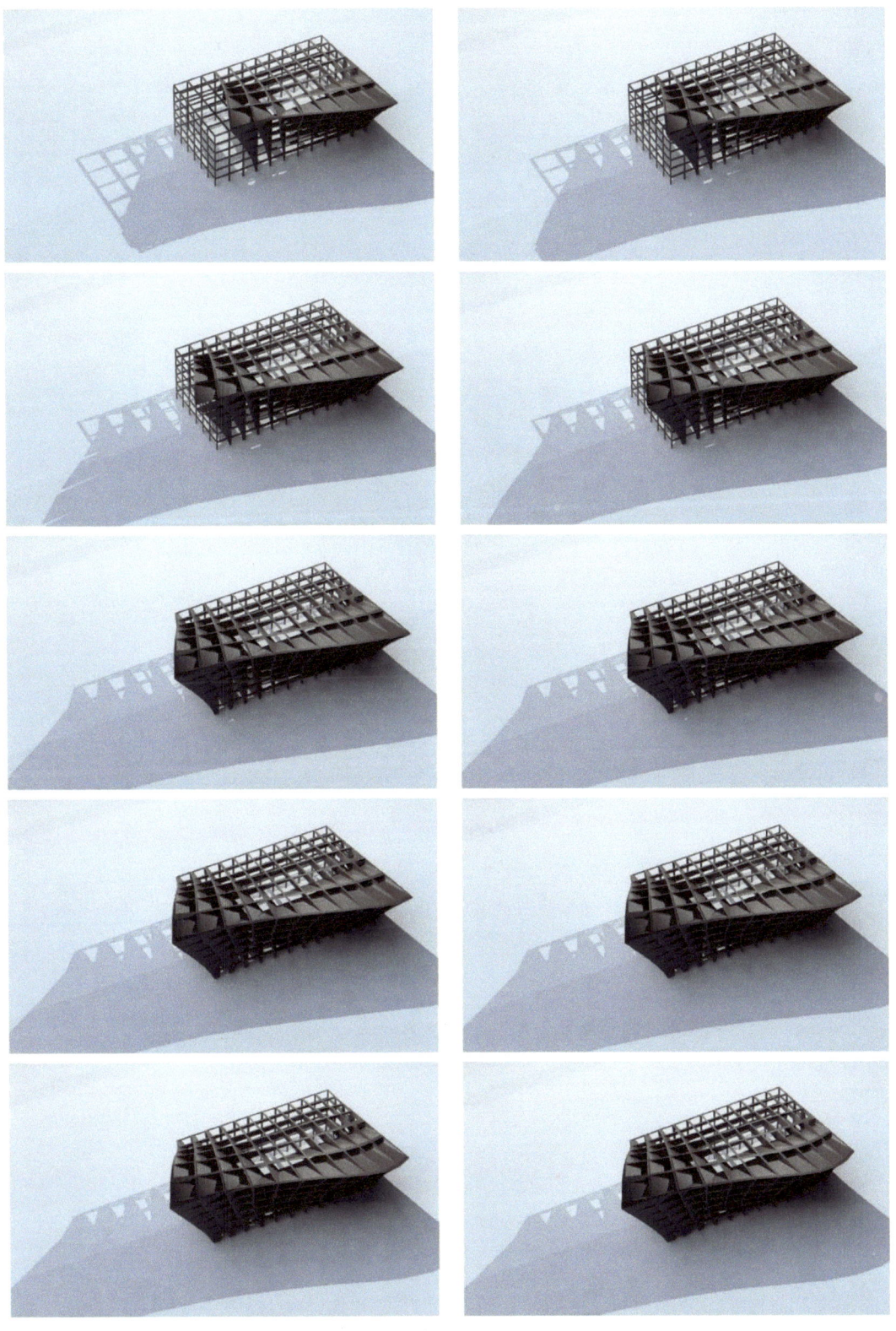

Picture 92

Picture 93

Sixth Part of Animate Design
Effect of a form on another form and vice versa

In the following project where "Morpher" instruction of 3Ds Max was used, demonstrates effect of a tea pot on four rectangular networks. As seen, when the tea pot comes near to the networks, the network was absorbed toward the tea pot and transforms. Transformation and dimensions of the tea pot create a similar effect. The tea pot is, in fact, an example of effect of different forces such as passerby, wind, etc. (Pictures 94 & 95)

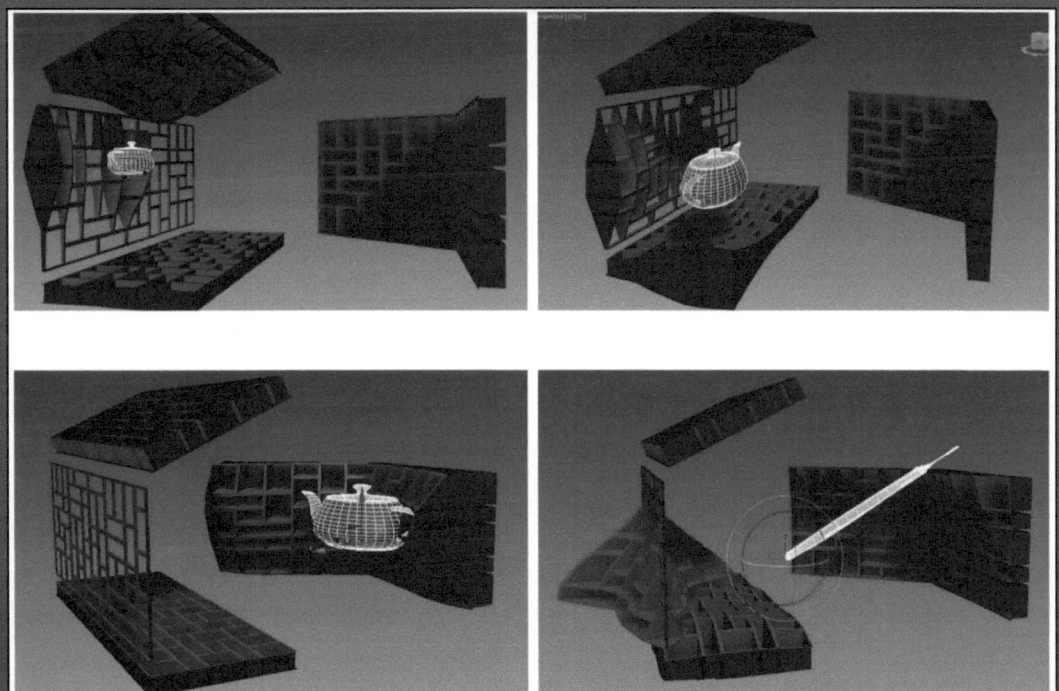

Pictures 94 & 95

In another experience, you will see lines attacking a wavy surface. However, they cannot penetrate or pass it. They transform considering structure and curve of the surface and continue their motion parallel with the surface. Here, the wavy surface also transforms and the lines and surface coordinately act as a whole (the first and second pictures were rendered from bird eye and perspective view, respectively). (Picture 96)

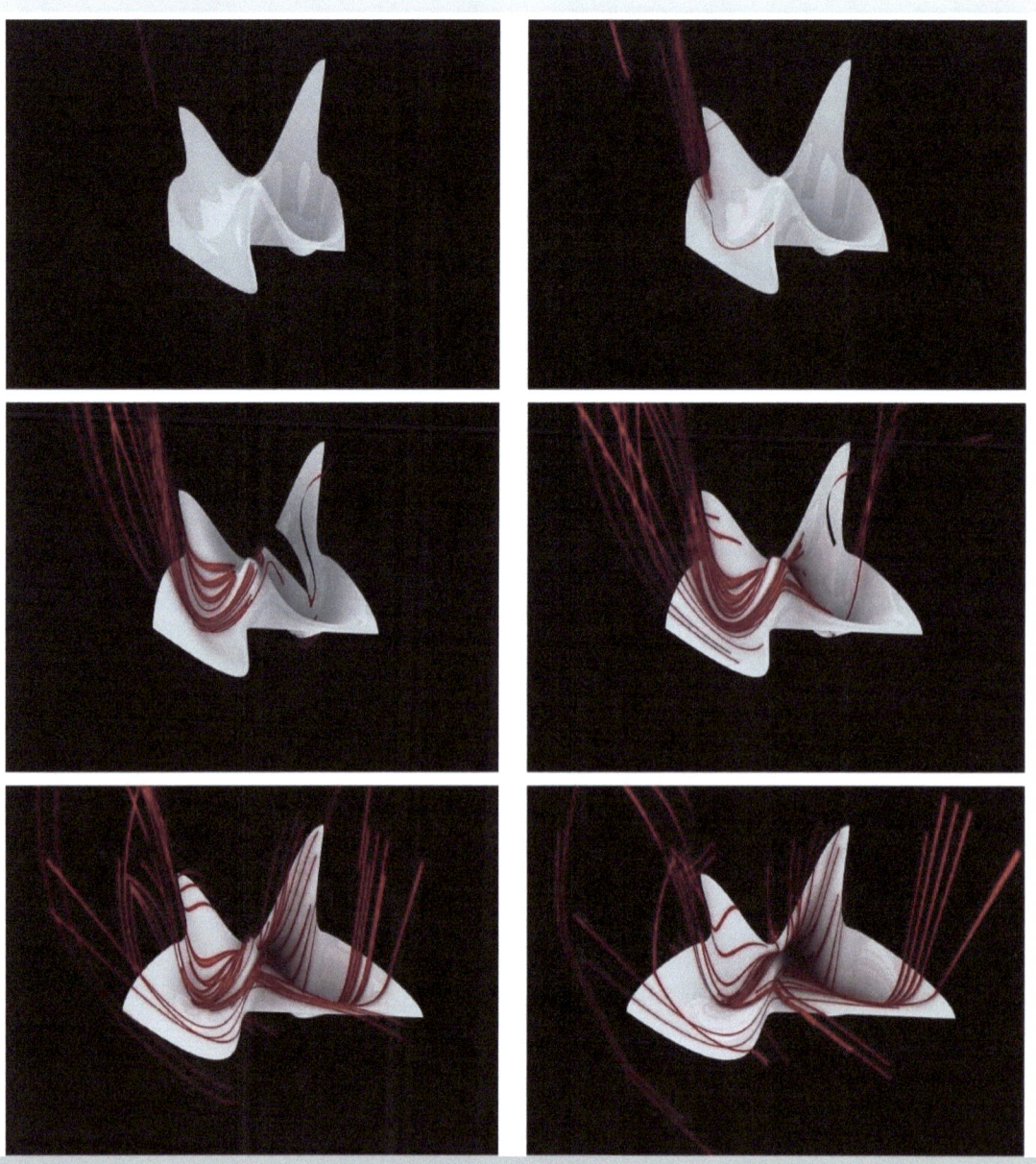

Picture 96

Animate Design Diagram

First diagram of animate design process (Diagram No.8)

- Design of the original volume based on the project requirements and in interaction with computer.

- **Animating (Capability to move, change and affect, converting to a living and intelligent form) the designed form and space.**

- Studying different forms of pictures and form animation.
- Studying and choosing or ordering to repeat the process.

Diagram

Digital Space (Software & Hardware)

Designer's mind

Designing and modeling of the original volume in interaction between the designer's mind and computer based on digital design process

Although designer plays an insignificant role in each of these stages, interaction participation and using of creative imagination power of the designer is of high importance

Flow:
- Original form and space of the project
- ↑ Animating
- ↑ Making animation — Different renders of changing of form and space
- ↑ Studying and choosing of the results by the designer
- → Developing & completing
- Ordering to prepare more pictures or animation from other angles or designing and re-improving the original form

Second Diagram of Animate Design Process (Diagram No.9)

- Making animate form or using ready models matching the project. Mcloth which was introduced previously is a sample of an animate object
- Locating the form in site position, effect of light, wind and other important effective forces of project design (e.g. reviving an old passage passing from middle of the site of gathering of trees, human, etc. in a specific part of the site, paying attention to a specific view from outside of the site to the building and/or vice versa)
- Preparing render and animation from the space variations
- Studying and making decision.

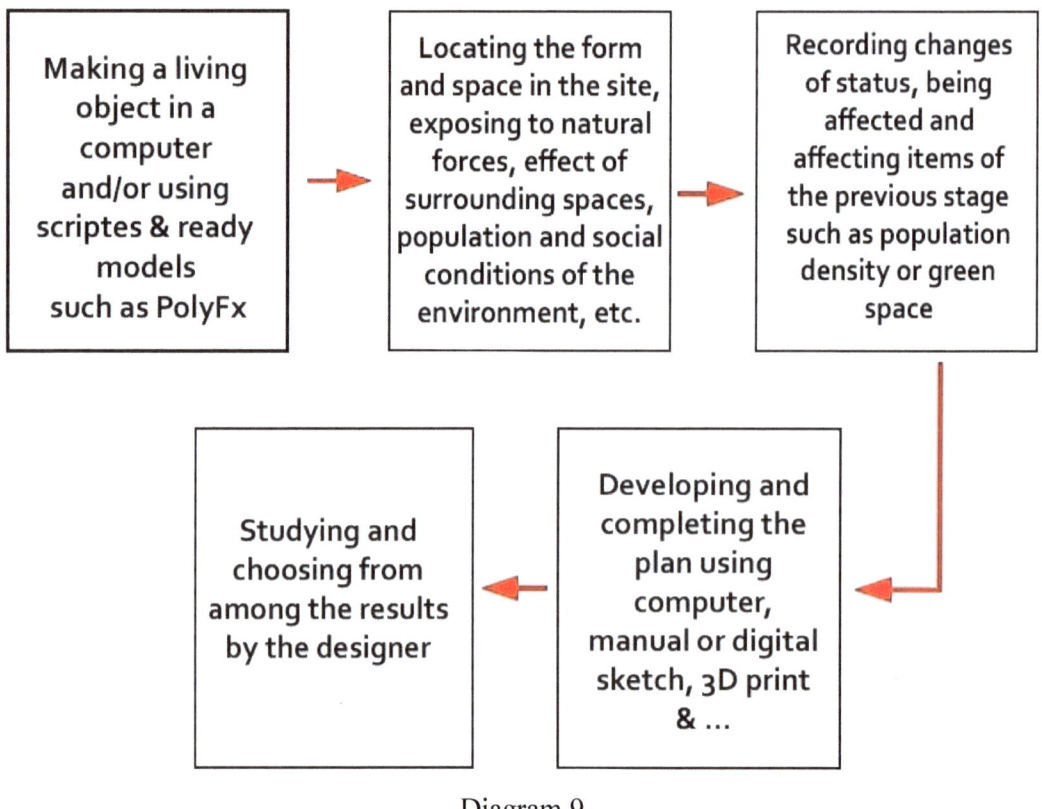

Diagram 9

Important point of animate design process

Integrating the diagrams 8 and 9, depending on idea and capability of the designer in using computers and managing design process, is an ideal technique of animate design process.

Animate Design & Sketch

This section does not aim at developing of manual design and entering it a new environment (there are few people to implement the frames created in computers using paper and pen), rather it aims at changing attitude of designers to non-digital works which have been done since a long time ago. Such changing of attitudes and watching sketches with a mind giving motion, animation and possibility of evolution and variation will be really helpful in understanding and using this technique.
- In a sketch, form is drawn as a set of pictures which transform or develop according to questions and requirements of the project. Do not suffice to one or more limited sketches of the project and make the project as sequences of a film to which the observer looks from different perspectives and imposes his/her comments on space.
- In a sketch, use light pens which are capable to record the design film and save your sketch as a separate layer. Meanwhile, you can easily change them using AutoCAD or Photoshop software.
In you sketch or design with an animate perspective, you will know that a sketch, even simple, is not a fixed and sole design and temporary experience or in better conditions a ring of design process chain, rather it may change to thousands of forms and live independently on both paper or computer. Sketches are not depiction of a fixed form. The designed form is opening of closing or affecting the environmental forces.
- Take a film of your sketch and select and develop different frames of it. Use the light pen to do it so that you can film and save the sketch process step by step.
- In manual design, you should leave your mind free to combine different events ad layers, involve left hemisphere of your mind (logic hemisphere) in design process, and use light pen and filming. Otherwise, it will be less possible to review your work or return and change the trajectory.
- In computerized design where you often work with a result-oriented attitude, you may be inattentive even though the pictures are available. Sometimes in parametric design where the amounts are changed repeatedly and involve different forces in our form and space design, we are not interested in recording the process, i.e. no animation is made of transformation or middle pictures are not discussed unless to justify and describe the final form.
Unfortunately, linear design process and result-oriented thinking occupy wide range of our thought in parametric design especially when working with algorithms. A created result or creativity which is different from our initial imagination is mainly result of facilities provided by computers rather than an intellectual process occurred without paying attention to result, or aiming at entering an unknown trajectory to discover ideas and new forms or evaluate the frames in detail and decide about it.

When we speak about animate design and sketches, we mean an animate attitude to form and space which may be created in sketches especially conceptual sketches. Otherwise, sketches are not included in animate design process. We emphasize it because we will encounter discussions in coming pages which may seem repetitive. But animate attitude toward other design methods and techniques especially digital ones direct us toward more recognition and power of action.

Light pens take film of your sketch and record your sketches step by step, depending of the designer. It is a great and even magic process provides us the possibility of review, play design process, delete a layer, complete or improve layers, and continue of sketch in another trajectory. The following sketch drawn using light pen demonstrates form design process in three layers.

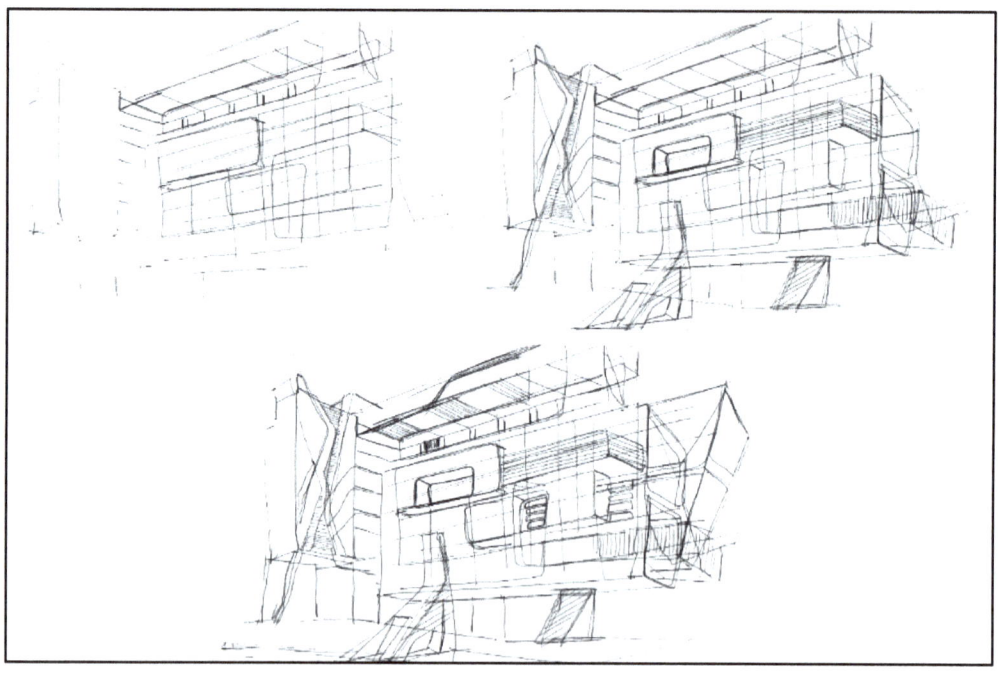

Chapter 4

Samples and experiences of facilities provided to designers by computers and software.

Pattern Design

Excellent application of animate design in designing pictures and patterns is of important achievement of the author during writing the book. Computers make it possible, instead of drawing by hand, to change parameters of the provided pictures (e.g. number of sides or rotation angle) to design several pictures and use their repetition in a specific surface such as facade of a project. It is really a helpful solution. When the designed pictures are designed with animate capabilities and arrange them,

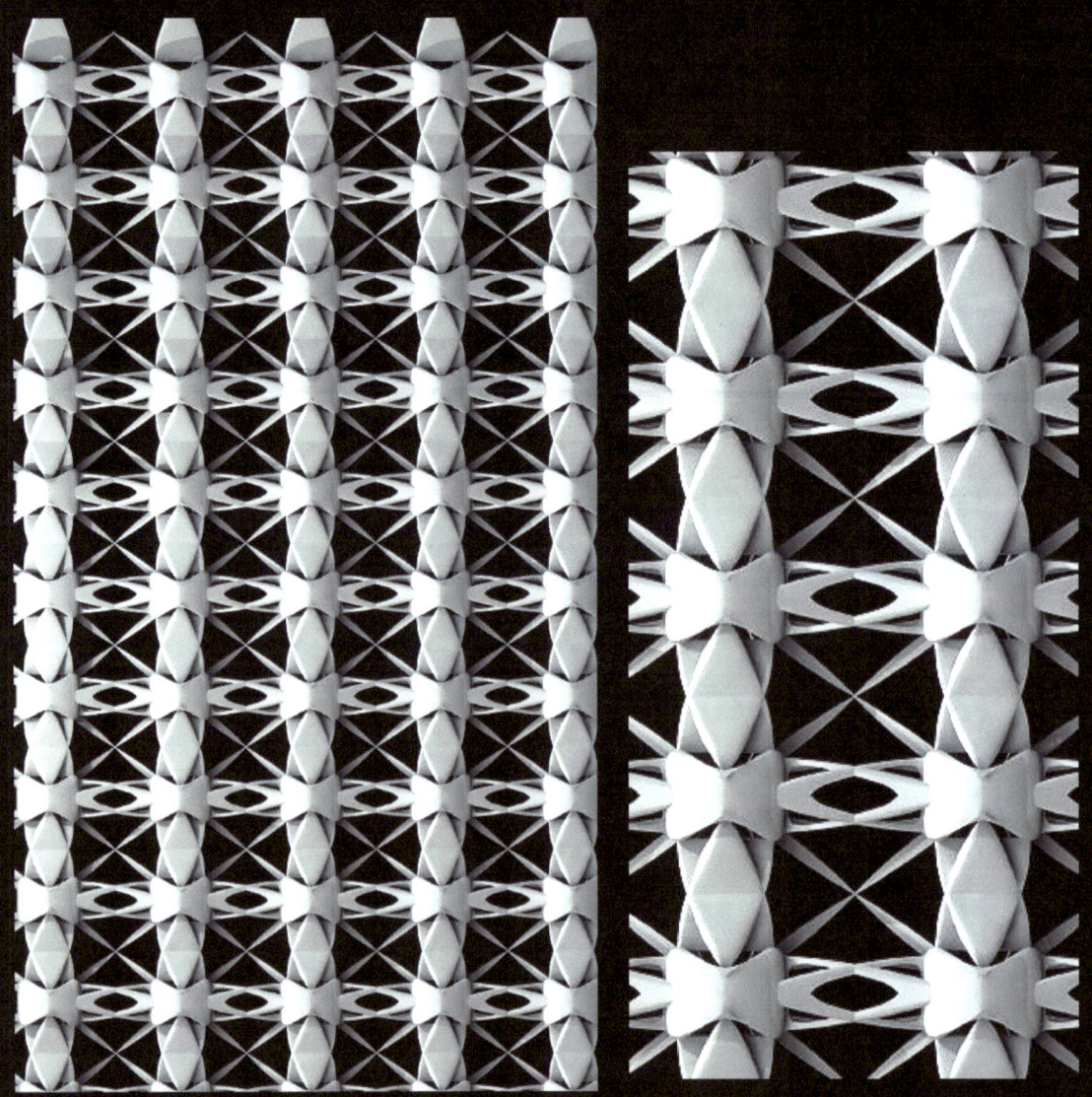

Pictures 97& 98 - The left picture is the final form of the designed pattern and the above picture shows magnification of the pattern.

Patterns selected of design process of the pattern observed in the last page. (Picture 99)

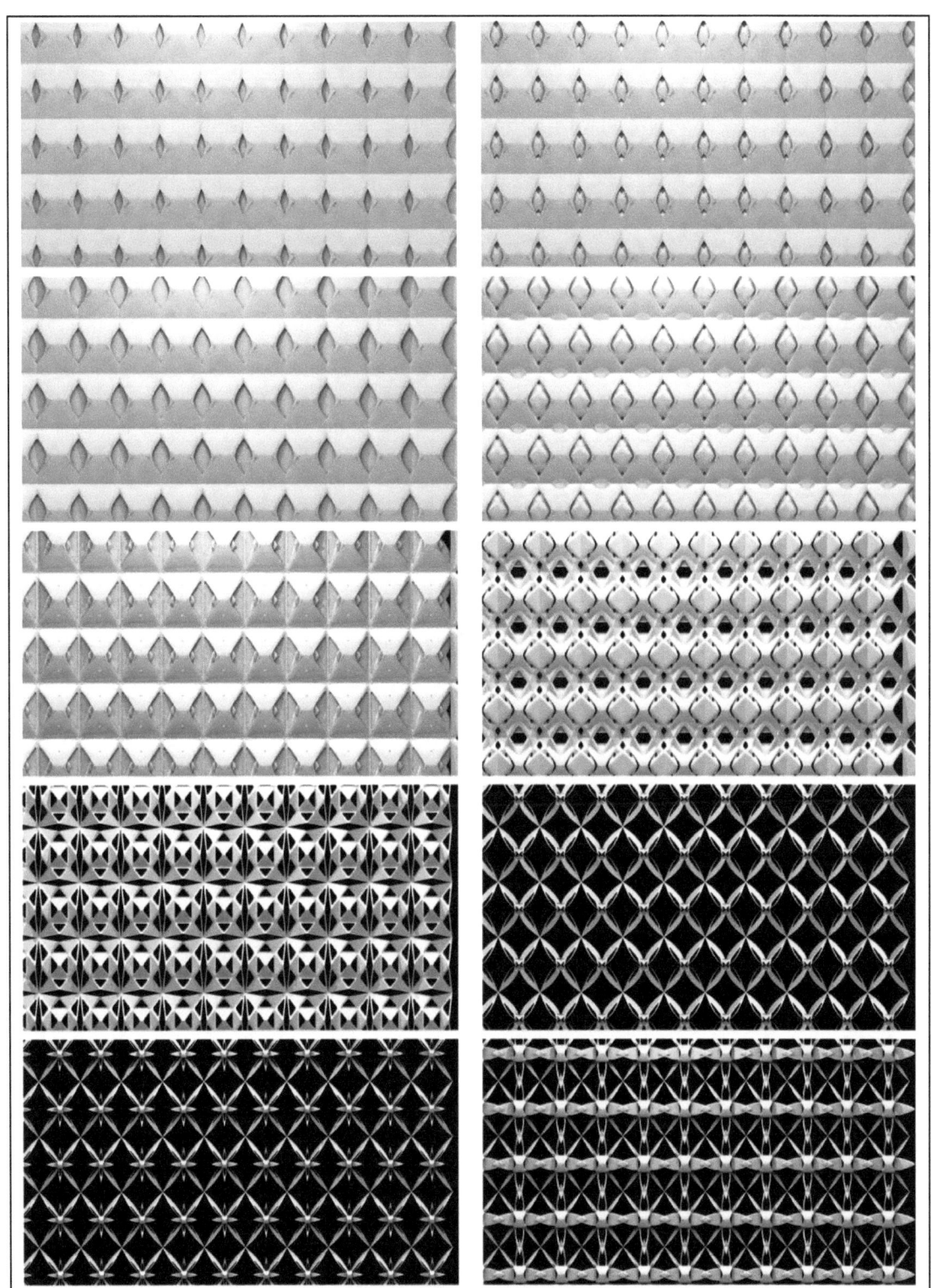

Picture 99

Severalty and variety of created patterns are of special features of animate design technique. (Picture 100)

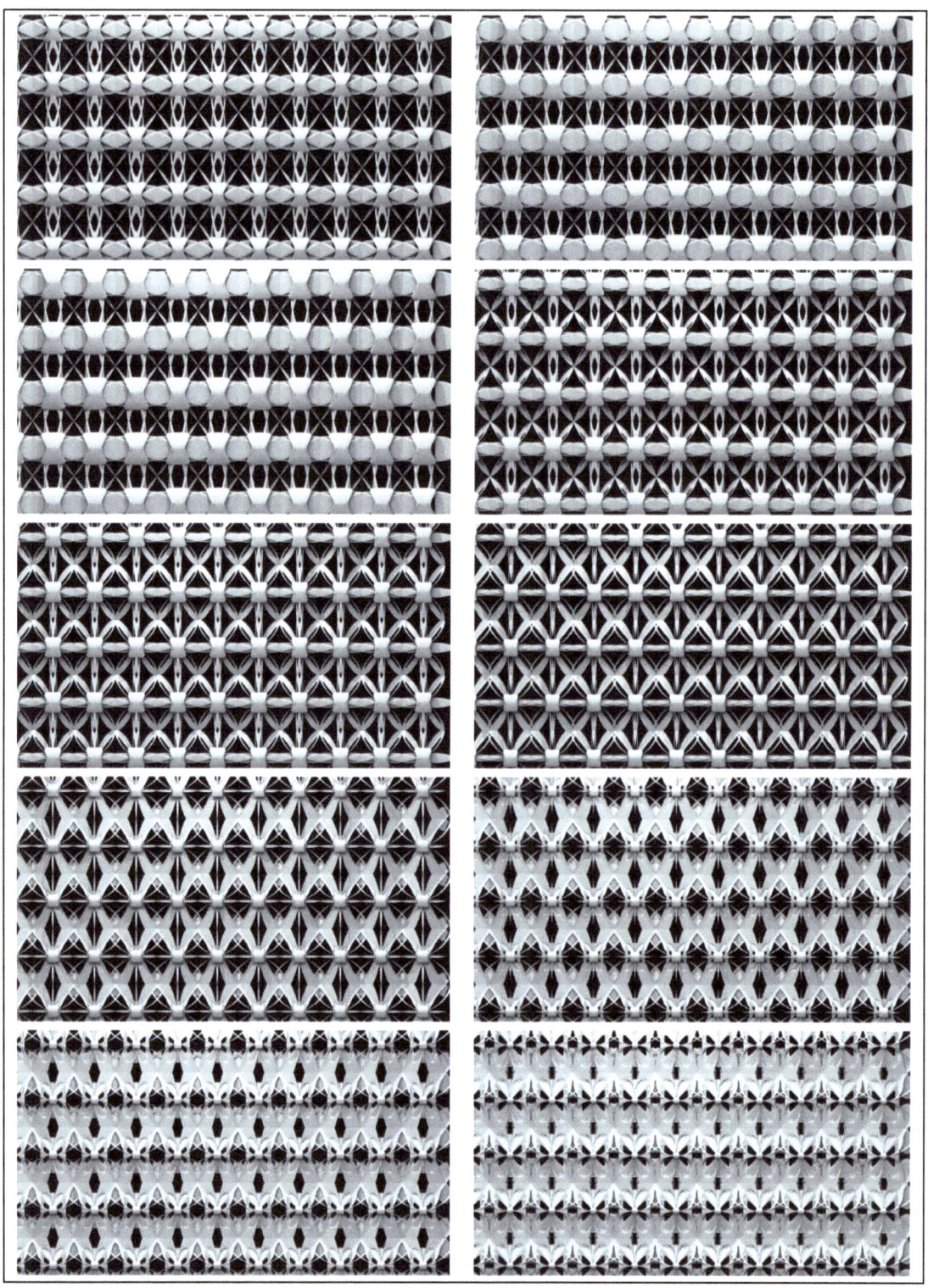

Picture 100

As seen, the surfaces are opened and closed, interwoven and their thickness is changed. (Picture 101)

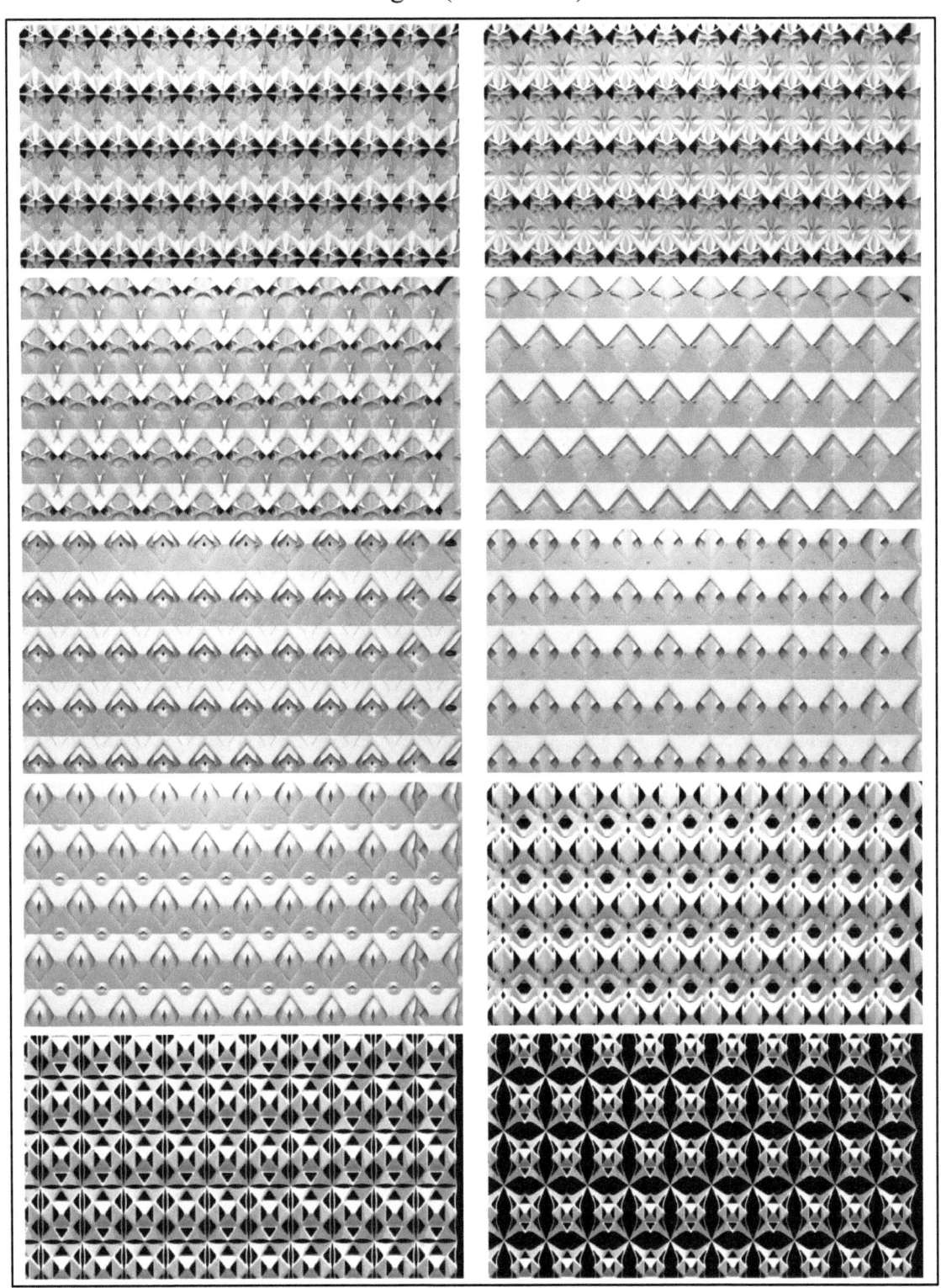

Picture 101

Another sample of changing of patterns in angle 90°.
Most surfaces move horizontally, are projected or retrogressed. (Pictures 102 – 104)
(Animation of the following file known as "<u>Animate Pattern Design Process</u>" may be seen in YouTube).

Picture 102

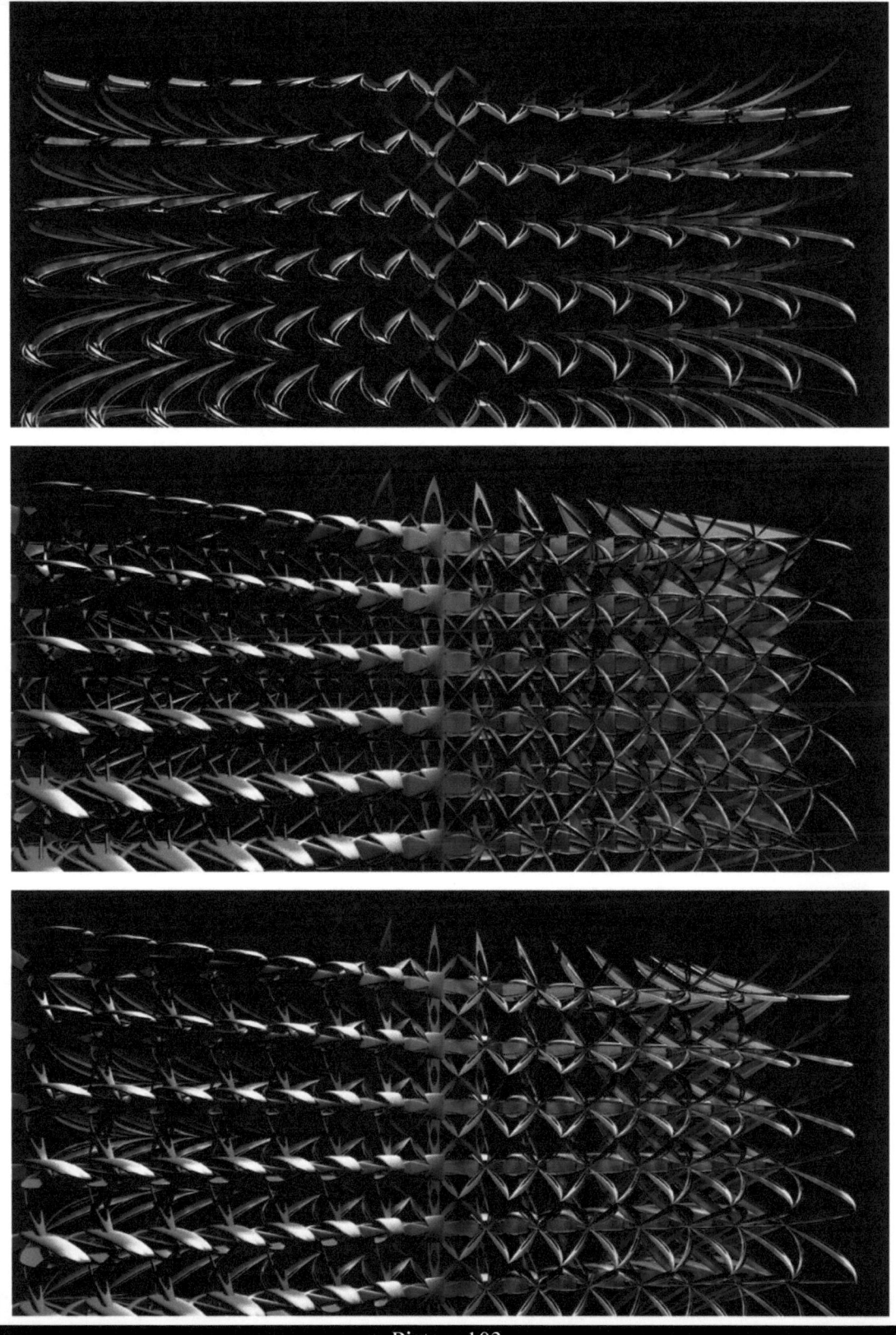

Picture 103

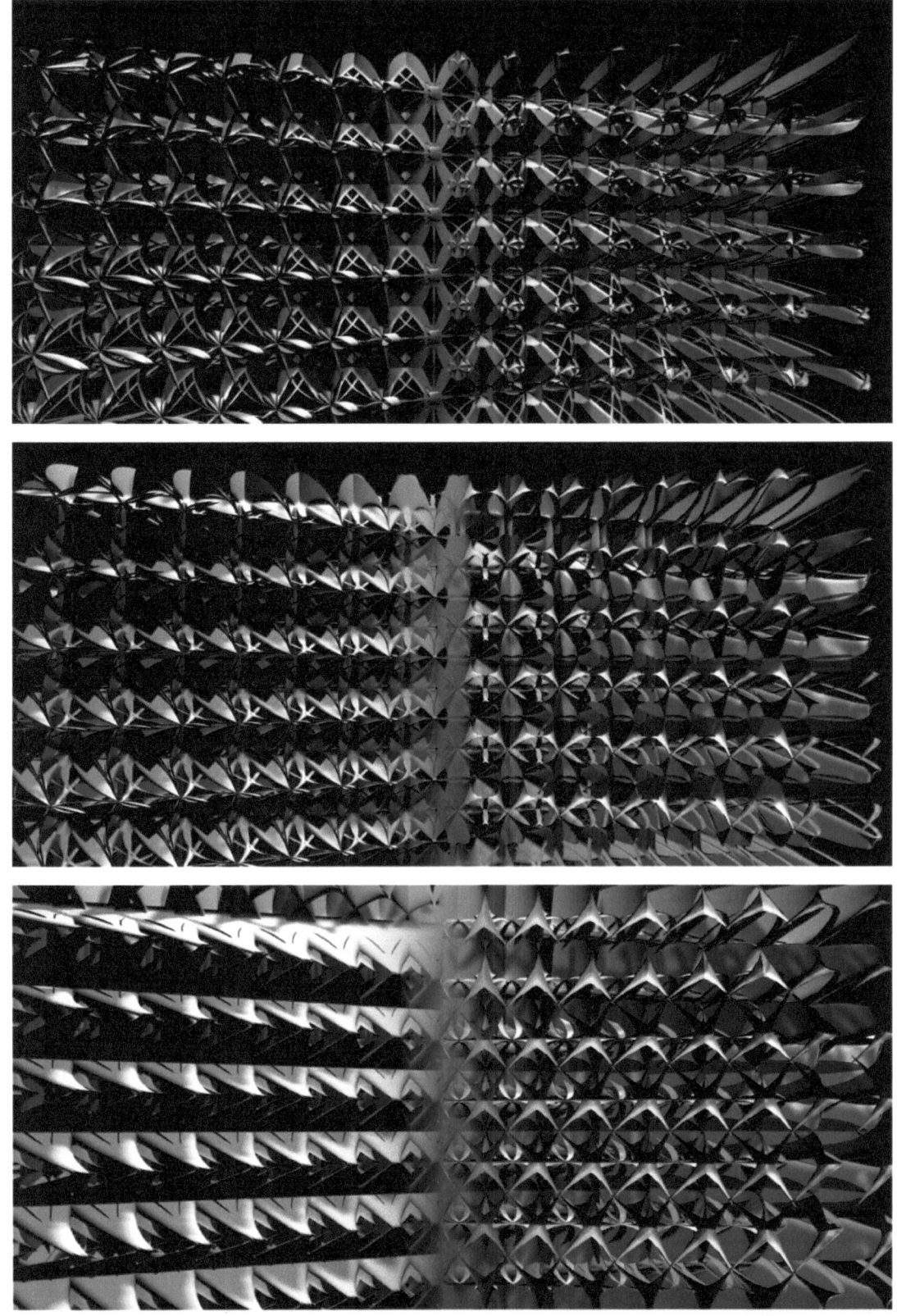

Picture 104

Second experience of pattern design

Third experience of pattern design

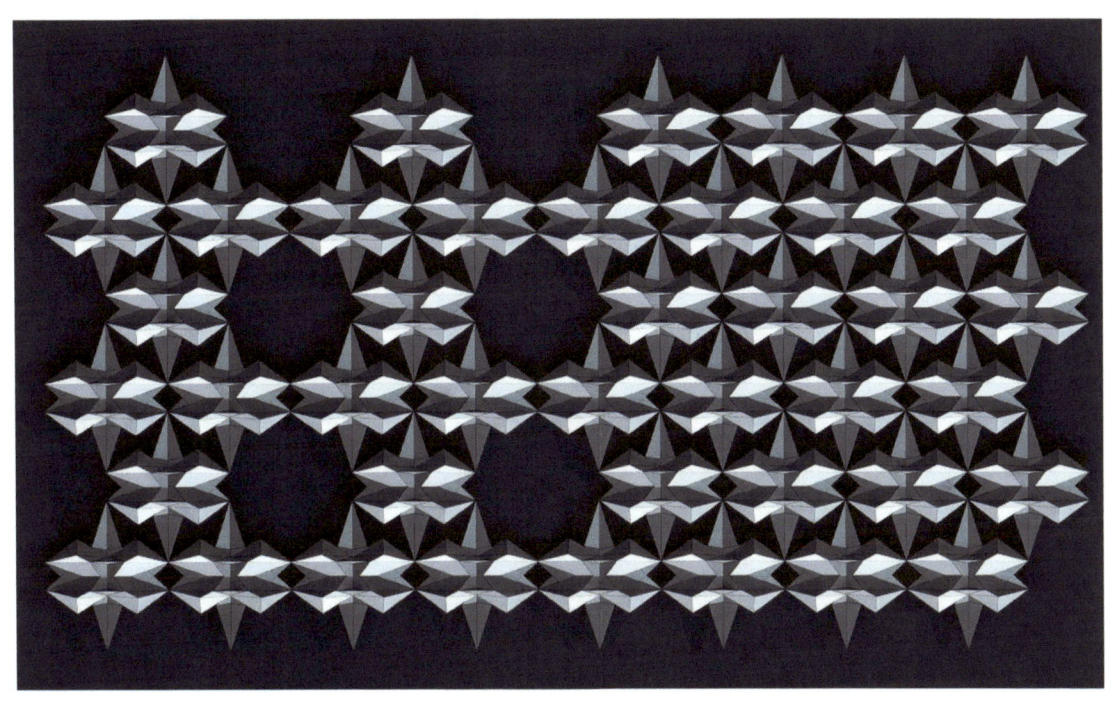

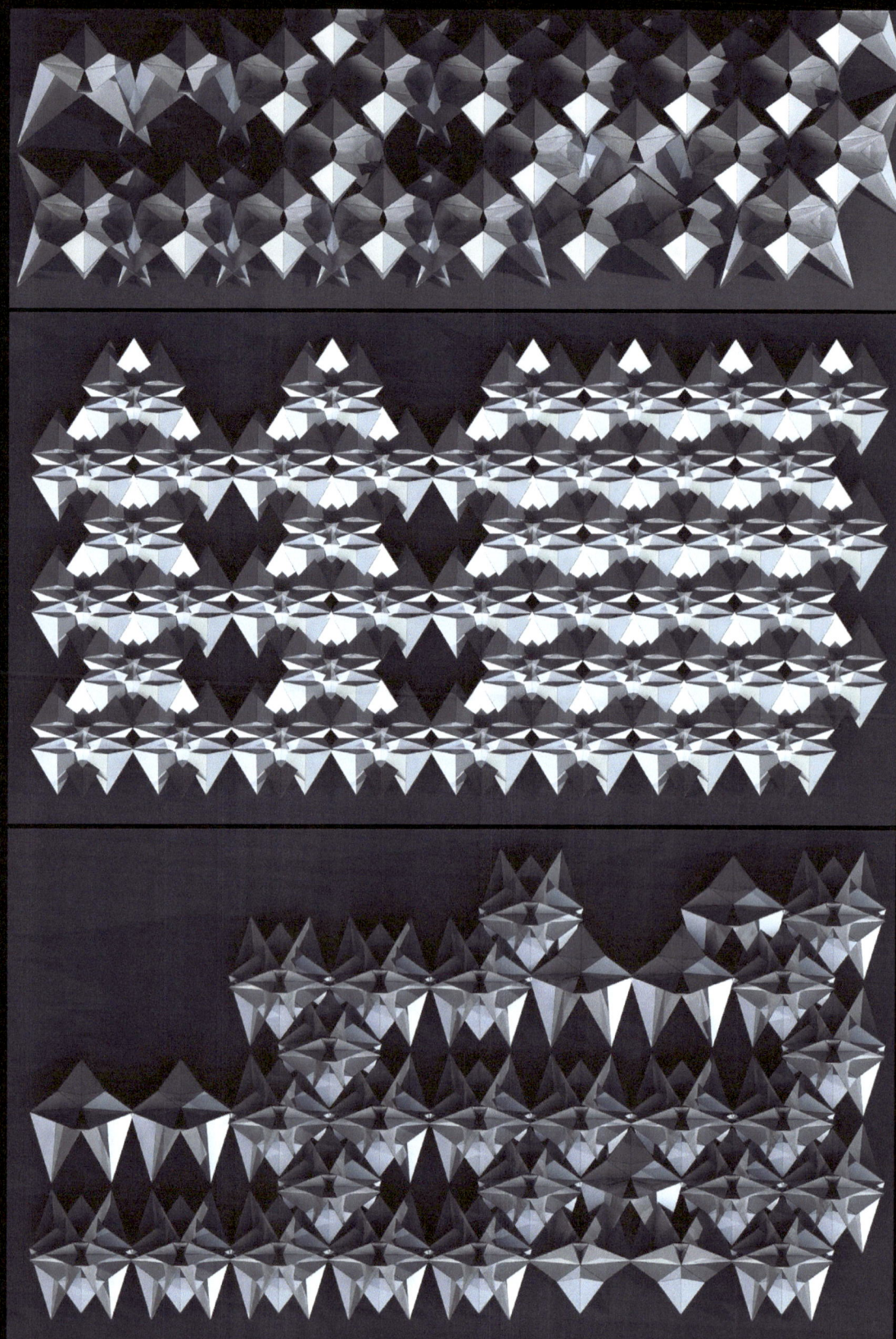

Forth experience of pattern design

Picture 103 – Patterns

Facade Design of Pezeshkan Tower

This project is related to design of facade of "Pezeshkan" tower in 23 stories in Tabriz. The original patterns are designed using parametric method. Making animations, arrangement and transformation of patterns (especially in interior views of the space) were studied to obtain the final pattern. The selected frames- out of tens of made animation frames- of parametric variations of patterns. (Picture 104)

This experience may be helpful in form of shades (considering aesthetic criteria) and controlling light intensity in indoor space.

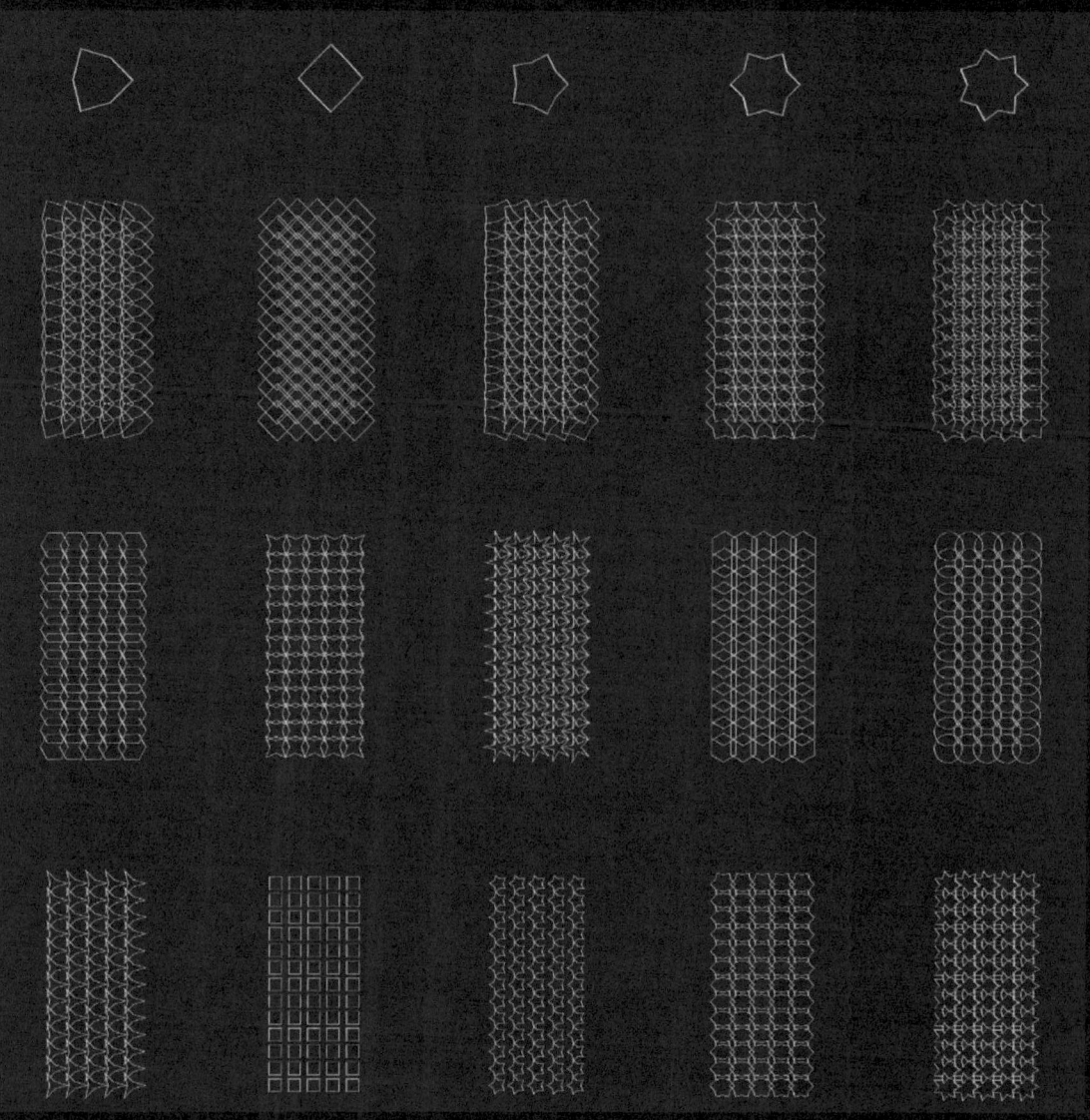

Picture 104

Picture 105 – Pezeshkan Tower

Picture 106 - Elevations

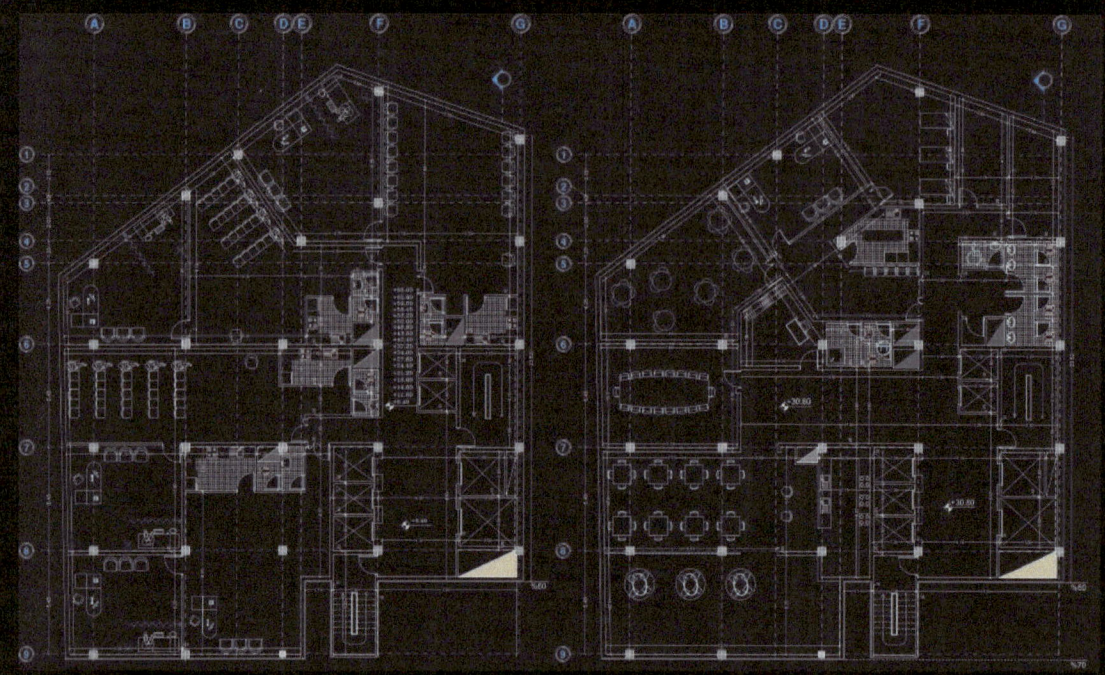

Picture 107- Plans

Eastern view of the complex which was designed simply to make two other views more salient due to contrast. (Picture 108)

Picture 108 - Eastern view

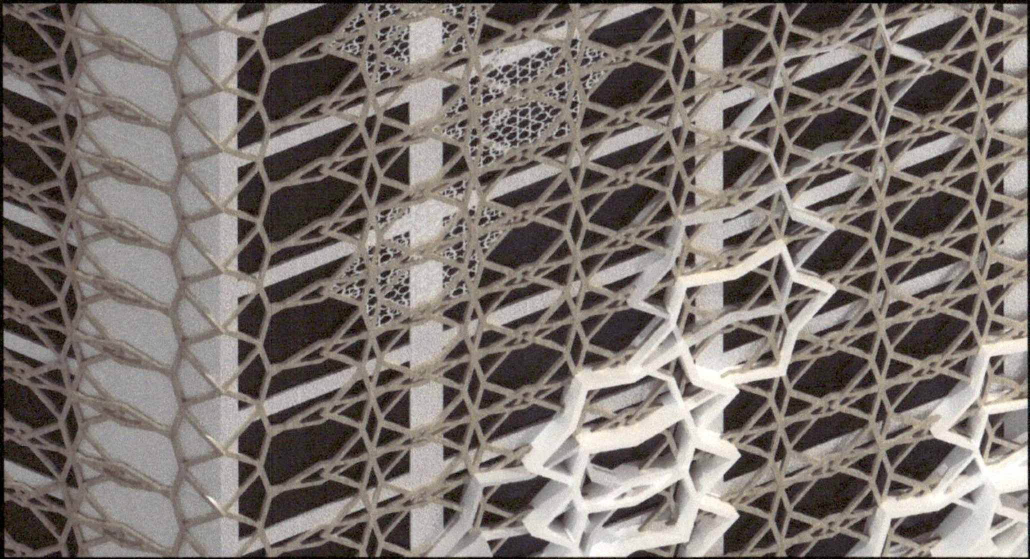

Picture 109 - A close view of details of the facade

Interior rendering of pattern changes and shadows

Studying different forms and shades created inside or outside of the building. In the pictures selected from animations made of curst formation and transformation, location and thickness of the lines indicating to volume and facade of the cube are changed, or they are omitted. It has an important and direct effect of facade form and created shades. (Picture 110)

Picture 110 – Interior renders

Change and Combine of Patterns
Conceptual Design of a Building Facade

Picture 111 – Frist Frame of Animation

Density of form & shade

In this experience, a line was scattered on the cube by scatter (an instruction of 3Ds Max where an object is scattered over another). After rotation and location of the lines, their density -in an ascending order- was made as an animation. I hide the main cube and only remained a mat-line structure. I put inside an "Omni" light to create share. Form, variety and density of shades are changed through increasing density of lines and interwoven of the mat. (cooperator: Sahand Latifi)

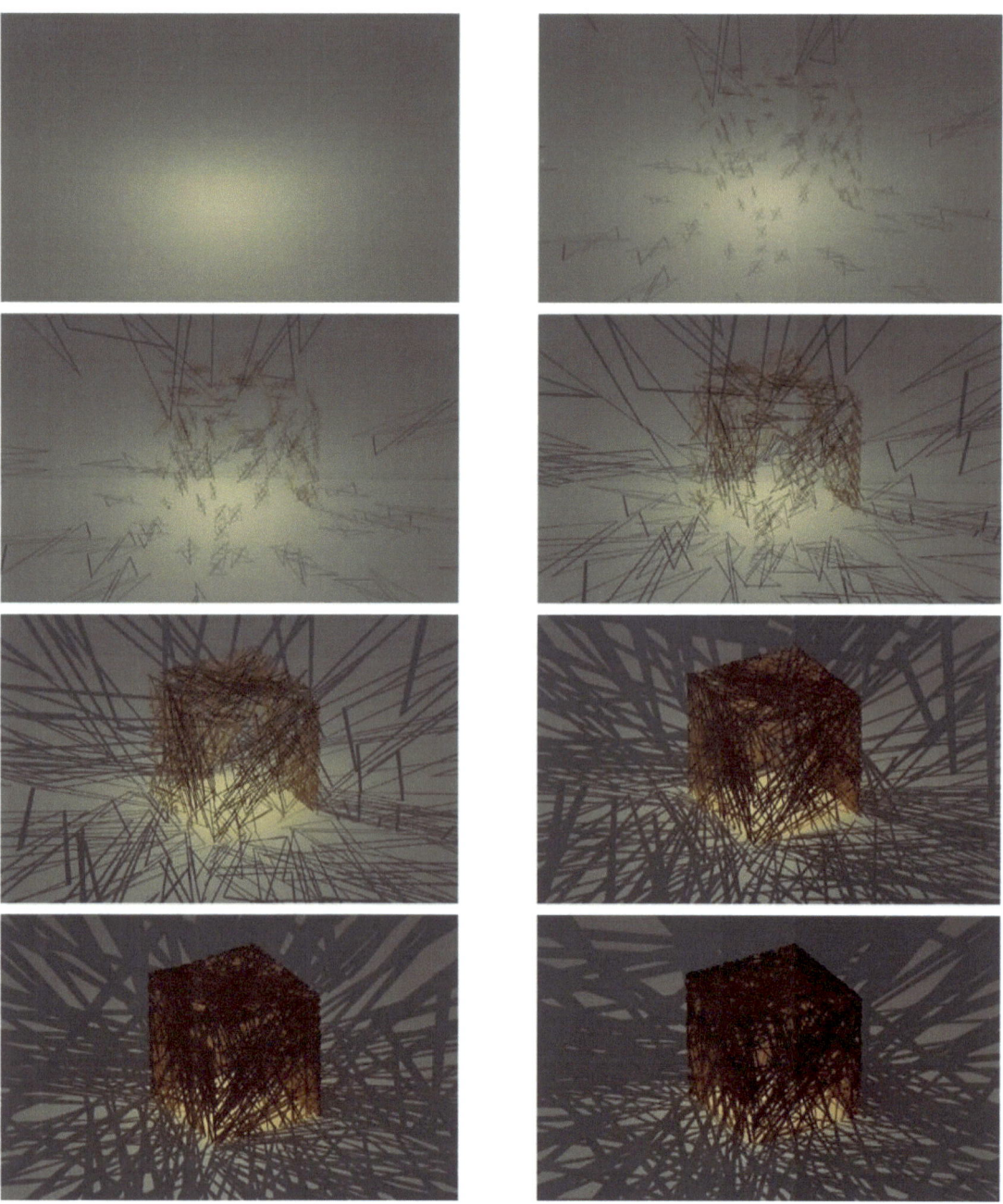

Picture111 - Density of form & shade

The previous practice was repeated vice versa, i.e. in a descending order associated with rotation of lines on surface of the main cube which is hidden. The variations made in the space through lightening and paying attention to shades is more and easier than working with form and volume.

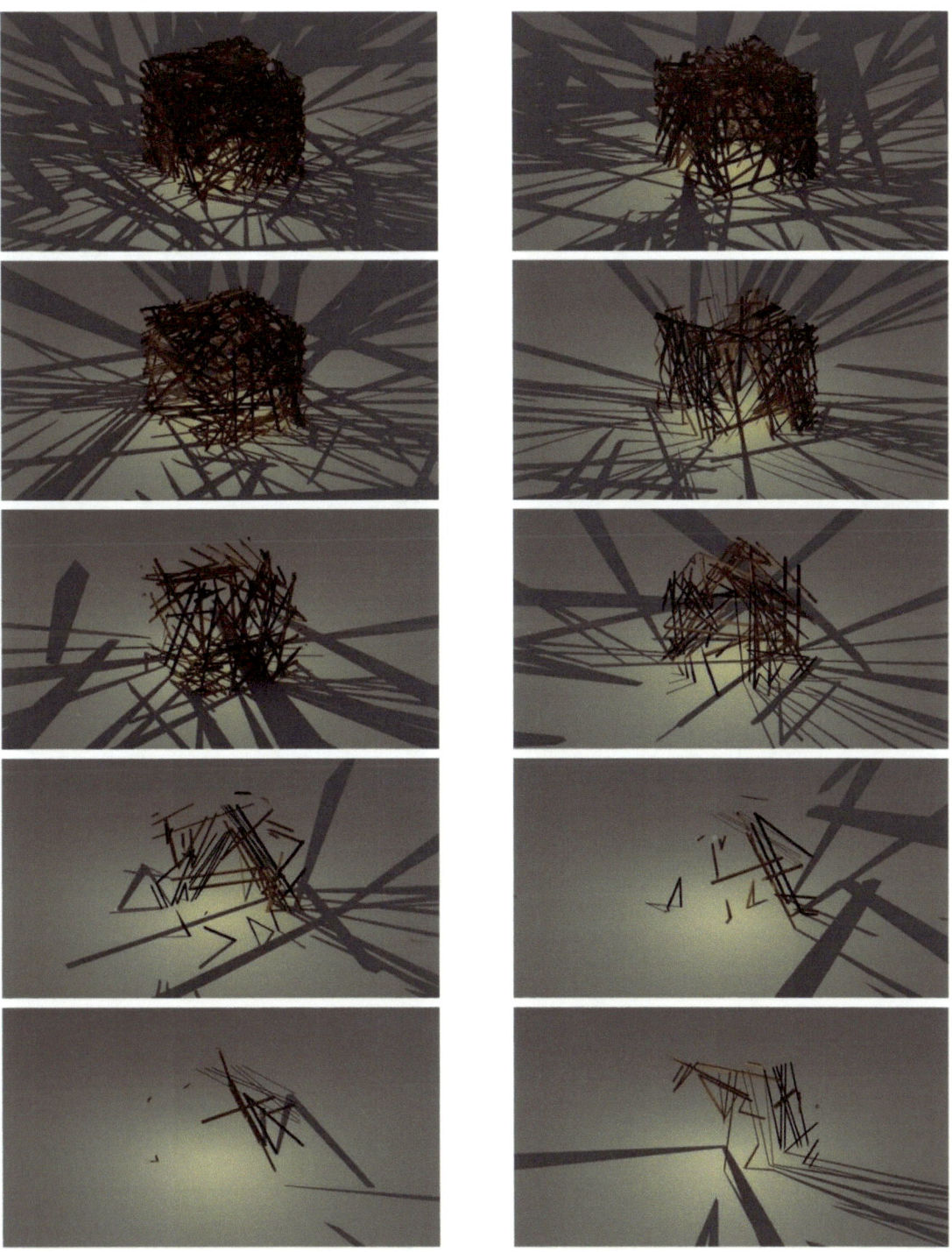

Picture112 - Density of form & shade

Daylight

Daylight in 3Ds Max is a light which makes it possible to designers to simulate radiation angle and intensity of sunlight at, for example, noon of May 2050.

Light address: Create> System> Daylight (Picture 113)

This light may be used in two ways: based on real location, angle, and intensity of sunlight or displacing light source manually

Choosing the "Date, Time & Location" option (according to the picture), parameters will be seen below to initially specify year, month, and time of sunlight radiation. Using "Location", you can choose location of the project on the world map (in this section, capitals of countries are mainly specified). Also, you can write longitude and latitude of the project opposite "Longitude" and "Latitude" options to exactly record sunlight radiation. Changing radiation times during different seasons, you can study orientation of the building, depth of light penetration, depth of sunshade, and dimensions of openings inside and outside of the building. Making sun movement animation, you can better introduce your project and clearly refer to climatic reasons used in the plan.

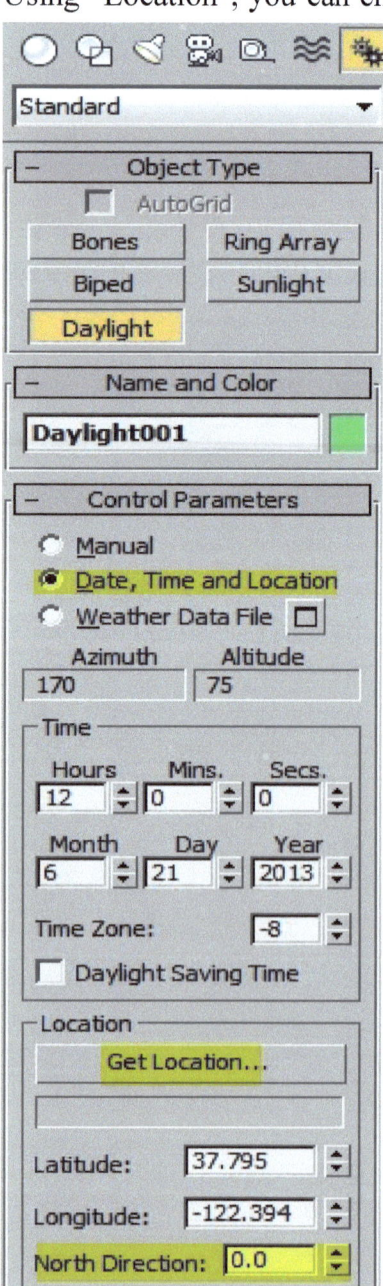

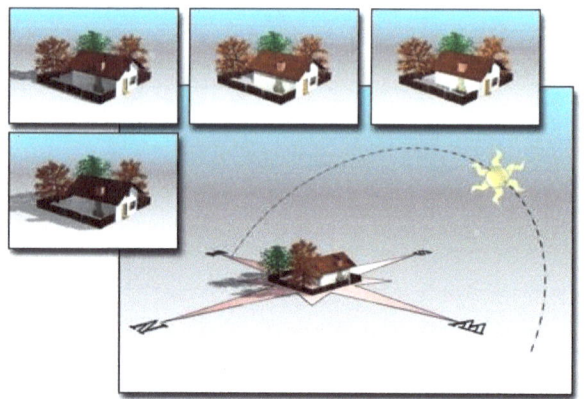

Picture114- In this picture adopted from http://knowledge.autodesk.com website (training of "Daylight"), sunlight movement and its effect on building and change of shades are seen.

<Picture 113

Chapter 5

Kinetic Architecture

Kinetic or dynamic architecture is practically a modern concept of buildings design quality such that a significant part of it is movable while its structural integrity is preserved. Such capability of the buildings adds to their beauty while it is accountable for environmental conditions. Therefore, the structure will have a function which is far away from a static structure. Movement in each elements of architecture is manifested in different ways.

This objective, i.e. animating part of a building, will be realized through knowing principles of motion and its governing rules, as the first step, and recognizing the required instruments to design and execute such principles, as the second step.

The concept of "Kinetic" in architecture has been used by nomad tribes. Movable structure of tent- as a foldup and portable system- has been still used in kinetic architecture. As another definition, kinetic architecture is defined as a building with changeable or kinetic location and/or changeable or kinetic geometry.

Foldup system is a kind of kinetic systems which controls the structure through moving all or part of it. Kas Oosterhuis, the researcher, completely defines kinetic architecture:

"Kinetic architecture refers to a building controlled by sensors and operators and is kinetically accountable considering the input data (Sherbini, 2004)"

Development of sciences such as mechanics, electronics and robotics which provided architecture with modern facilities led to more practical application of kinetic architecture at end of the 20th century. However, it does not negate historical records of "Mobility" thought. Drawbridges of the middle ages and before it, are samples of such thought. Ancient romans used combination of vela structures in their sport fields (Afzali, 2015). Combination of opening and closing mechanisms and animating are of modern ideas used in modern architecture. They may be used in combination with different parts of a building or as part of it. In the first and second samples, the system plays the role in combination with an architectural element, i.e. facade, and as part of the building, respectively, like what has been occurred in the building of Milwaukee Art Museum designed by Calatrava (Taraz, 2015).

Picture 115 - Milwaukee Art Museum, 1994

Simulation of Kinetic Structure No. 1

Simulation of Kinetic Structure No. 2

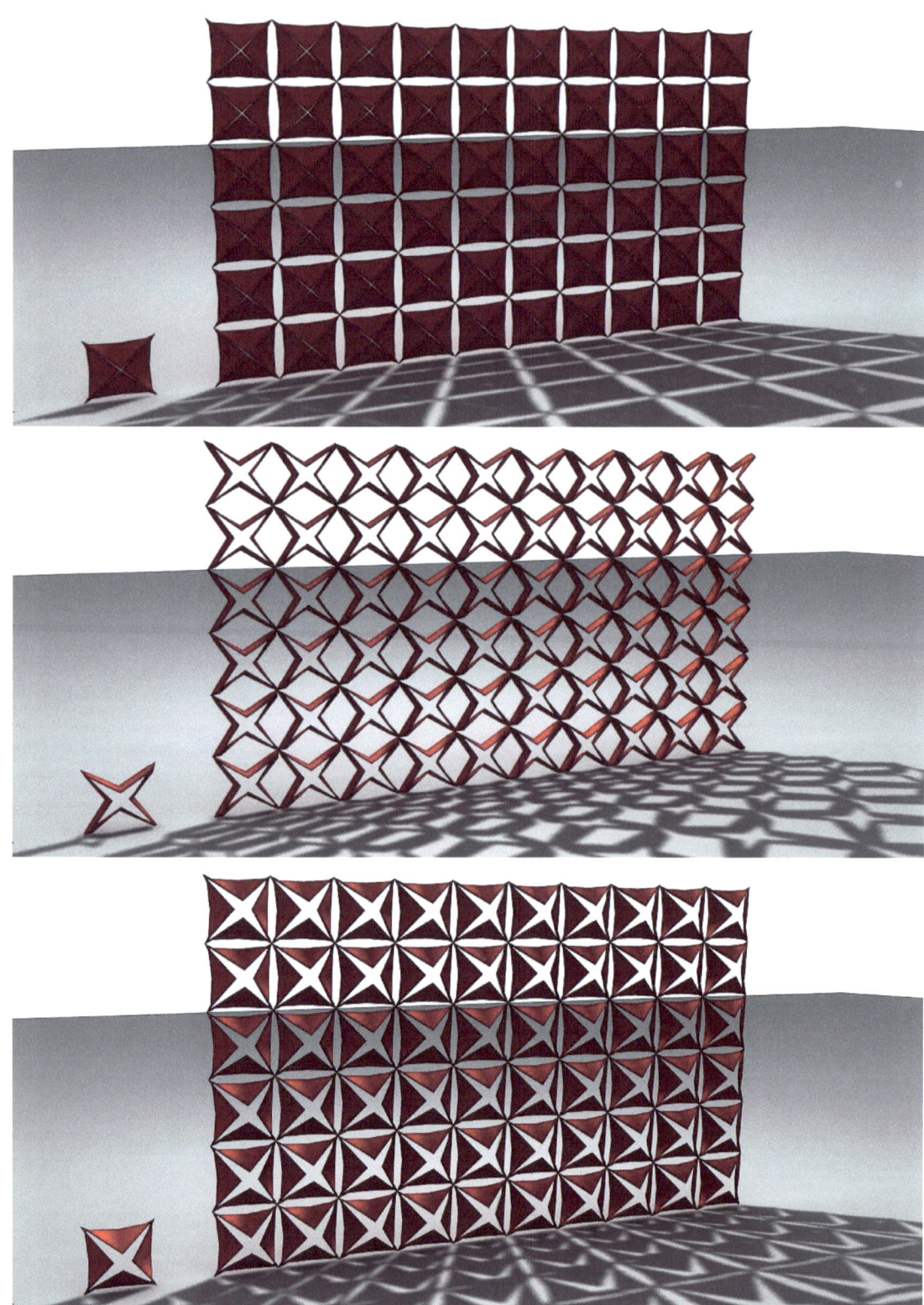

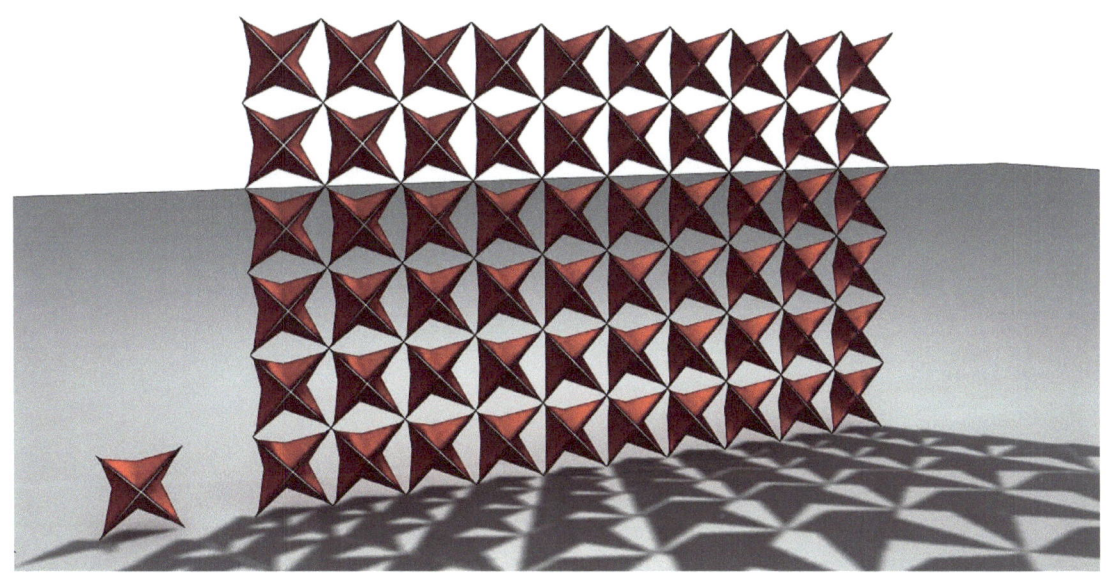

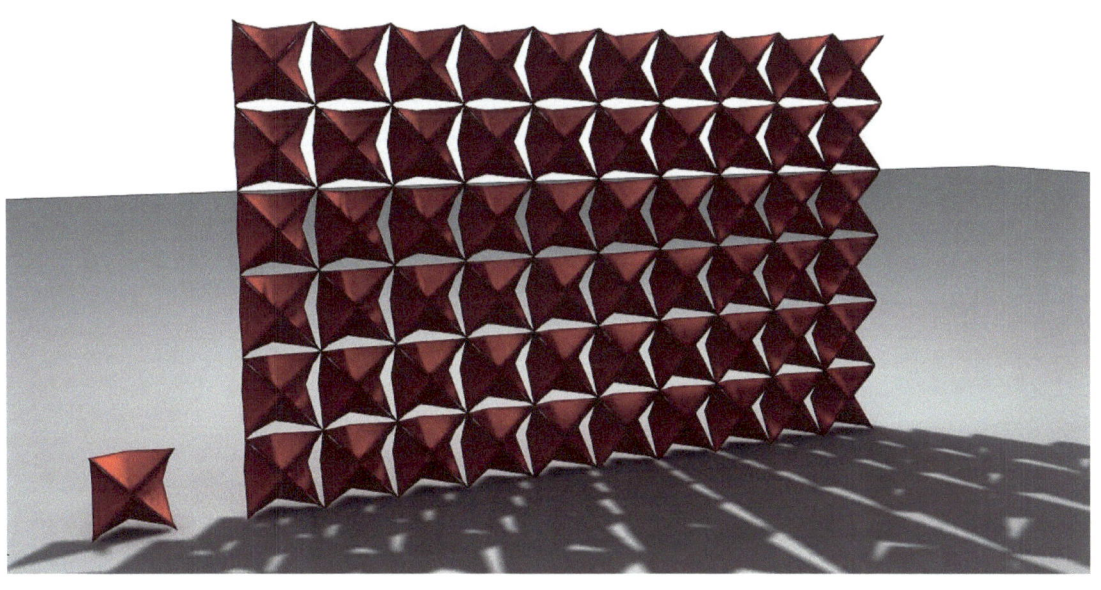

Design of Facade of Diba Bags & Shoes Market (Tehran, Iran)

In another project designed for facade of "Diba" Bags & Shoes Market of Tehran, we simulated opening and closing of patterns (the idea of opening and closing of the designed patterns were adapted from Al-Bahr Tower project).

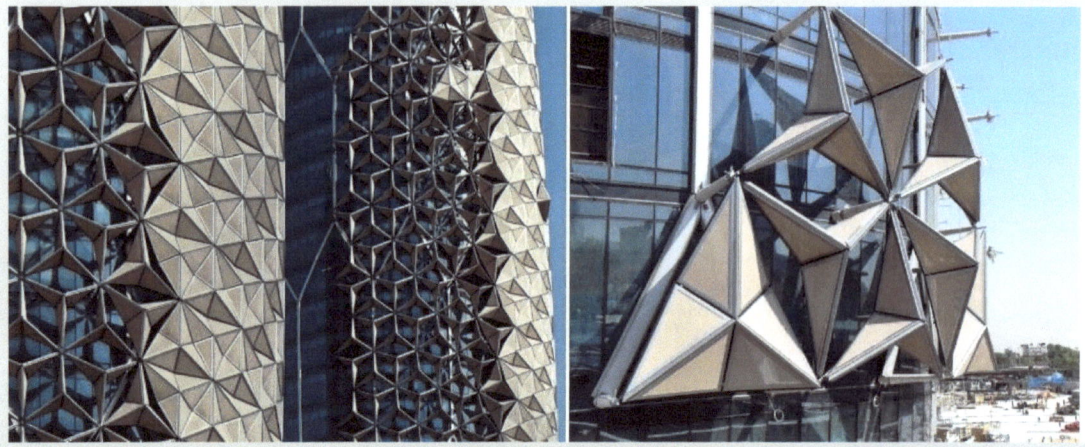

Picture 116- Al-Bahr Tower

Patterns design process.

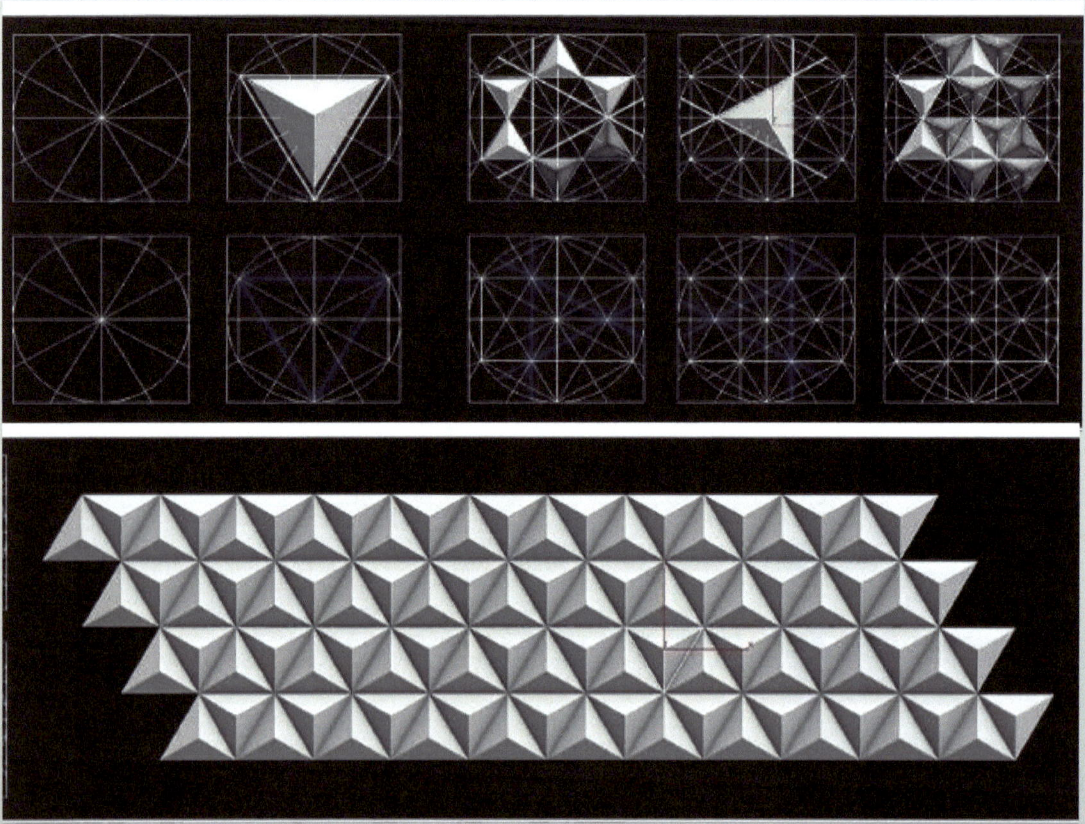

Pictures 117 & 118

Parametric Analyze of Patterns.

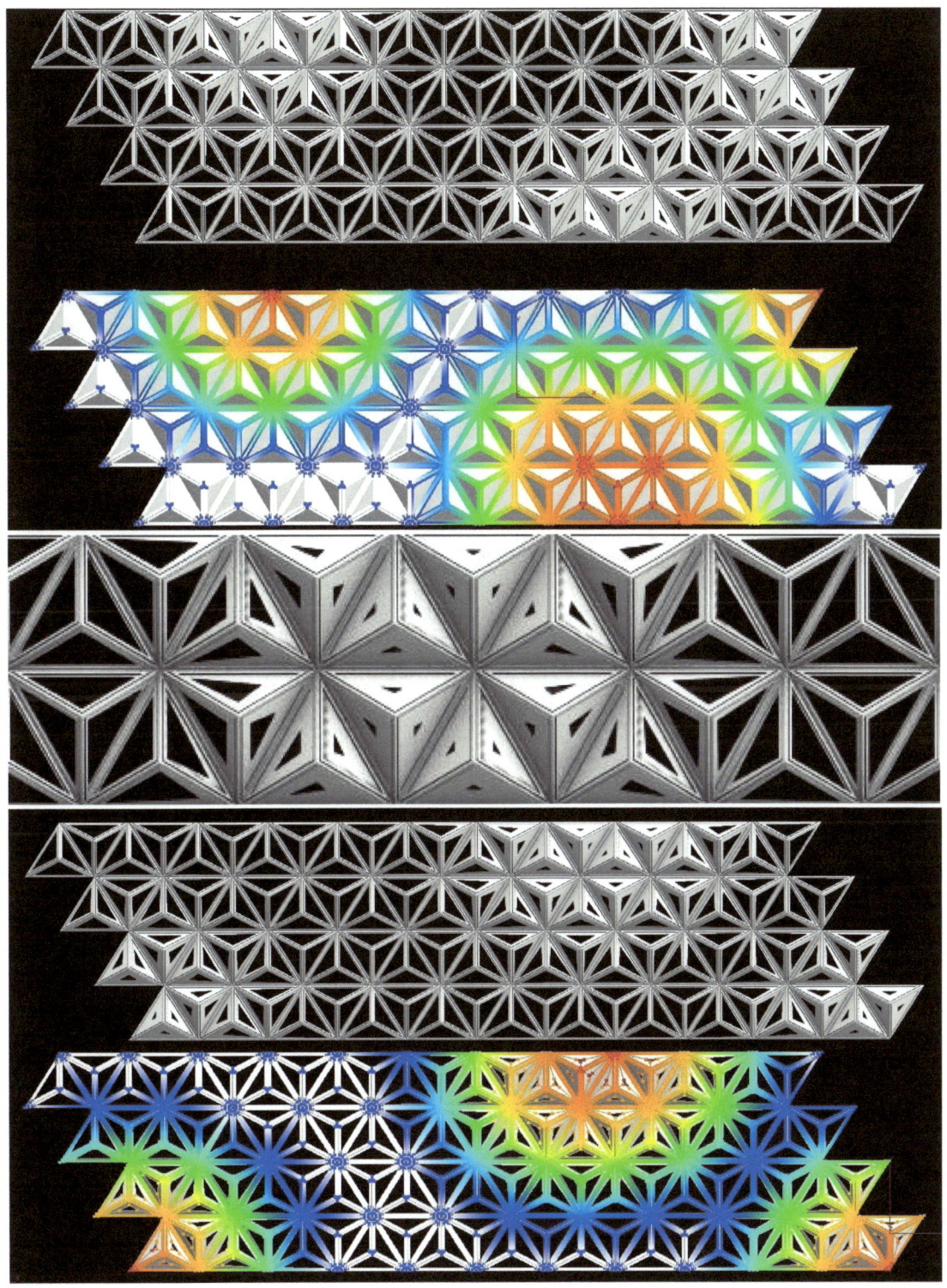

(Picture 119)

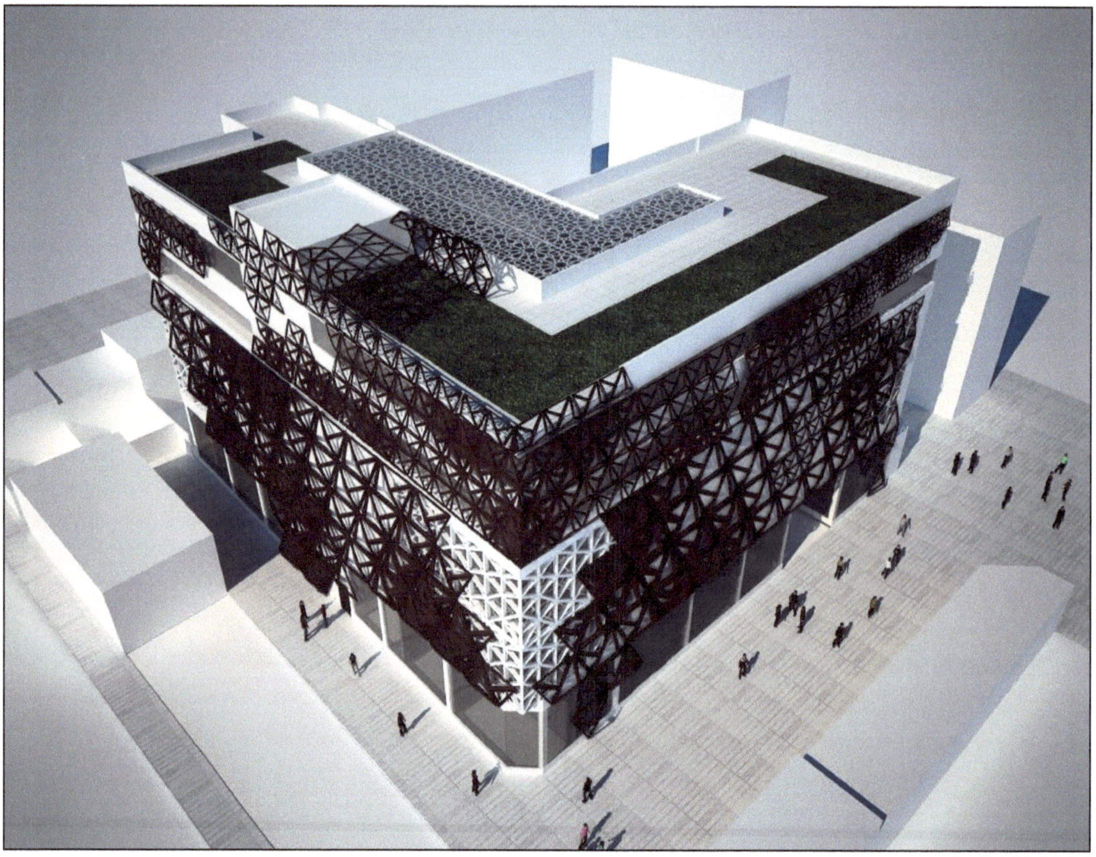

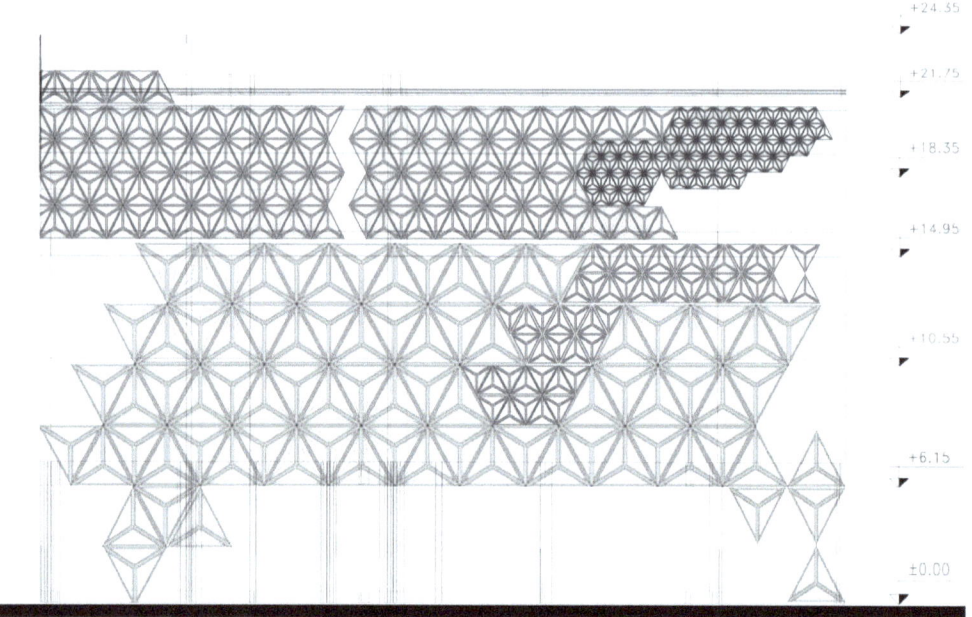

Picture 120 – Perspective

Picture 121 – Elevation

Indoor renders of the complex show different forms of opening and closing of patterns in facade, creation of various shades, and controlling of the light enters inside space. (Picture 122)

Picture 122

Examples of Kinetic Surfaces & Crusts

- Design and construct structures which can change according to behaviors or requirements of human
- Design facade or dynamic crust which transform according to human movement.
- In a more developed state, virtual and even real walls are moving intelligently and parts of a house can rotate according to requirements and needs of its residents such as Sharifiha House (designed by Eng. Taghaboni). This project won the first rank of residential spaces of Architect Award 2013 and Middle East Architect Award 2014. (Pictures 123 & 124)

Pictures 123 & 124 - Sharifiha House (The pictures were selected from Eng. Taghaboni's office site (www.nextoffice.ir)

Virtual walls with changeable and dynamic nature

As another example, focus on an old factory with a big hall and high height divided with virtual walls and ceiling where the walls disappear and a new arrangement appears on festival days or other celebrations only through pressing a button.

Windows, rooms or buildings which move and rotate are important events. The most important, but, is the virtual walls which will be dealt with in plan division in real world. Form of walls or height of the ceiling will be changed through displacement for a special celebration.

Flowering
Conceptual experience of kinetic architecture
Design team: Samira Mahoutchian, Negin Hosein Alizadeh

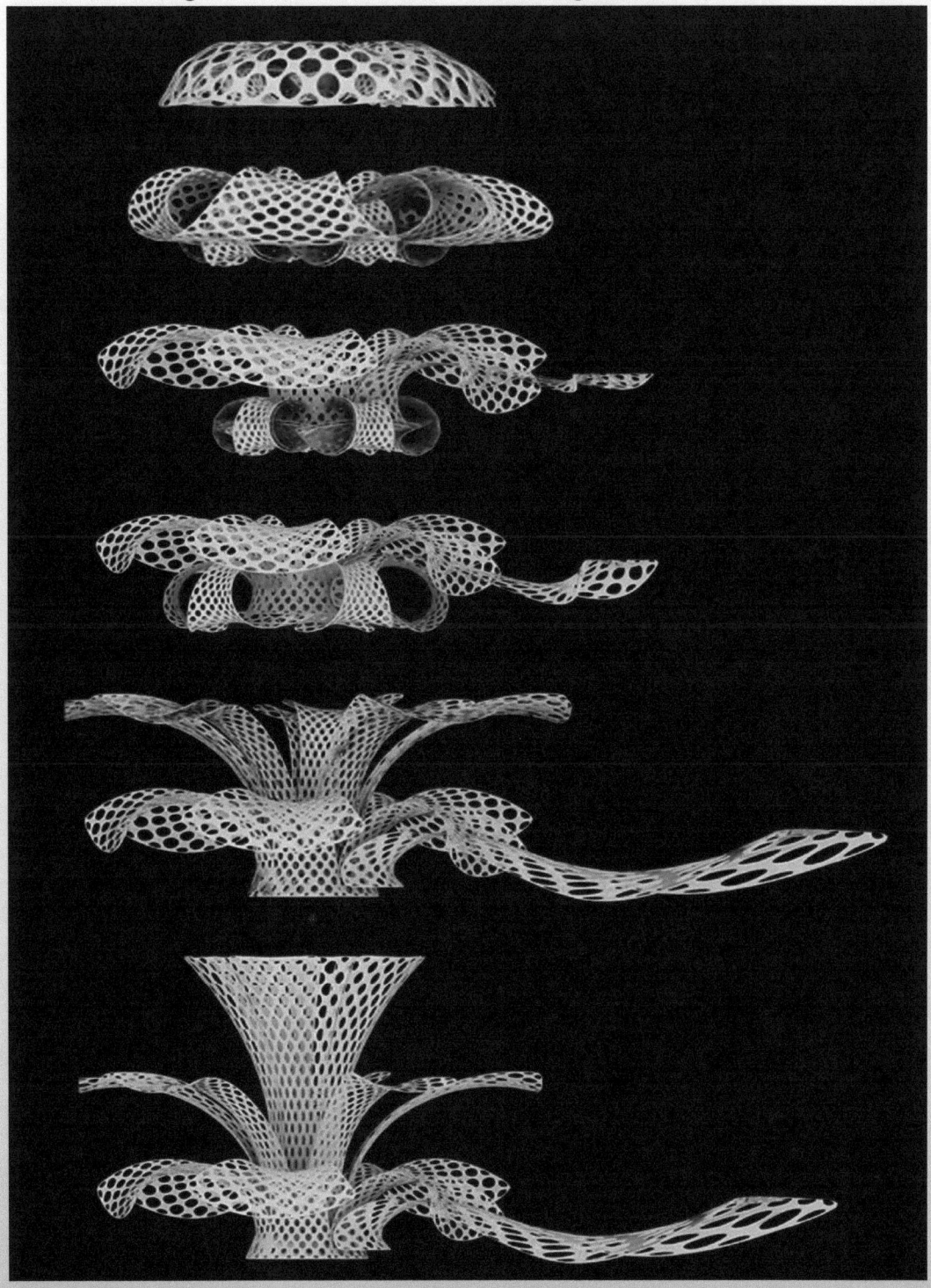

Picture 125 – Front View

Picture 126

Picture 127

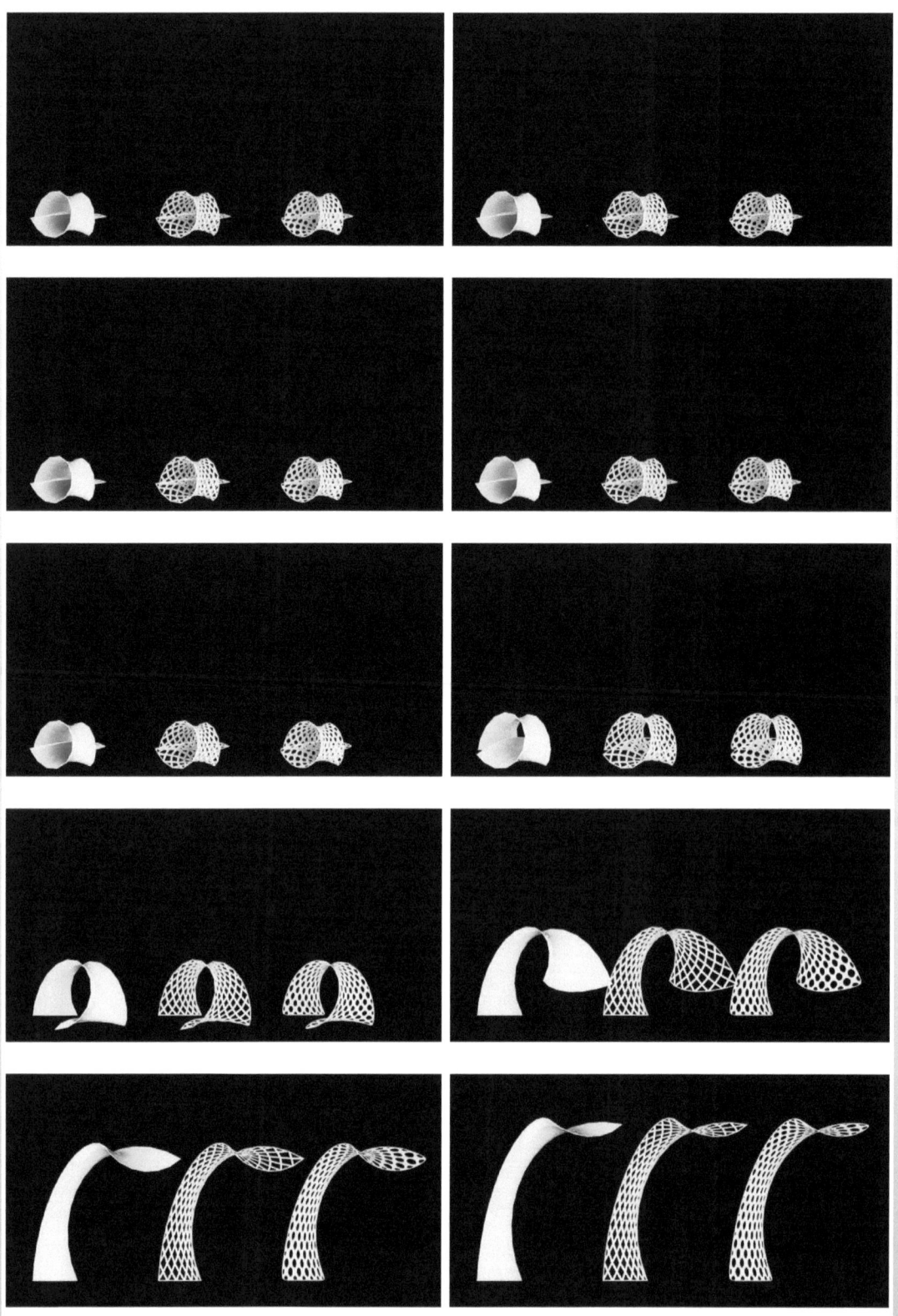

Picture 128 – Opening a surface

Pictures 129 & 130 – Final renders of project

Symmetry Tower
Conceptual experience of kinetic architecture

Picture 131

Symmetric evolution process

Chapter 6

Growth and Metamorphosis

Metaballs

Metaball is another technique recently used as the main structure of a project by architects and is based on forms generation similar to drops falling from a liquid. It has an animate structure where speed of bubbles scattering, dimensions, adherence or severance of bubbles and their cohesion may be determined.

After production of Metaballs sciences in mathematics and physics and then its completion in computerized graphics, the knowledge entered modeling software. Therefore, the designers have the opportunity to produce forms arising from metaballs technology calculations using this technique. The forms arising from this technique are similar to modeling of behavior of high density liquids in vacuo where liquid drops absorb each other and are stretched in in-between distances. In this clear example, transfer of knowledge of other fields to architecture resulted in production of new ideas and methods and imposing its behavior which is a result of mathematical algorithm (Khabazi, 2014). It should be mentioned that the technique was previously and repeatedly used by animators to show waterfall, water flow, coffee or any liquid poured in a glass and so.

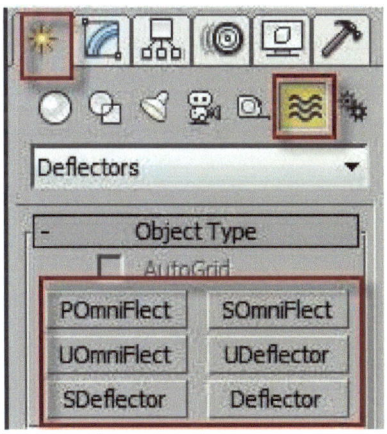

3D software makes it possible to control behavior of particles or drops. Defining "Deflectors" in 3Ds Max, for example, you can define a gravity to direct the drops downward. According to the pictures, the produced drops fall down and scatter upwards when they class the floor.

You can define different similar forces to control and direct the particles in encountering with specific limits such as site of adjacent buildings. (Picture 136)

Picture 136

In "Vray 3.6" plugin, a section known as "Vray Metaball" has been added to 3Ds Max 2018 which is completely compatible with Deflectors of Max and makes it possible for the user to render fast with high quality. The renders you will see are prepared using this plugin.

Pictures of the animation made using Metaball

Picture 137 - Metaballs

Growth

Conceptual experience of growth of the curve forms. (Animation of the following file known as "Animate Form (17) - Twist" may be seen in YouTube).

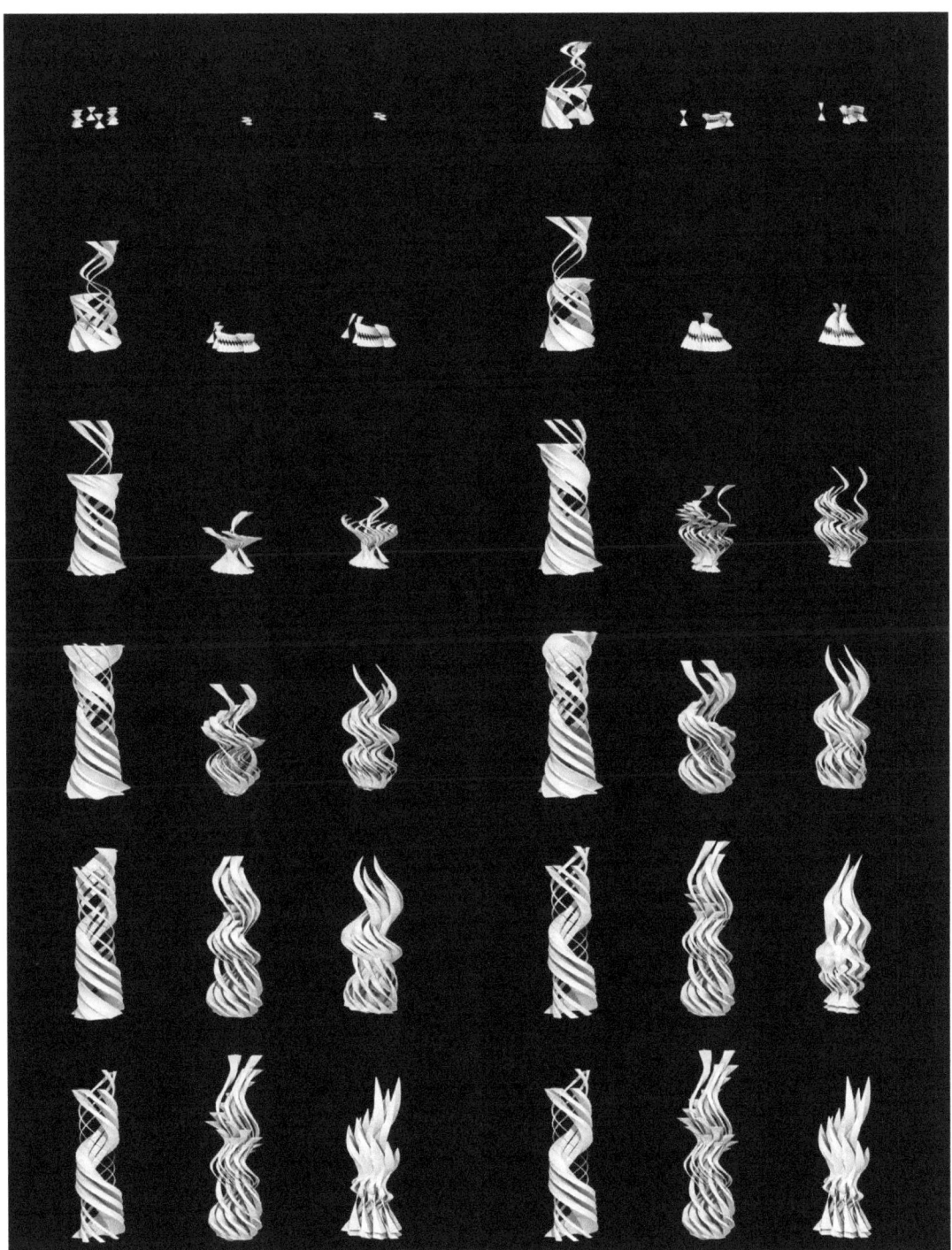

Picture 138 –Process of Growth

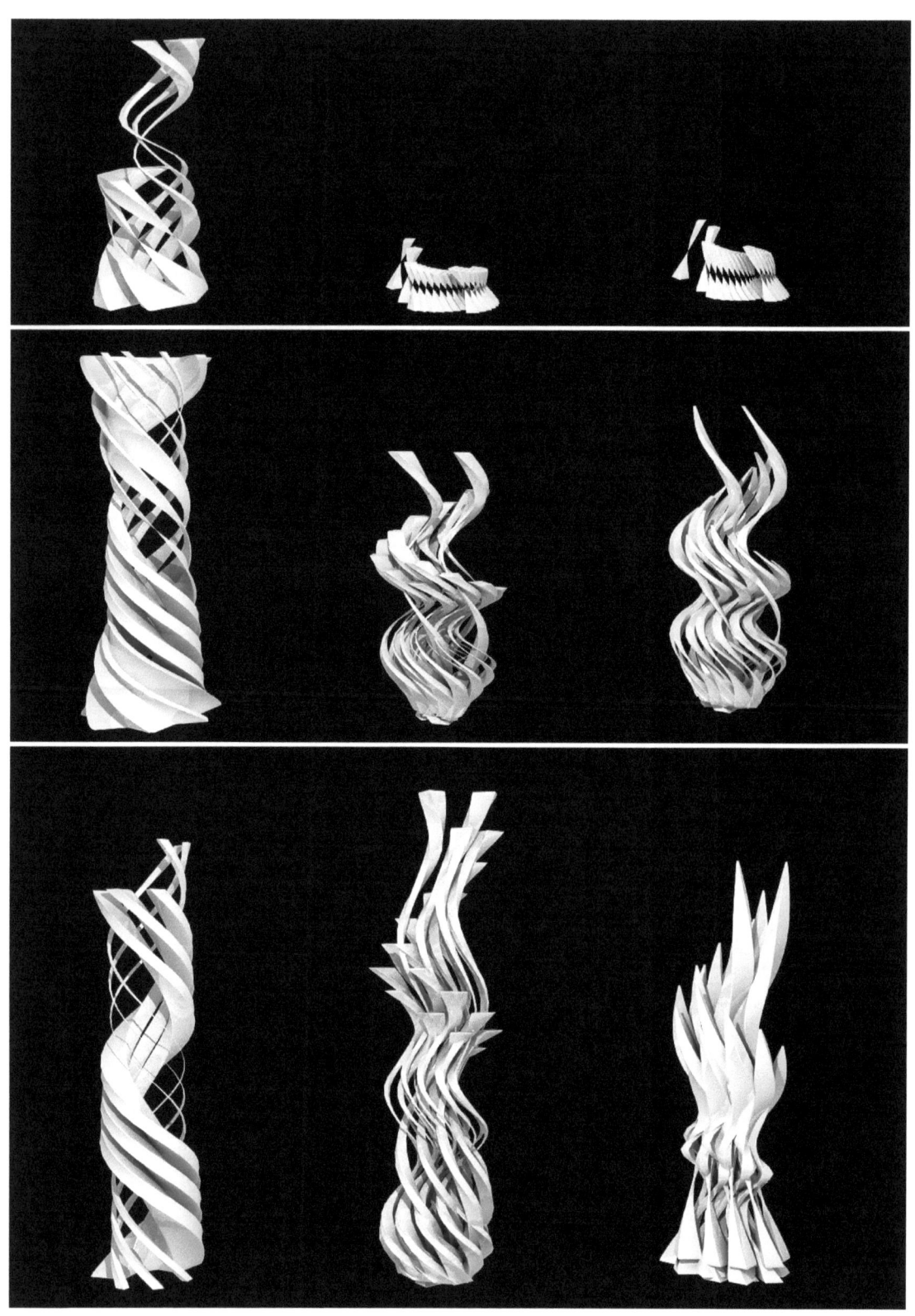

Picture 139 – Selected frames of animation

Twist

Conceptual experience of growth of the curve forms

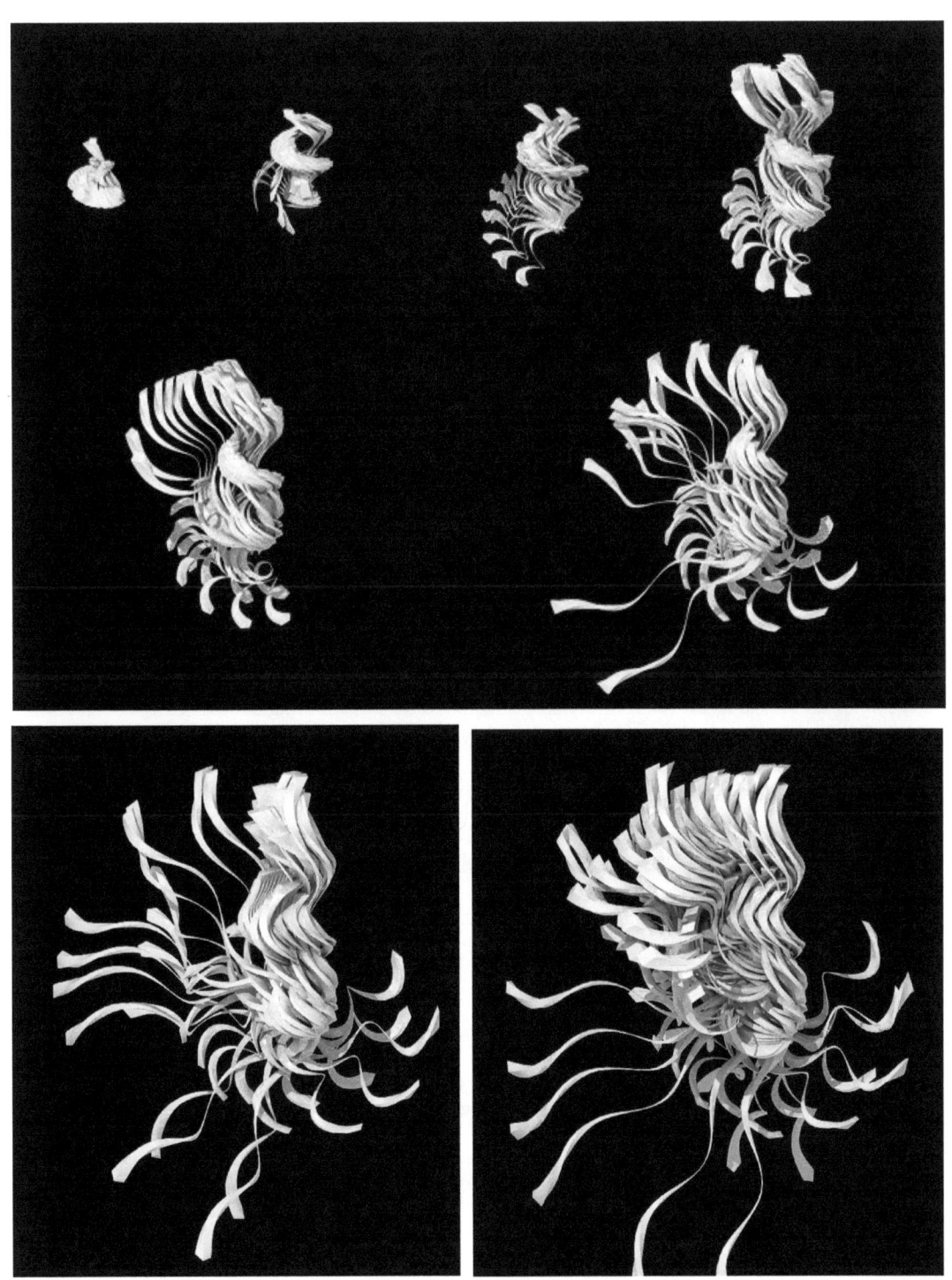

Pictures 141- 143 – Primary frames of animation

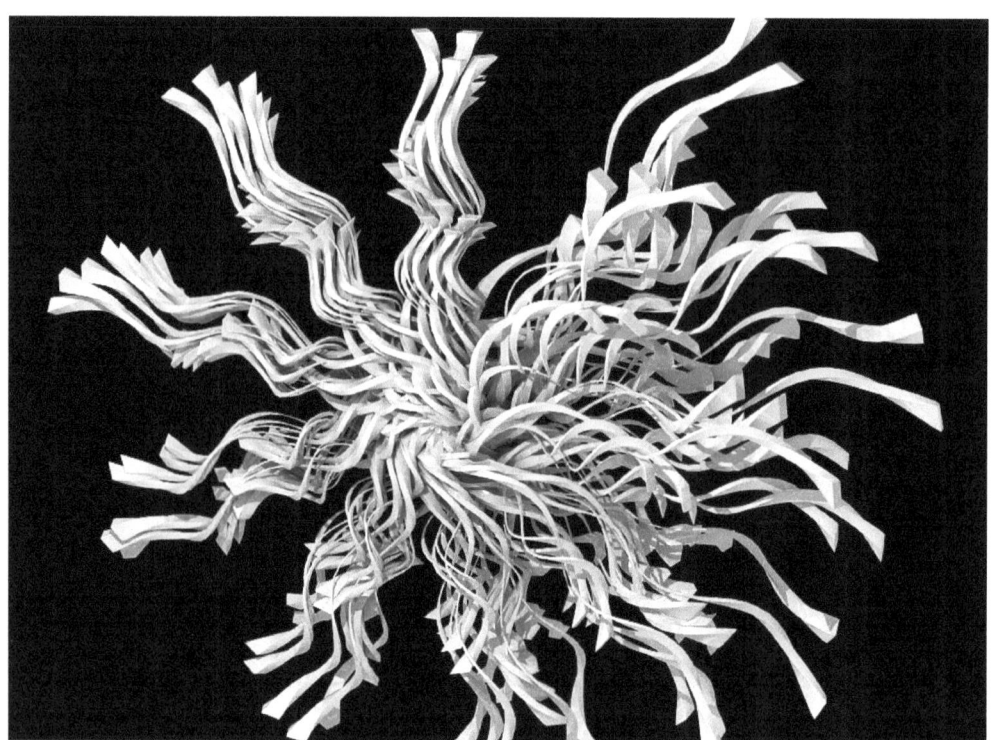
Picture 144 - Final frame of animation

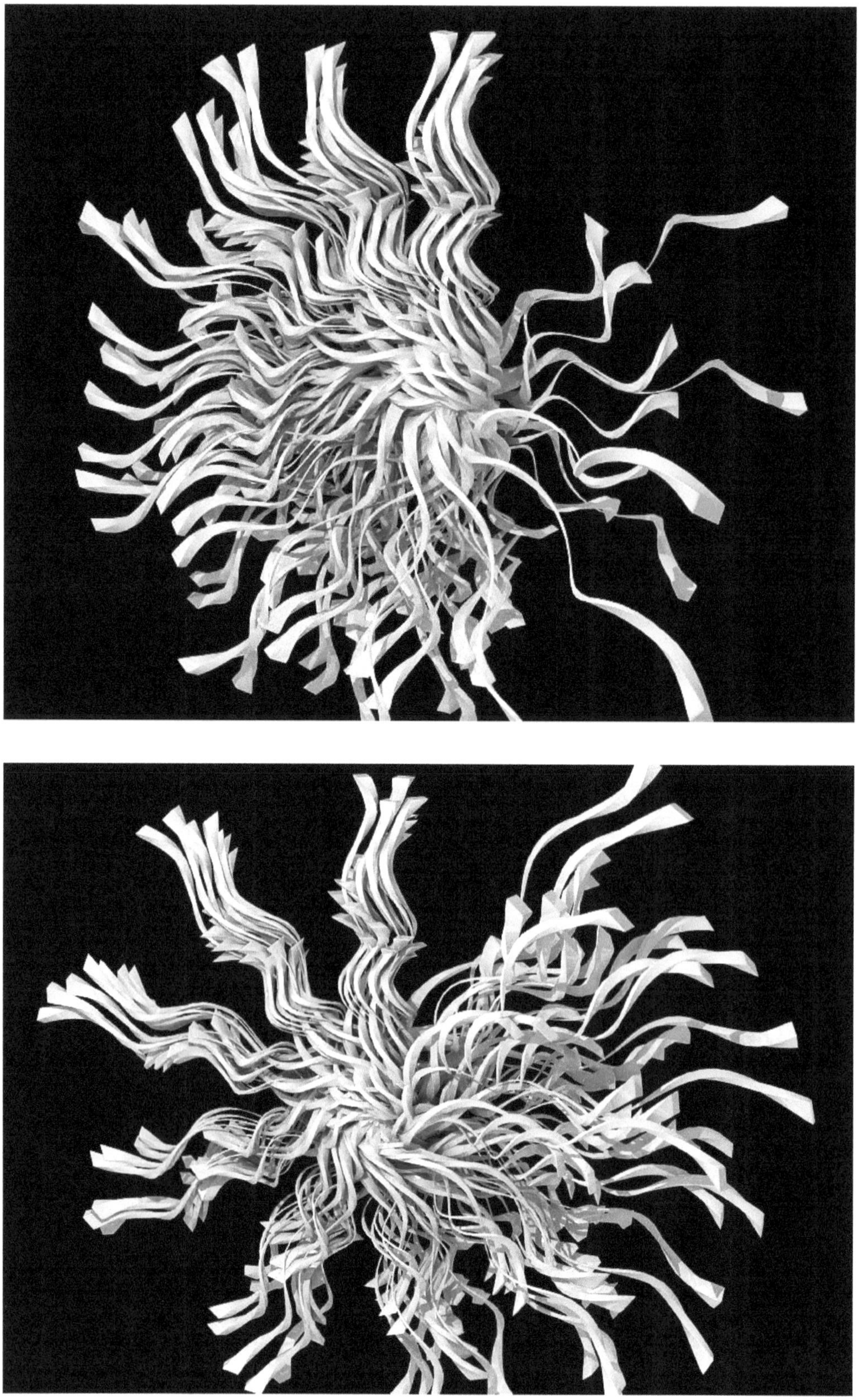

Another experience of changing of a volume from vertical to horizontal structure
The following pictures are 20 selected frame-renders out of 200 made frames.

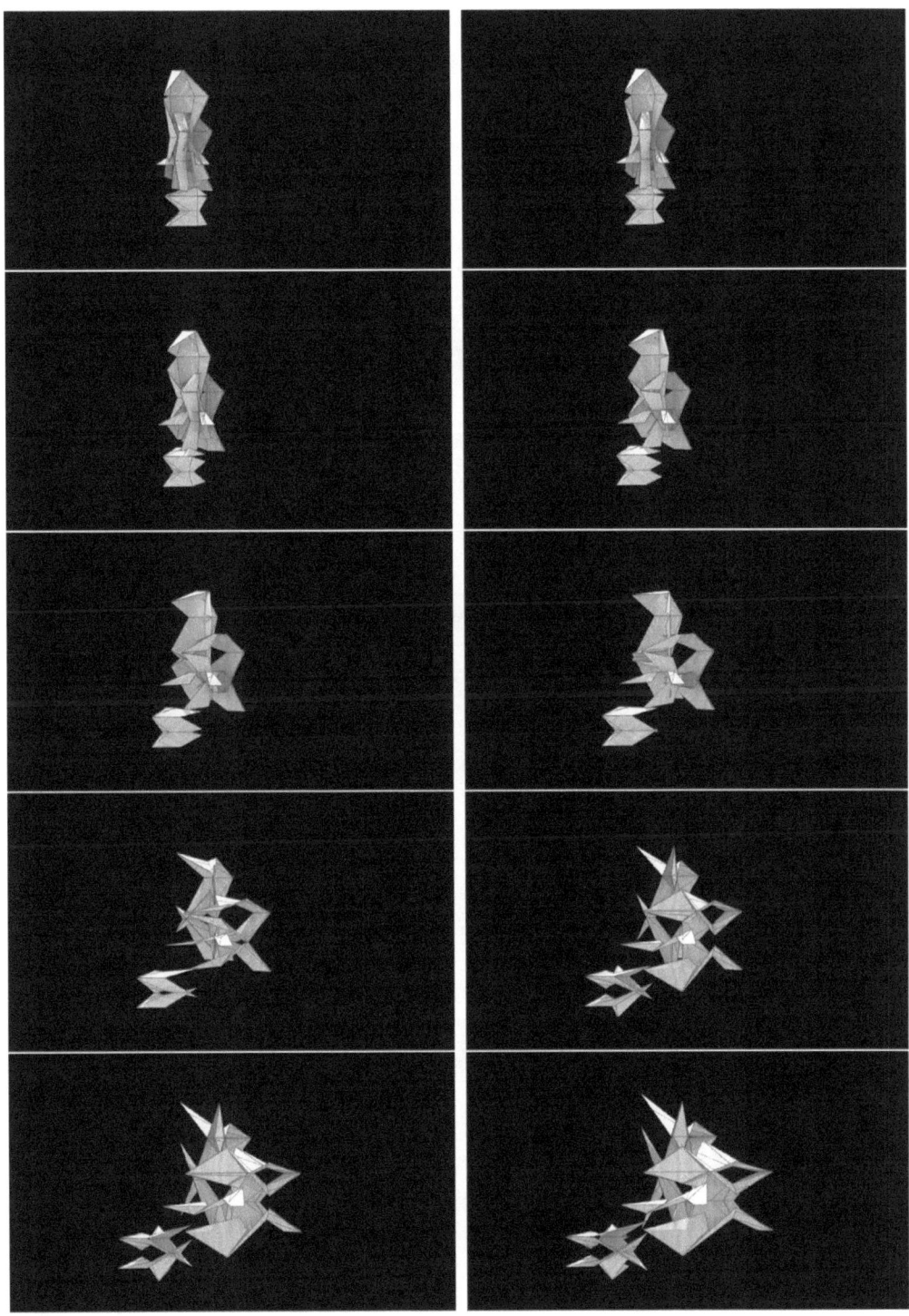

Picture 145

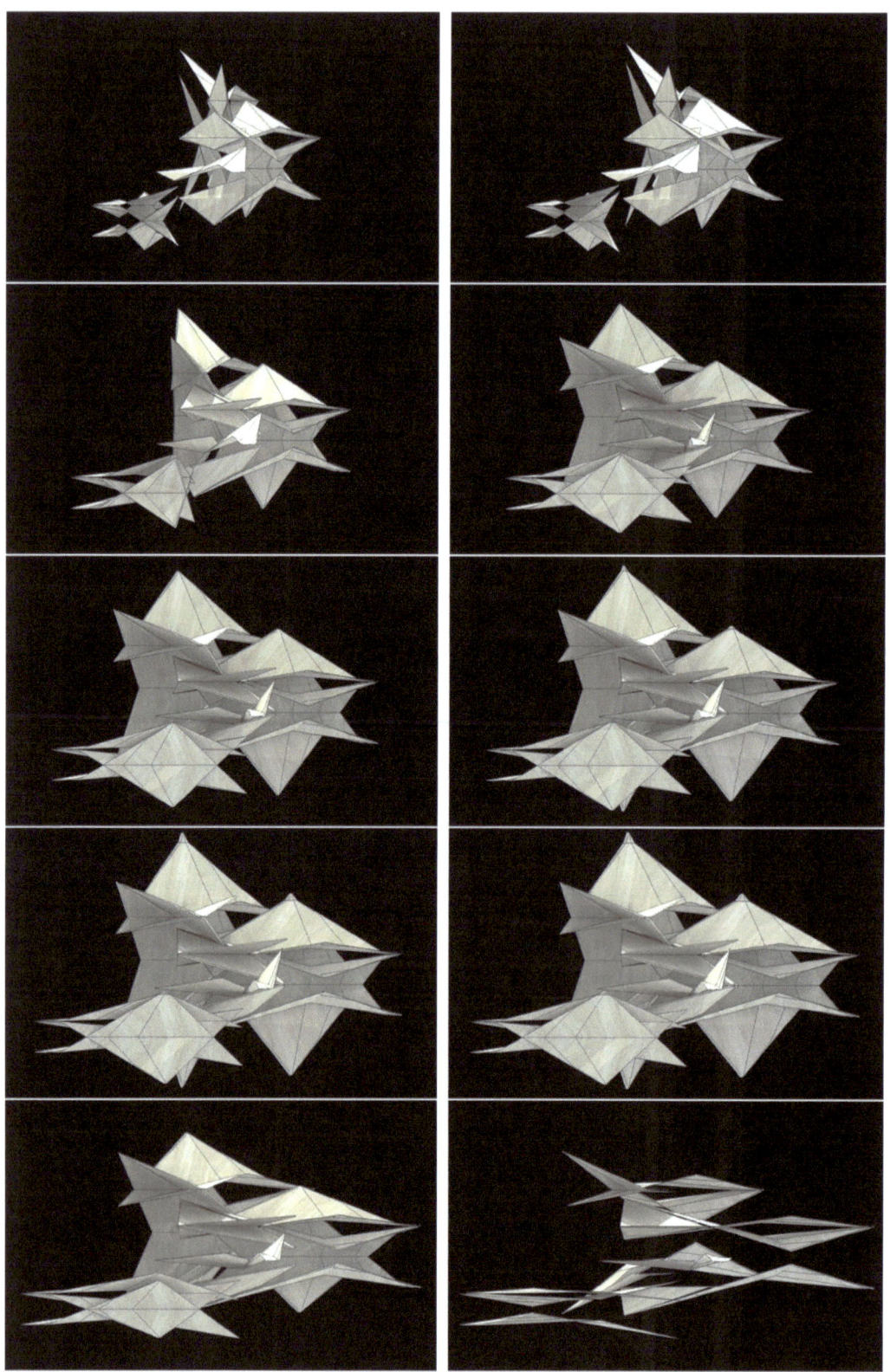

Picture 146

Transformation

Another experience of form conversion and changing from curvature to a broken structure. Design team: Samira Mahoutchian, Leila Manzouri

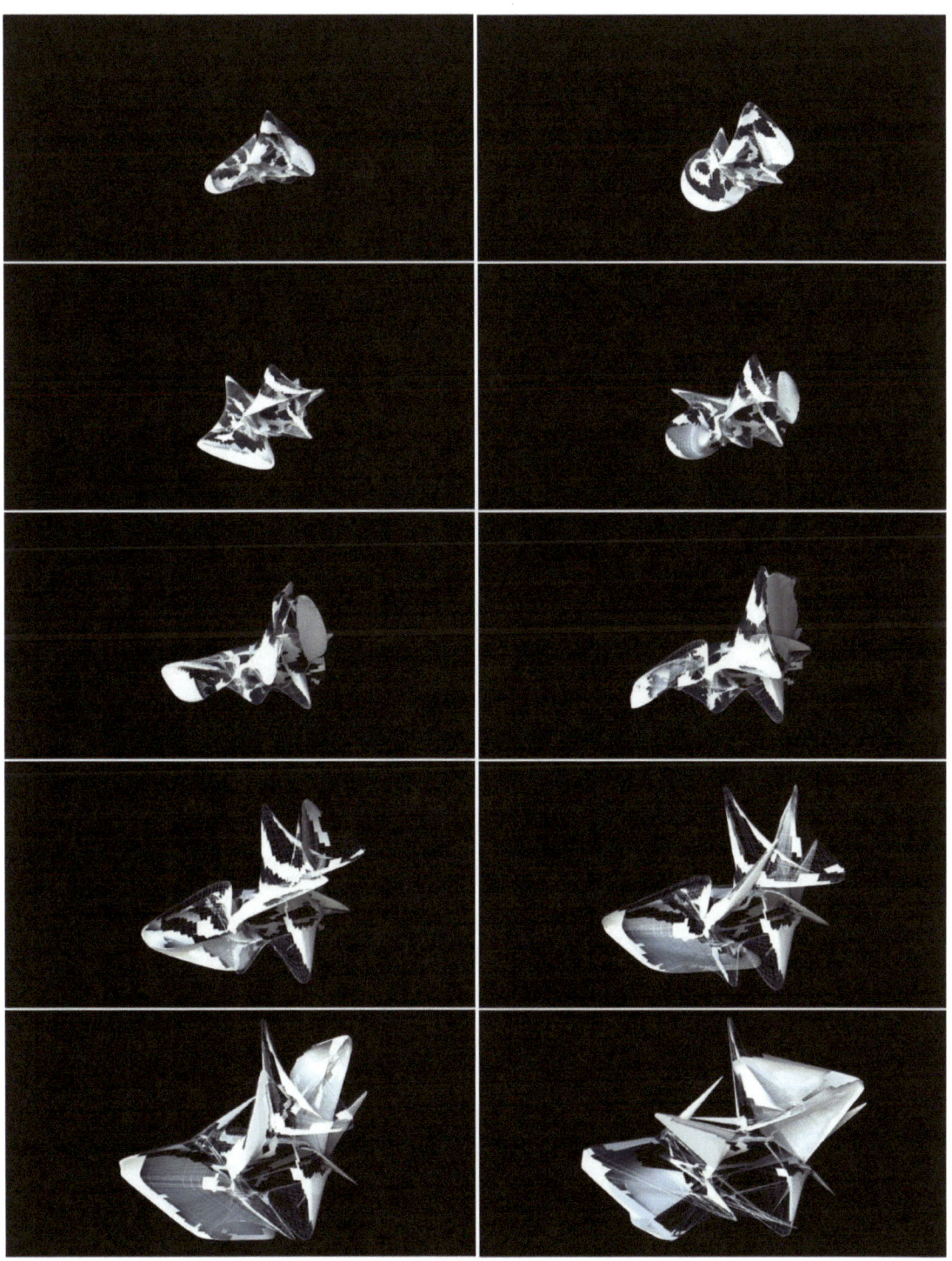

Picture 147

Re-study of form through showing the form in a wire form

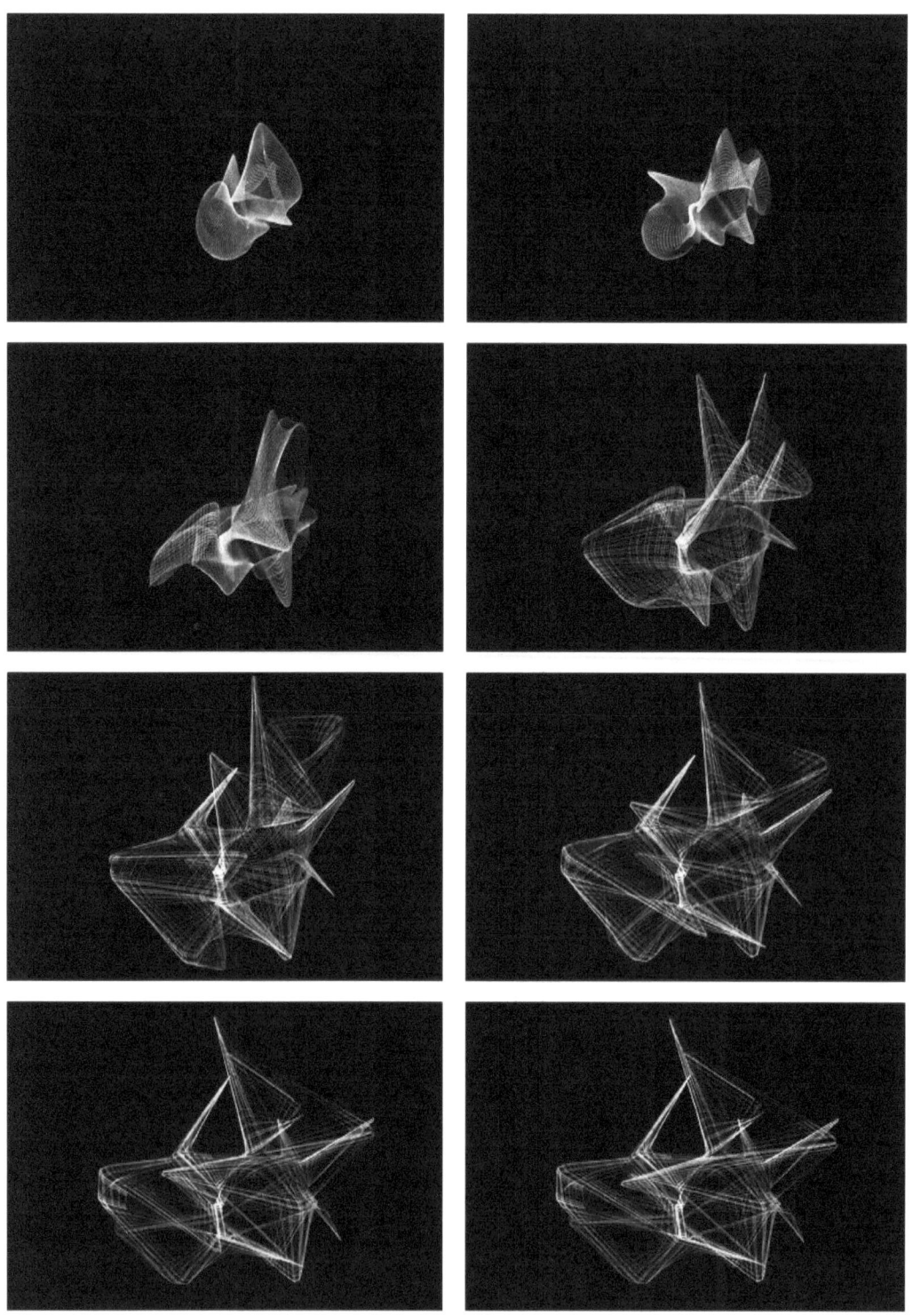

Picture 148 – Wireframe renders
Tree

Growth
Conceptual experience of growth

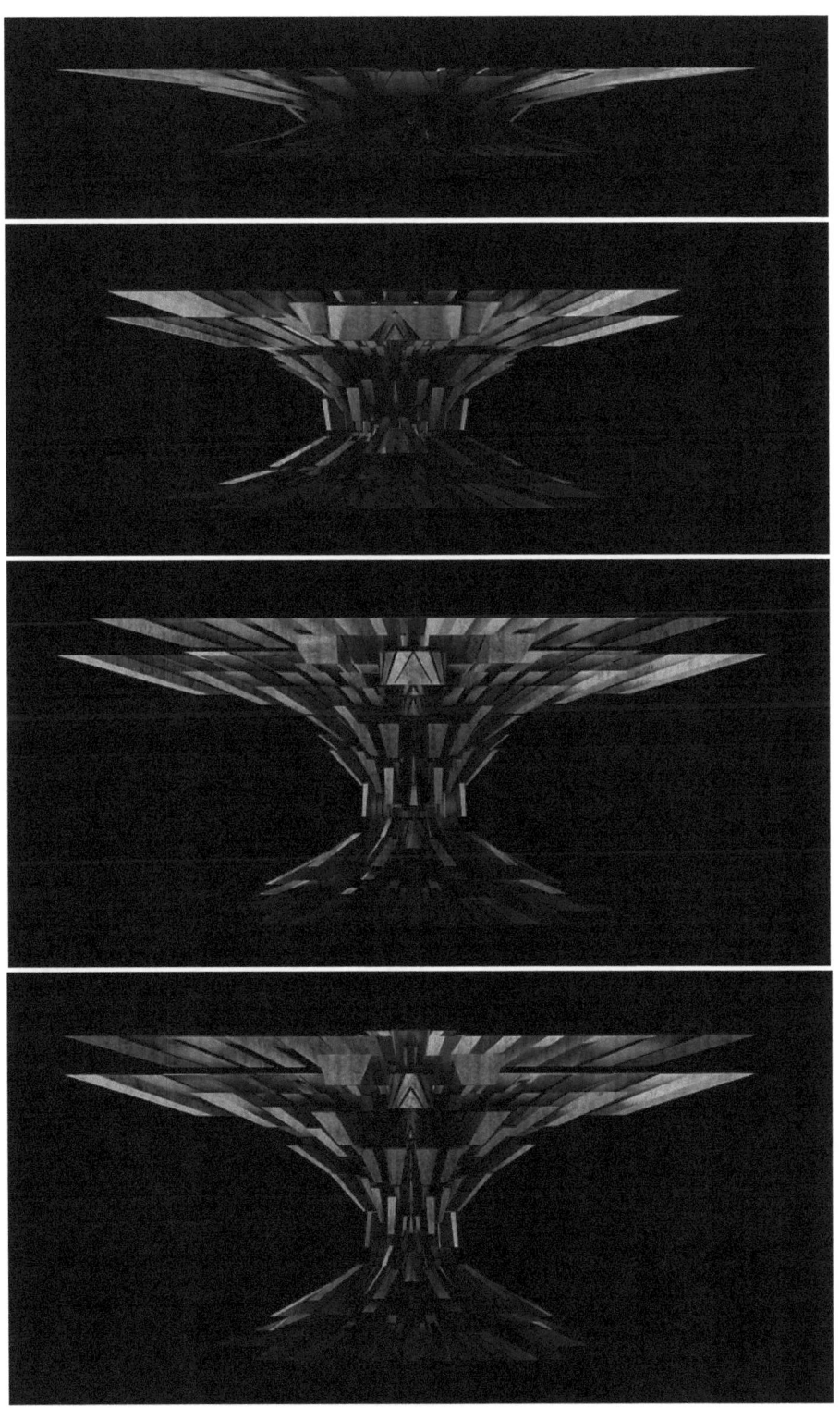

Picture 149 – Renders of Growth

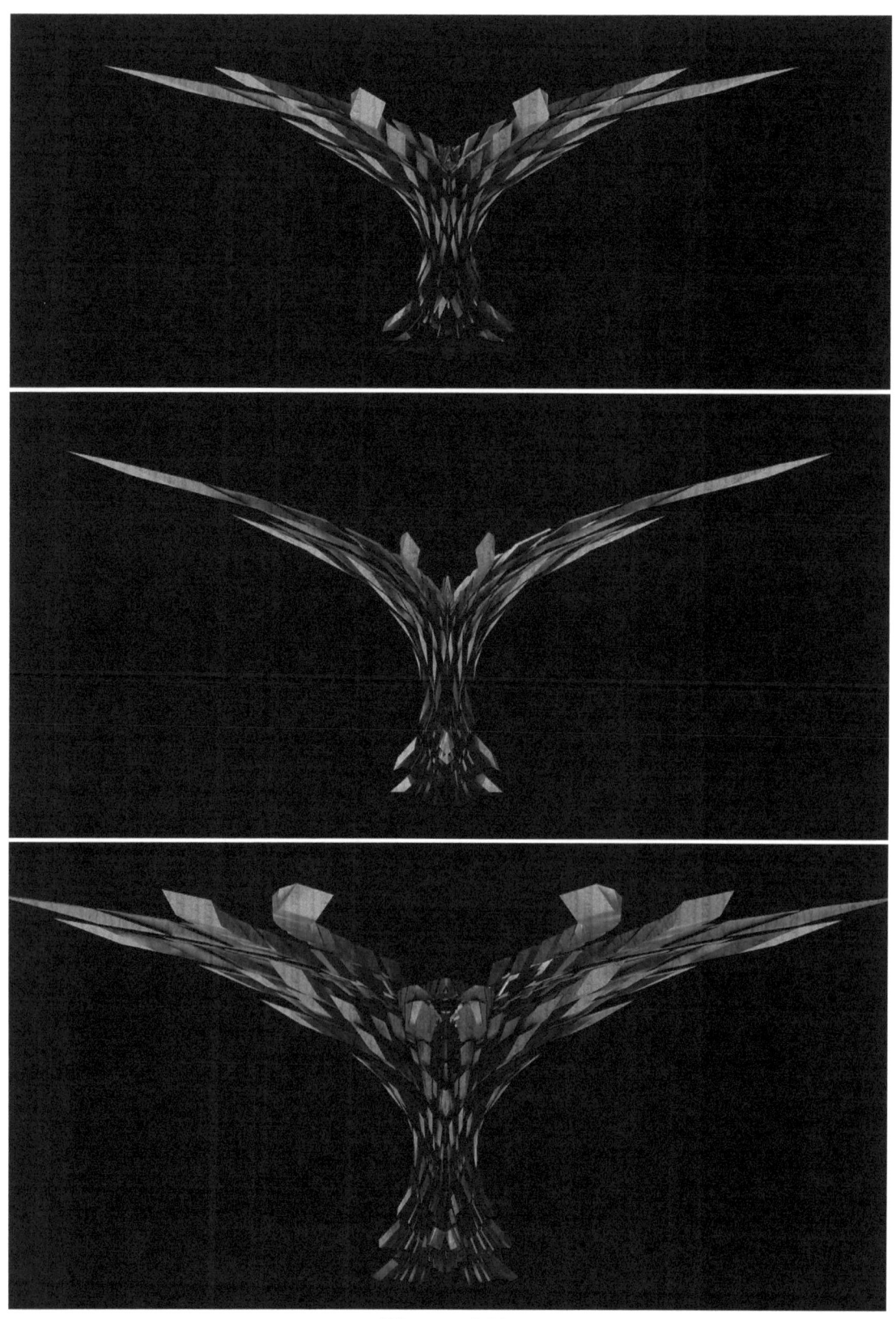

Picture 150

Metamorphosis
Conceptual Design

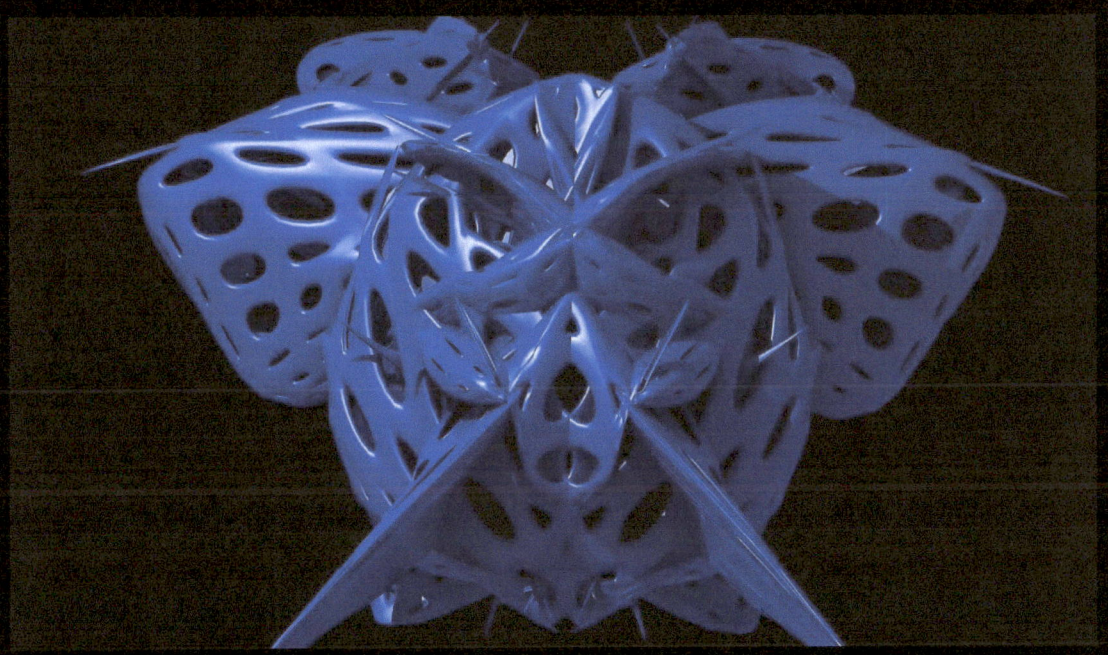

(Animation of the following file known as "Animate Form (22)" may be seen in YouTube).

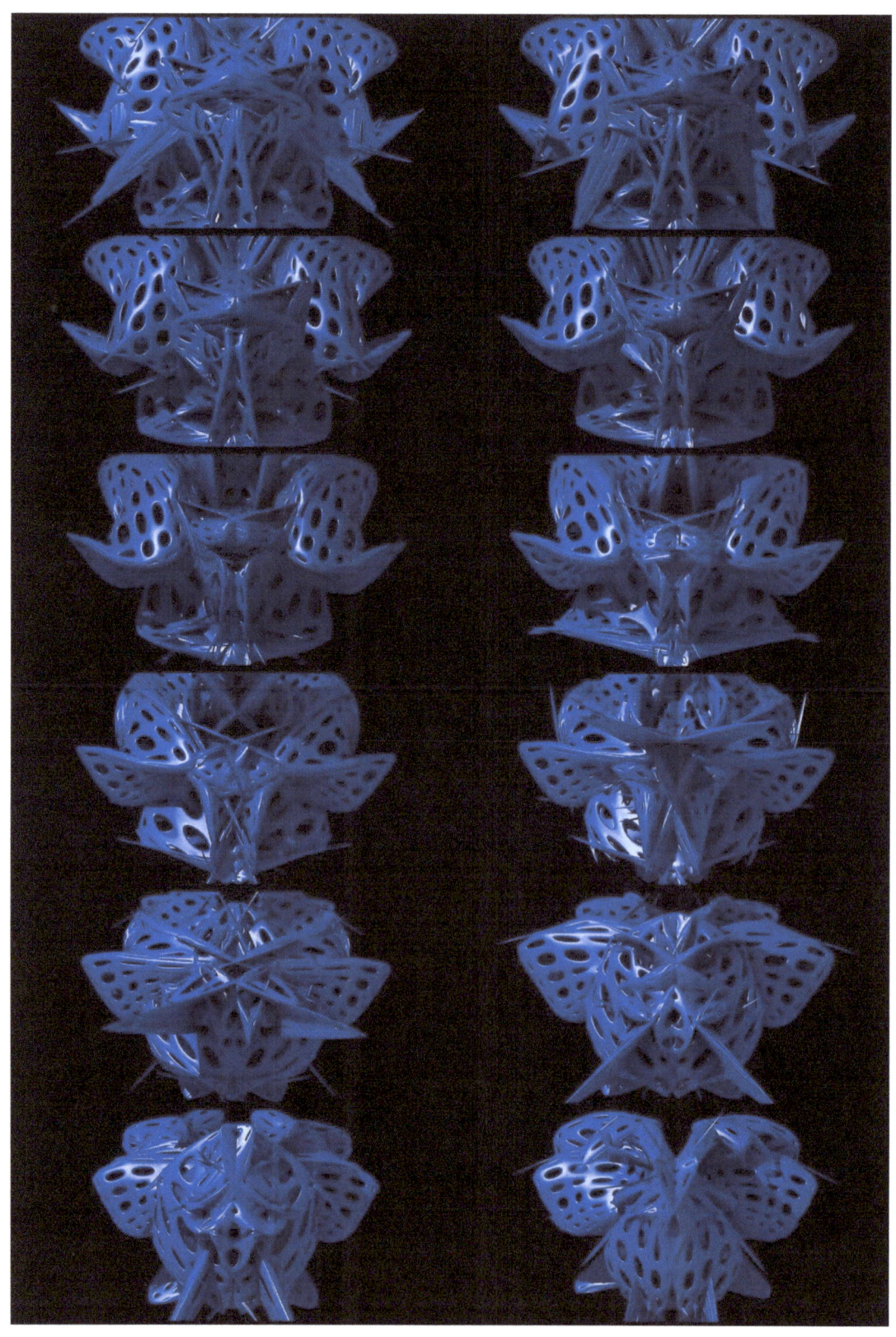

Picture 151 - Metamorphosis

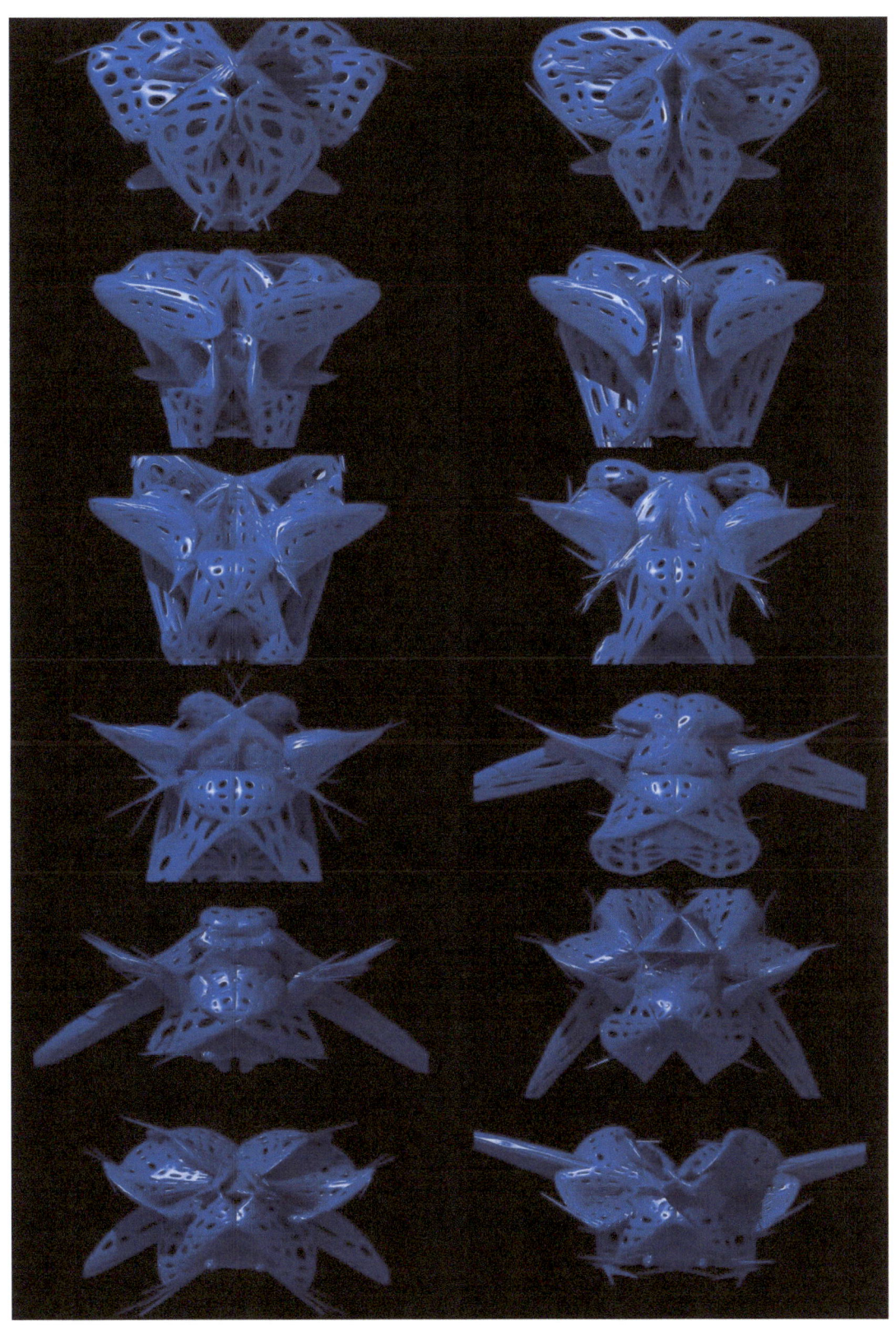

Picture 152 - Metamorphosis

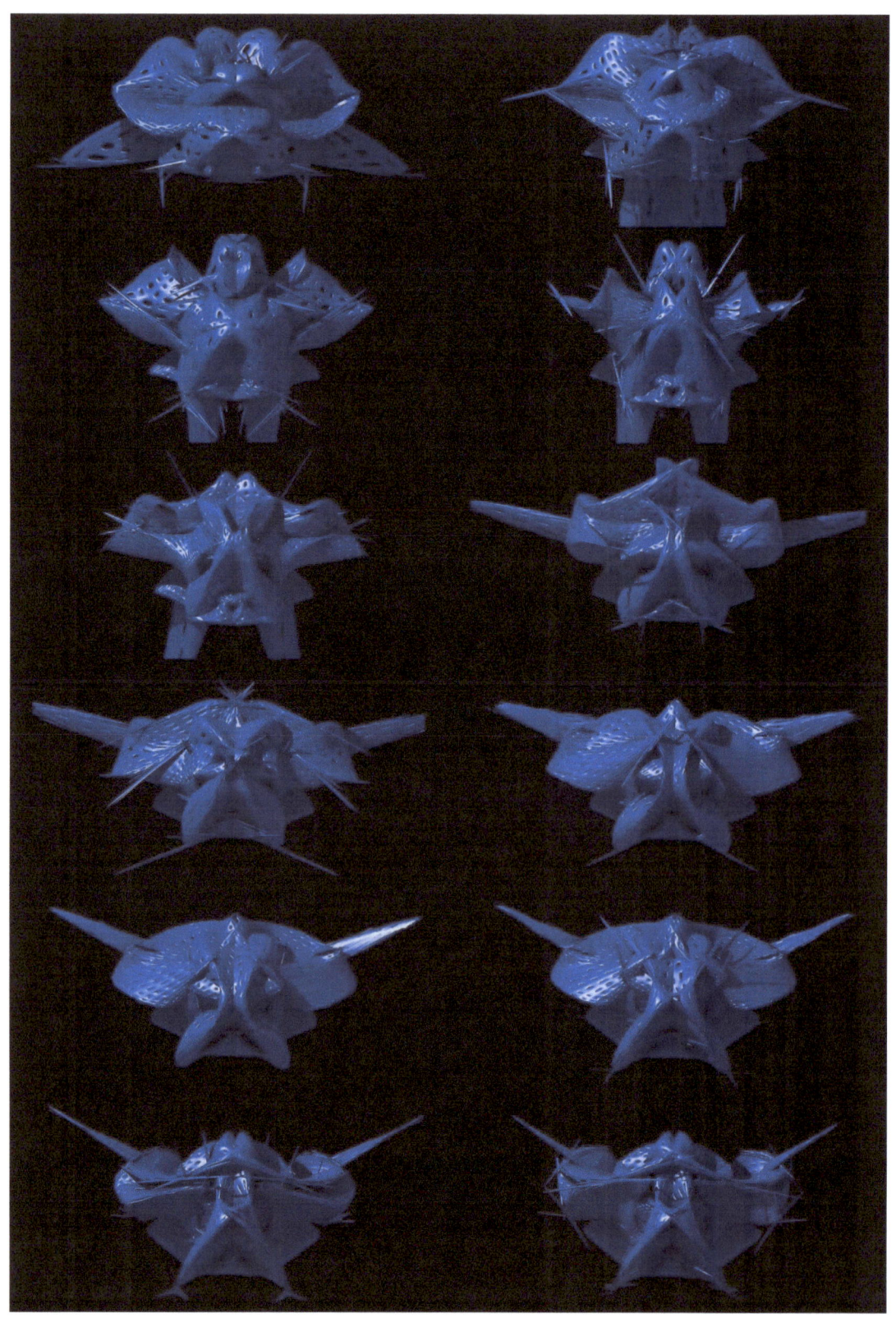

Picture 153 - Metamorphosis

A dance in middle of city

A conceptual model of an animate form, a set of Mobius strips move, transform, open and close in interaction with each other, stretch and change the environment with any variation, an idea which will be executed in a near future.

The model may be made dynamically and transform upon interaction and behavior of people. In fact, this animate form or the next work go beyond theories of Greg Lynn and challenge form and structure with a prospective attitude. The work animation known as "Animate form in the city" may be found in YouTube. (Picture 154)>

Concept of the work is based on animated sculptures of Mohsen Vaziri Moghadam, a prominent character of world modern art. Mohsen Vaziri Moghadam created the first sample of Iranian interactive art. His brachial volumes are an endeavor to create art in it's the most numerous form, animate volumes made in hands of the addressee and accepts thousands of designs. Vaziri Moghadam designed them in form of sharp knives in space which are only used to cut final nature of the volume as a static work[1]. Picture 155 >

1- Part of article of "honaronline" website with subject of "Maggi's Vain World and Interactive Art of Vaziri Moghadam", on the occasion of his exhibition at Etemad gallery on November 08, 2015 (http://www.honaronline.ir/)

Animation of the following file known as "Animate Form in the City" may be seen in YouTube channel.

Picture 156

Picture 157

Urban design elements

A concept of growth and evolution of an element in urban space. Animation of the following file known as "Urban design elements based on the animate design" may be seen in YouTube.

Picture 158

Design of trade-office tower using animate design technique

The original structure of the tower was made using animate technique, a structure which moves in computer, goes up and down, stretches, and/or concentrated in parts. Several renders were taken and several animations were made of different states. After each stage, the forces imposed to the structure were changed and/or improved. Forces and animation of the structure were based on size of openings, voids between the stories, relation with site plan and two cube buildings of north of the site, aesthetic criteria of form, lightness and adhesion of form, interactive and sometimes interwoven form and space, etc.

Finally, the main volume was chosen from among the made animations after several evaluations. Of course, voids to place windows were included in the original volume and their location was determined in the final result after required edits. The following pictures concurrently show volume variations from three views.

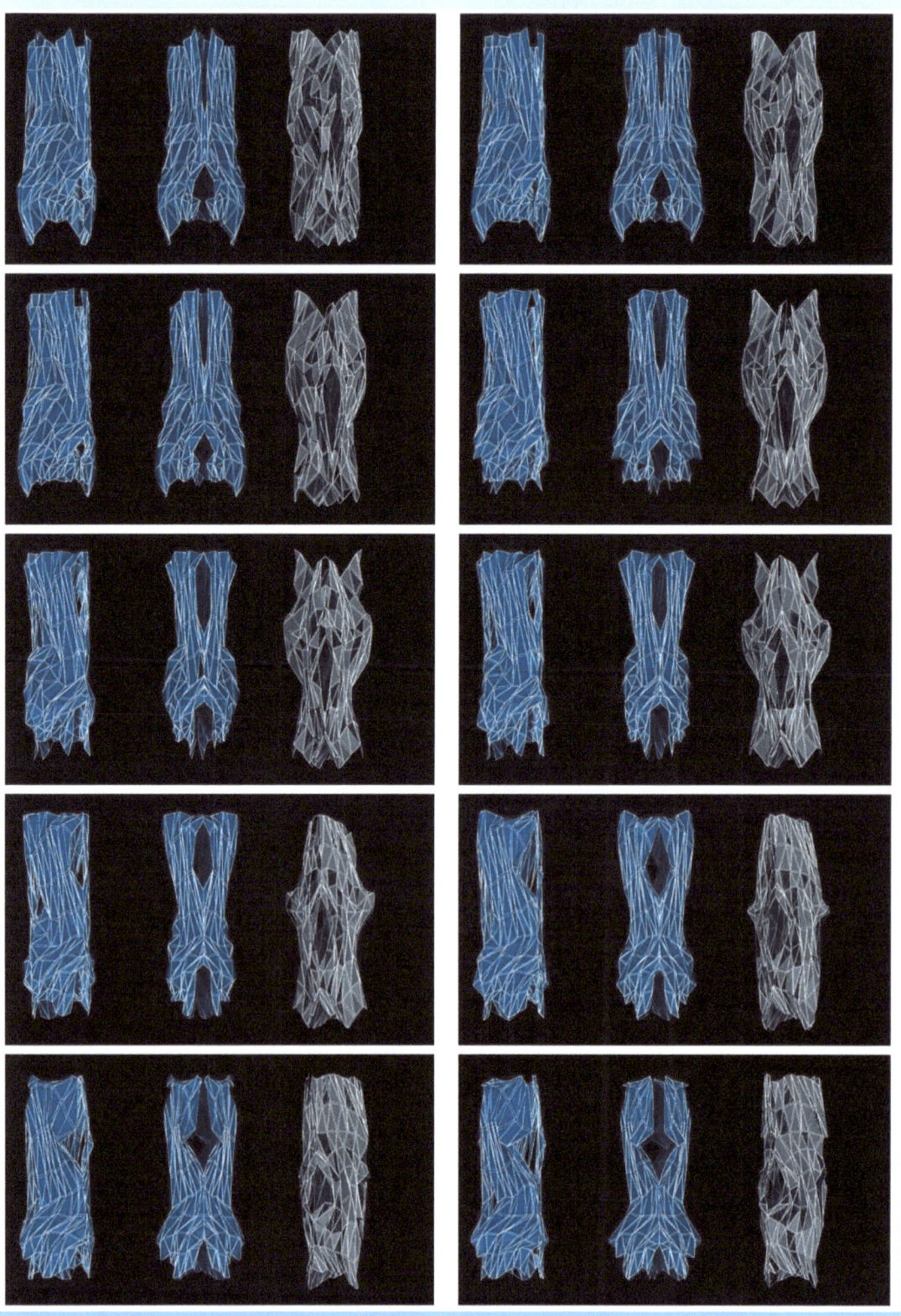

Picture 159 - Selected Frames of Animate Form

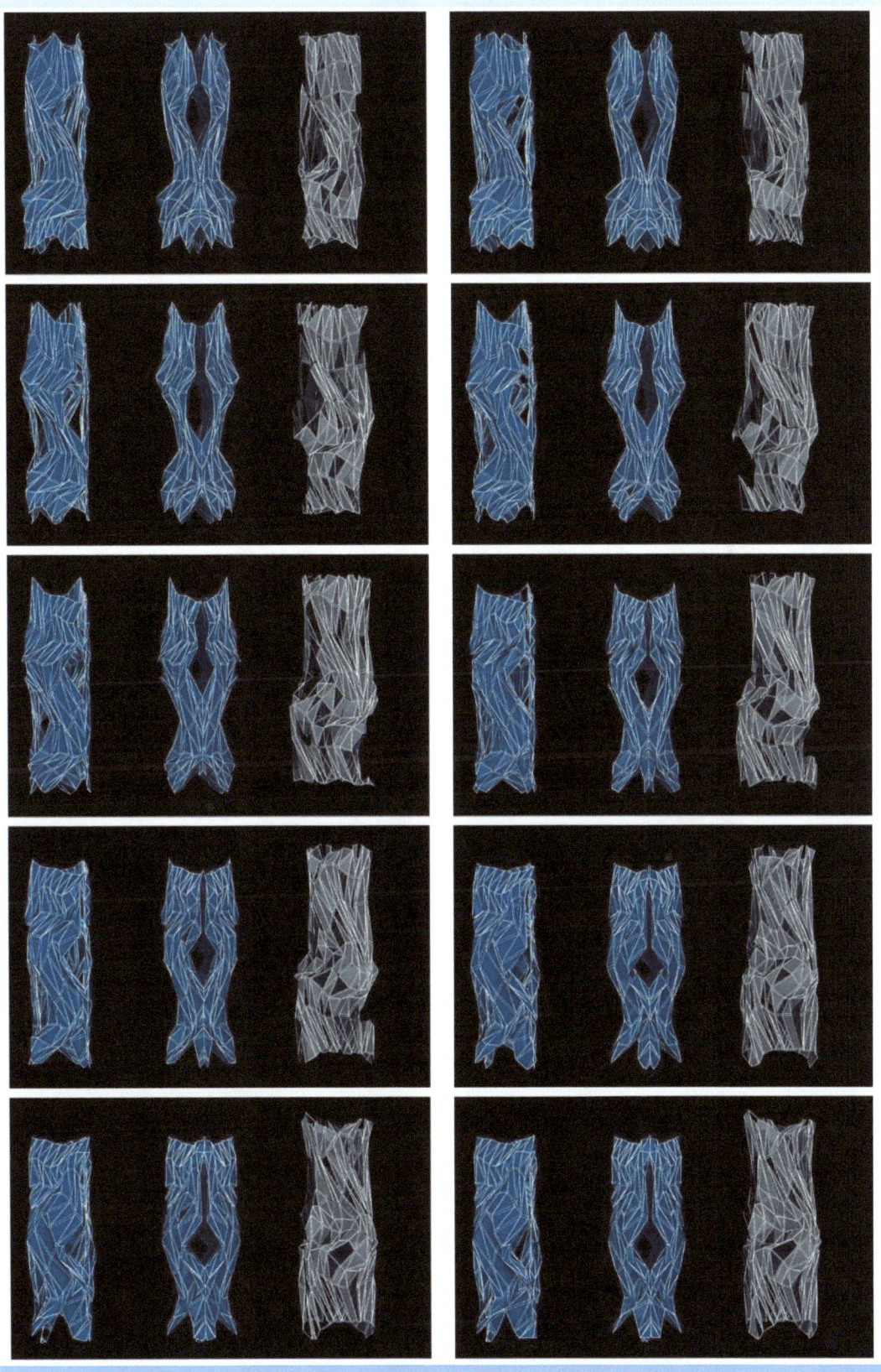

Picture 160 - Selected Frames of Animate Form

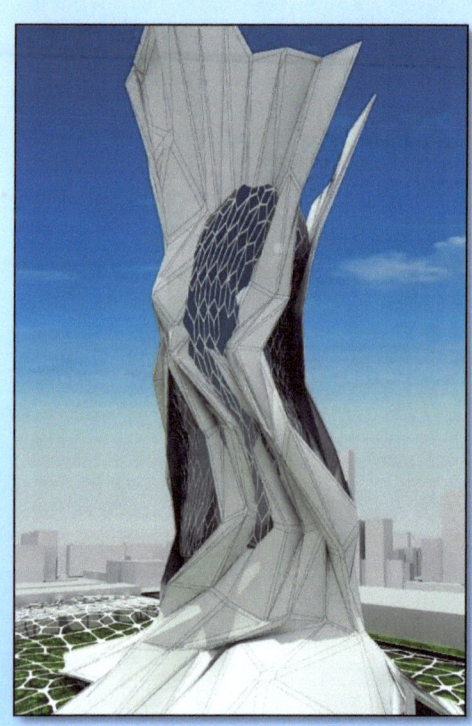

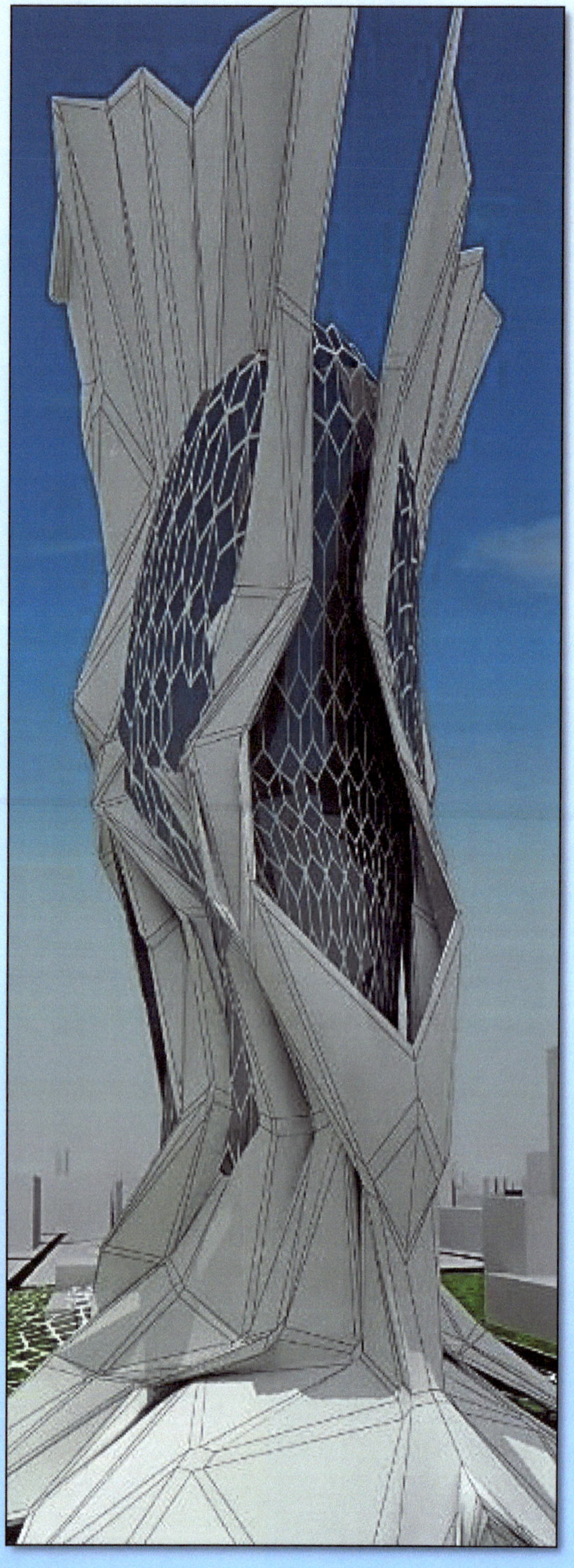

Pictures 161 – 163 - Final Design

Pictures 161 & 163 – Perspectives of Site plan

Animate Thinking

The world will not stop motion and varies and evolves constantly. But, what about our thinking?

I will not speak about changing and development of thoughts. But, how human thinks and produces thinking are important for me. We suffice to a religion, ideology, party, etc. during our life and there are few people who change their position. It originates from how we think and how our mind works, a technique making our mental world, we make decision and choose based on it.

In fact, it may be seen clearly in few schools and groups. In a world which is full of excitement, variation and transformation and constantly shows a new appearance, we live invariable, look at our surrounding events with an invariable attitude, judge about life, God and the world with beliefs experienced the least variations during decades. We will not leave such freezing thought until our life and properties are not at risk or values of the society are not changed. Our exit is also interesting! There is not any trajectory of what we were and to what we will change.

We change only our perspective and do not still see more things. This is one of the main problems of human being looking an answer during the history but was not successful in finding a convicting answer. There were several tried to find the answer but they found answer only to some aspects of life problems. We are not able to understand our neighbors, students and clients and complain about non-understanding of the world and its complexity.

"Animate thinking" is a thinking technique which is completely dynamic and unstable. It is not kind of a special thinking method trying to answer some questions or solve some problems; rather it is a technique to think. Animate thinking is a kind of process thinking, stops never, and variation, evolution and even transformation are defined as its essence.

No question has one or limited answers remaining unvaried for years.

In animate thinking, it is not compulsory to scrutinize the objective or problem. The problem should be known completely and it is repeated in every stage or location and periods. Possibility of variation of the achieved recognition mainly differs with supposing basic rules and regulations stable which may be found in most philosophical schools. Instability and supposing the findings relative exposes them to variation and evolution and, for this reason, the thinkers constantly experience renovation or refresh. Refreshing himself and the discussed phenomenon is the main issue in animate thinking.

In a simple word, we accept that phenomena and behaviors change and there is dynamism and freedom of action in this type of thinking looking for variation, welcoming them, acting in interaction with them, trying to understand and conform with phenomena, and new thoughts are born from constant association.

Animate thinking is not a linear process. It is a wide field where different questions, ideas and problems are brought forth, evaluated by an independent mind without any background, different cases are connected and completed and a space is provided to reach answers and produce new ideas.

In animate thinking, we encounter with expansion of human power of imagination. Imagination is the most important lever of a person who wants to think in this method. Imagination makes it possible to suppose the desired phenomenon as an animate and accountable, discover and renovate the relation between the phenomena and finally imagine evolution of phenomena, ideas, volumes and spaces.

- You will find another solution when you want to solve a problem.
- Fir example, animate thinking imagines and evaluated the brought up idea in a dynamic frame.
- Animate thinking is not a technique separate from other kings of thinking rather it is a kind of thinking such as critical thinking and so. Presence of animation in thinking, refreshing of findings, flexibility, uncertainty, freedom of action of the thinker in bringing up new questions or different answers and the last but not the least, thinking in a specific evolving process which may be changed in future and should be evaluated again even after reaching a result. For example, creative thinking is adapted or developed in form of animate thinking. In his "Creative Thinking and Creative Solving of Problems" book, Haerizadeh defines creative thinking as follows (Haerizadeh, 2003):

Creative thinking means the process of understanding problems, issues, deficiency of information and accepted factors, guessing and hypothesizing about such deficiencies, evaluating and testing hypotheses and guesses, improving and re-evaluating them, and finally, presenting the results.

Here, they are evaluated and developed in conformity with animate thinking

- The above definition refers to a specific process directing us to a result after passing some stages. This is a linear process but creativity or, generally, thinking may not be included in a linear trajectory. Human mind is highly capable to connect different issues and evaluate several issues concurrently. Defining a linear process for thinking limits at least two important features of our mind.

- One applied way to guess and create a new thing is to connect seemingly unimportant things. To connect, the things should be made available or put them in mind or at least do not omit them from thinking desk and do not limit ourselves to special subject.

- Reevaluation is an important act and is often ignored by architects. In architectural design, a linear process is usually used and findings of, for example, recognition stage are gradually faded and replaced by comments of designer or employer. As mentioned, animate thinking is regarded as a wide range where the things are scattered and there is not any hierarchy. However, reevaluation is not enough at end of the work and the designer or thinker reviews and refreshes it after completion of each stage of act or even when an act is practiced.

- Involving the addresses in thinking process and avoiding from unilateral judge is another issue which may be helpful in progress of creative thinking technique. When we want to offer a new plan to re-animate an urban square, we do not pay serious attention to physics of square, residents and those trafficking there.
To make the discussion more clear, suppose yourself as a thinker who is going to evaluate architectural training system using the mentioned technique.

- Evidently, the method which will be codified finally will be an open system where there is not any certainty and should be reviewed in a specific time interval.

- Thinker should have a dynamic mind and look at each architectural training technique as if he wants to develop or complete it. He should imagine beyond what is available or, in other words, evaluate what is available beyond its presence or current possibility.

- Animate thinking may be called developer or evolutionist thinking.

- How flexible will be the system you will codify? Will the instructors or students be able to essentially change the system? How much freedom of act is found there? Codifying specific semesters with courses and syllabus not providing freedom of action for the instructor is similar to what happens in our architectural higher education system and will never result in presence of creative or critical thinking.

- Is education and architecture regarded as an animate, accountable and variable creature or as an invariable and neutral one? Are we going to discuss with students, instructors and educational personnel and hold different tests of the defined courses? And hundreds of other questions …

- Will our defined system be used as an unchangeable order for years or will conditions be provided to use comments of people and consider cultural and global variations, pay attention to future requirements? As you know, several variations have been made in architectural design within the last recent and entered or connected it to other mental and technological fields. Unfortunately, they may not be entered architectural education sue to our frozen architectural education structure.

- Does our current educational system require injection of new attitudes, books and philosophies or recognition, communicating and interacting with its addresses?
In animate thinking, the thinker discusses with his/her addresses and tries to establish a creative relation with them. It does not look for injecting or imposing any comment or technique. Rather, thinker and his/her addresses are connected to each other as fields of force and have a connection of force type where variation of one of them will affect another and will result in their response.

It is not enough an idea in brought up by a thinker or designer and it is polled in his/her statistical society. Such plan or idea should be brought up due to communicating and interacting of the fields (addresses). Note that animate thinking is a process and includes our thinking method. It is not kind of thinking rather it forms the bed where the thinking should be completed and knows the tools which should be used by the thinker. What mentioned above refers to such attitude. Accepting or being familiar with tools and facilities as well as renovating his/her mental space, the thinker begins to think. Certainly, he/she will not focus of specific kind of thinking and will use their combination evolutionarily.

Another example:

Architecture instructors do not provide their students with enough freedom of act in design. They suppose students as empty minds without any belief, requirement and idea and suppose themselves as a person who is responsible to fill and explain these minds. They do not discuss with their students, do not look at their plans with an evolutionally viewpoint while a simple plan may be changed to a complete work through more work and a little creativity. They impose their ideas and regulations to the students and are bound to a specific architectural style or technique and other cases which have been mentioned in detail in "Creativity in Design Process I".

As an architect and author, I never followed a specific style or technique. I experienced different viewpoints with a free mind. "Creativity in Design Process II", "Creativity in Design Process III" and "The Role of Brain Hemispheres in Architectural Design" include various works of different styles. A dynamic, free, and creative attitude toward design encouraged me to write books instead of translating a specific book. Evolutionary attitude, mental renovation and refresh of findings and ideas were the main reasons to publish volumes II and III and other supplementary books. I imagined myself as a child freely following butterflies in a garden in a wide bed of excuse, attractiveness and need to design and education. Usually, I do not follow a specific objective and any scent or noise makes my mind absent. However, I move in the design garden and find my way since roots of all techniques and creations of art and architecture end to a point which is a single bed, i.e. I finally can connect different subjects.

The present book is a good sample confirming this thinking technique. Animation, motion of volumes, their variation and conversion were really attractive and I spent much time to make abstract and architectural animations following my wantonness. I still do it. I was not aimed at compiling a special book or technique. I made and saved them in computer. Finally, I could exhibit them in cyberspace in recent years and followed it up more seriously because of their reception by the addresses. I passed evolutionary process stages its end and result was not known for me. In architectural design, I often try to create a space for presence of such thinking in spite of restrictions. For example, I do not suffice to one or two alternatives and show my special ideas to the employer beside other works. In most cases, I recompleted or changed a work even after publish, presentation or construction of it. Evidently, animate thinking has a lot in common with critical thinking.

Animate thinking, not as a kind of thinking rather as a kind of thinking process, may include kinds of thinking and compensate their gaps through creation of connection and interaction between them. I hope I could find opportunity, facilities, expectation and incitement to study and write in this field in future.

Thinking and Creativity Pavilion

Conceptual design Based on Animate Design Process

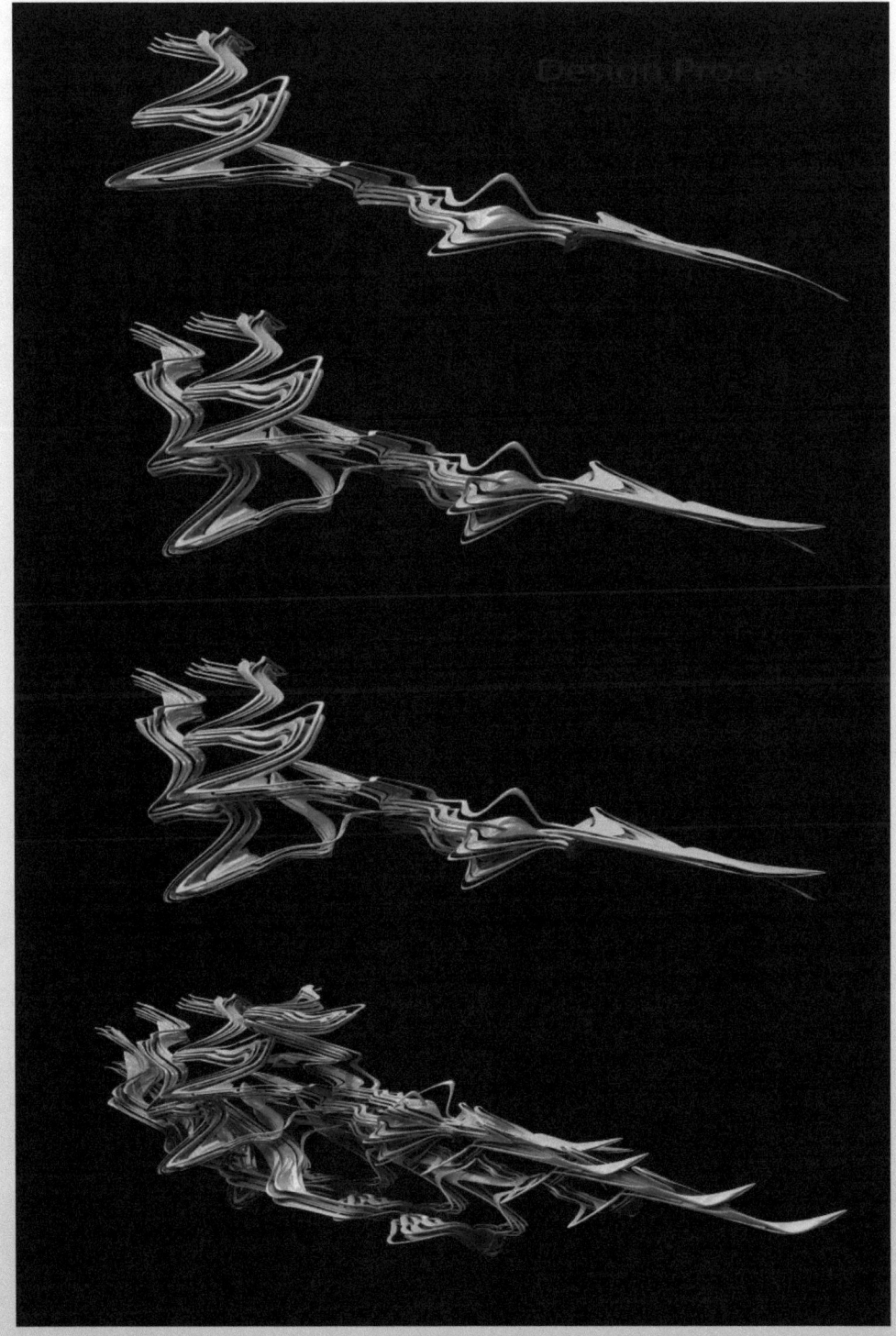

Picture 164 – Design Process

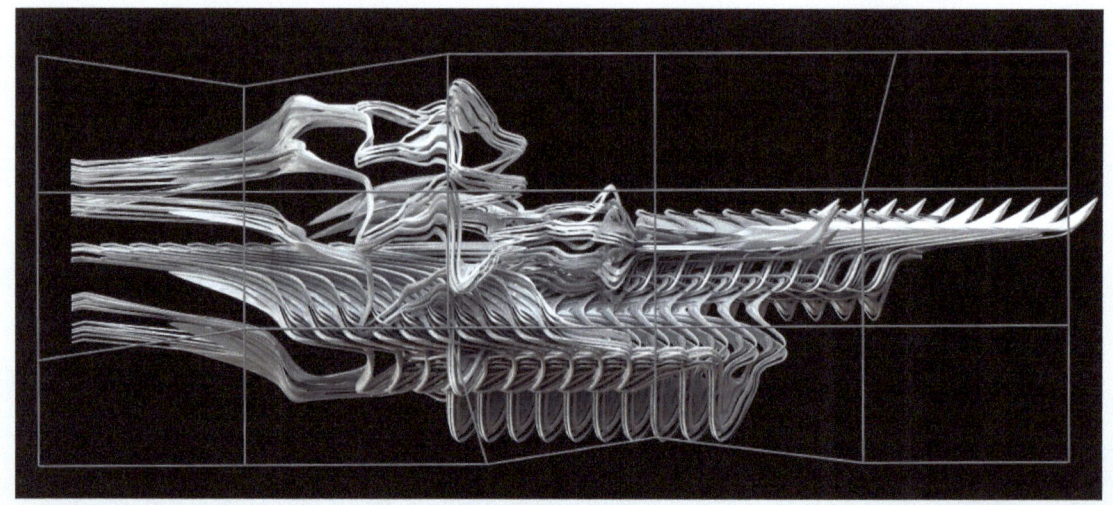

Picture 165 – Elevation

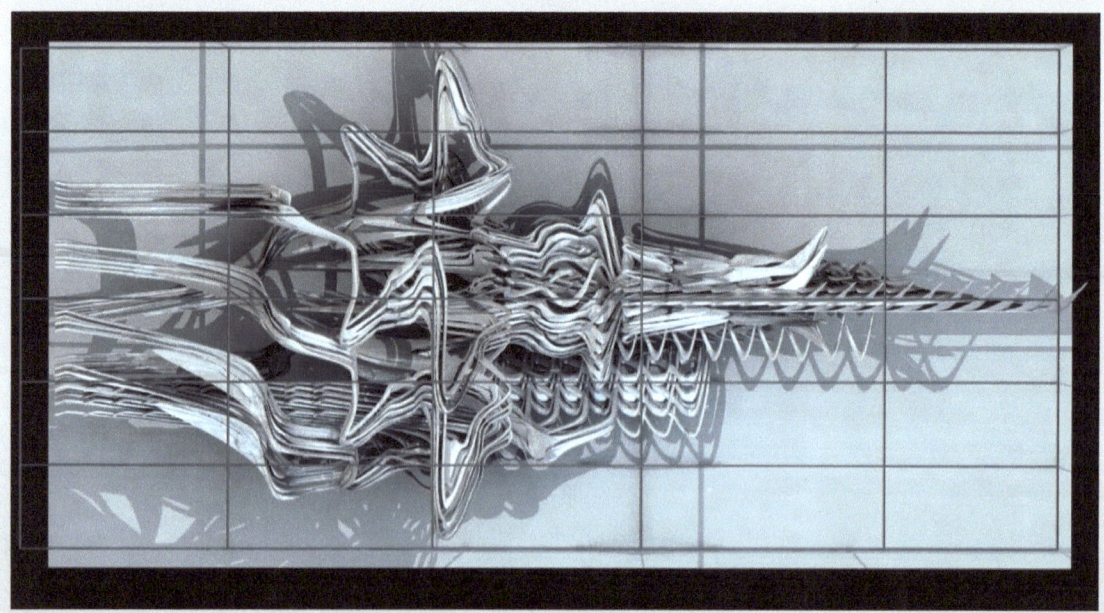

Picture 166 – Roof Plan

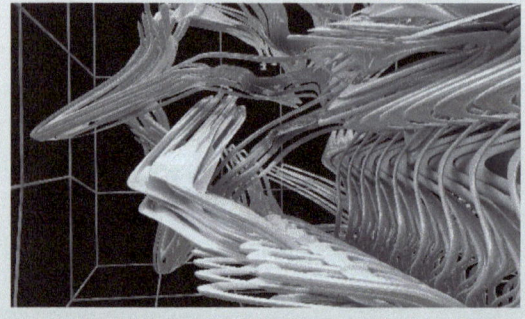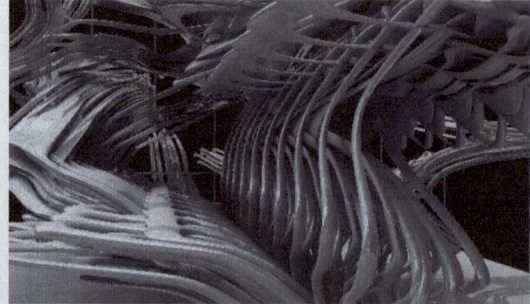

Pictures 167 & 168 – Interior Renders

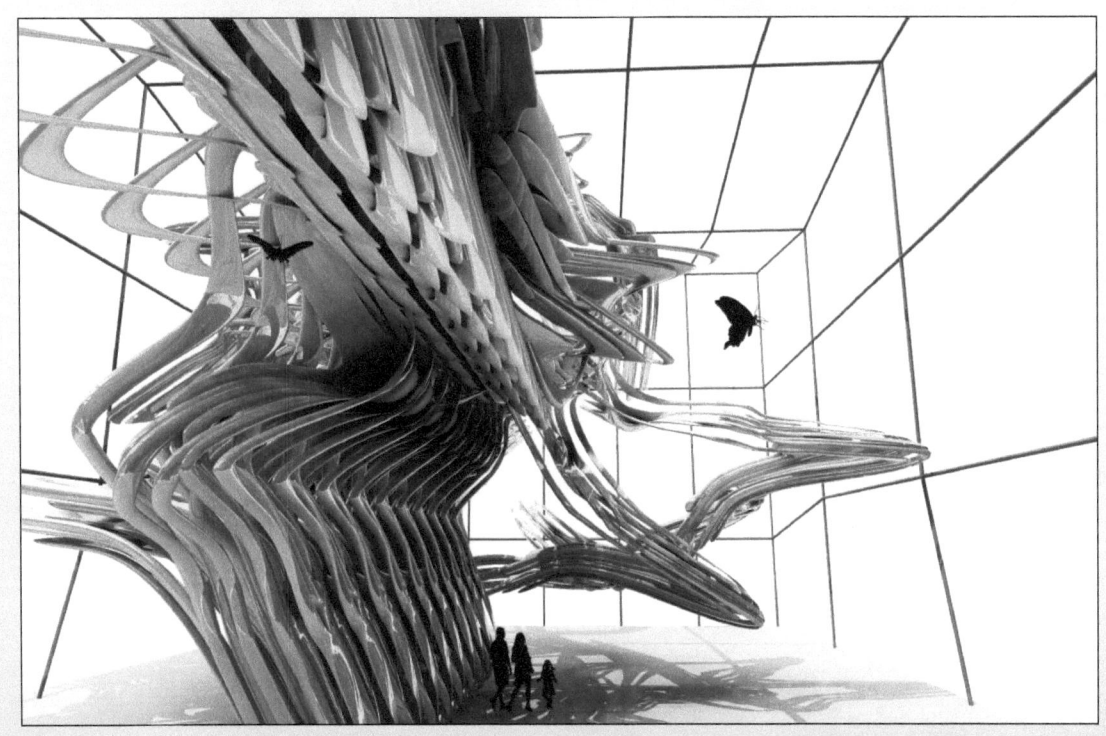

Pictures 169 & 170 – Interior Renders

The last words

Probably, some readers who have studied the book wonder that they have read some of these techniques and ideas in other books or have seen works similar to what are included in the book. It is noteworthy that the author tried to collect the viewpoints in a specific and comprehensive frame which can include most techniques and ideas, provide conditions for their communication and interaction, provide conditions for its development through the tools provided to thinkers and designers, and provide conditions to encounter with realities, requirements and needs of life and society.

- Obtain a world where no specific design style or attitude will govern or will be regarded better than others.

- Before any event, pay attention to requirements and needs of human and society and our duty.

- Make ideas for future and avoid from guiding it to a specific direction.
- Study outcomes of our design.

- Suppose culture, materials and nature as animate, accountable, variable and evolutionary creature.

Motion and transformation of buildings in two future decades will be inevitable whether due to requirement, climate and energy saving, or charms offered by technology to live differently. The designers, with any attitude and belief, should pay attention to undermine of structural stability of buildings. It will go beyond activity of smart buildings managing the building energy or displacement of some surfaces of building, lights, etc. and will direct us to a point where every element of the building will interact and dialogue with their residents, the building will transform according to their requirements, and whole building will appear in a new form within some minutes through executing a plan modeled by the architect and programmers. Therefore, animate design should be seriously taken into account and buildings should be designed in a way such that we encounter with a living, animate and fluid creature running in time and looking for transformation. As we eagerly accept awards of technology god, the human being will be enthusiastic to accept variation and transformation and most people will be interested in having a virtual model of an old palace or castle in Europe virtually appearing in a location in Iran or India!

Stable and economized use of nature is another important issue and significant actions will be taken in this regard at presence of cyberspace. The issue that we will need 30% of current materials to construct or repair a building and facade, space division, walls

and virtual crusts will be done and will be responsible to control light penetration and will serve as thermal insulation will be enough to damage nature less.

Fortunately, we observe significant progress in the mentioned field (though too late). However, future is more complex than what we encountered in the past and we should expect for mental, belief, technological and cultural mutations, diversity, conflict and complexity of imaginations of design ideas. As you know, the concepts of time and location are changing and we should expect their transformation in a near future. It is better to realize our thoughts before occurring of any important event in the field of technology, culture, philosophy and life and change our design technique and attitude.

References

- Afzali, N. Hoselou, S. Motion in architecture and parameters affecting kinetic architecture design, 4th international conference on civil, architecture and urban development, Tehran (Shahid Beheshti University), 2016
- Taraz, M., Taghizadeh, K. Energy analysis and efficiency of an animated view in Tehran, Naghsh Jahan research-scientific periodical, Tehran, No.5-2, P.55, 2015
- Haerizadeh, Kh., Mohammadhossein, L., Creative thinking and creative solving of problems, Tehran, Ney press, 2003
- Khabazi, Z., Digital design process, Kasra press, Tehran, 2014
- Khiabanian, A., Creativity in architectural design process I, Mehr Iman press, Tabriz, 2009
- Khiabanian, A., Creativity in architectural design process II, Mehr Iman press, Tabriz, 2010
- Khiabanian, A., Creativity in architectural design process III (parametric architecture), Mehr Iman press, Tabriz, 2012
- Khiabanian, A, The role of brain hemispheres in architectural design, Supreme Century, USA, 2015
- Fathzadeh, N., Articles of global conference of electronic and internet cities, Kish Island, 2001
- Anders, P., Envisioning cyberspace; designing 3D electronic spaces (MsGraw Hill:New York, 1999), pp.47, 49
- Manovich, L, The Language of New Media (MIT Press: Cambridge, Massachusetts, 2000), p.112
- Manovich, L, "Liquid Architectures in Cyberspace" in Cyberspace: First Steps, Ed. Michael Benedikt (MIT Press: Cambridge, Massachusetts / London, England, 1993), pp. 248-251
- Novak, M, "Liquid Architectures in Cyberspace" in Cyberspace: First Steps, Ed. Michael Benedikt (MIT Press: Cambridge, Massachusetts / London, England, 1993)
- Negroponte, N, Being Digital (Vintage Books: New York, 1995), pp. 60, 117
- Jenny, H, Cymatic: Wave Phenomena, Vibrational Effects, Harmonic Oscillations with their Structure, Kinetics and Dynamics, volume 2 (Basel: Basilius Press, 1974), 58
- Sherbini, Kh. Krawczyk, R. Overview of Intelligent Architecture, 1st ASCAAD International Conference, e-Design in Architecture, Dhahran, Saudi Arabia. pp.137. 2004
- Virilio, P Open Sky (Verso: London, 1997), p. 103

Internet References

- http:/dezeen.com/
- http://eabiennial.com/
- http://fineartamerica.com /
- http://.formz.com/
- http://nextoffice.ir

Books published by Ali Khiabbanian

Poem and Painting
- Shades dance
- Leili & rain man
- Song & silence, USA, 2016
-

Architecture

Creativity in architectural design process I
- Creativity in architectural design process II
- Creativity in architectural design process III (parametric design)
- Reflections of awake mind
- Ideas for facade design
- Conceptual Sketches in Architectural Design, Supreme Century, USA, 2014
_The Role of Brain Hemispheres in Architectural Design, USA, 2015
– Impact of parametric design on young architects, USA, Supreme Art, 2016
- Box in Digital Transformation, Supreme Century, USA, 2018

www.ingramcontent.com/pod-product-compliance
Lightning Source LLC
Chambersburg PA
CBHW041521220426
43669CB00002B/15